Y0-CAR-383

3 1611 00289 9745

BECOMING A STRONG
INSTRUCTIONAL LEADER

BECOMING A STRONG INSTRUCTIONAL LEADER

SAYING NO TO BUSINESS AS USUAL

Alan C. Jones

FOREWORD BY
Robert V. Bullough Jr.

Teachers College
Columbia University
New York and London

LB
2831.82
.J64
2012

Published by Teachers College Press, 1234 Amsterdam Avenue, New York, NY 10027

Copyright © 2012 by Teachers College, Columbia University

All rights reserved. No part of this publication may be reproduced or transmitted in any form or by any means, electronic or mechanical, including photocopy, or any information storage and retrieval system, without permission from the publisher.

The author would like to express gratitude for use of the following material:

Table 6.2: Two Traditions of Pedagogy is adapted from P. W. Jackson, *The practice of teaching*, 1986, New York, NY: Teachers College Press. Copyright © 1998 by Teachers College Press. Adapted with permission.

Table 7.1: Great Implementation was inspired by J. C. Collins, *Good to great: Why some companies make the leap . . . and others don't*, 2001, New York, NY: HarperBusiness. Copyright © 2001 by HarperBusiness. Adapted with permission.

Table 7.6: Acts of Interpretation is adapted from R. L. Daft & K. E. Weick, Toward a model of organizations as interpretation systems, 1984, *Academy of Management Review, (9)*2, pp. 284–295. Adapted with permission.

Table 10.2: Western Versus Toyota View of Problems is reprinted from J. K. Liker & M. Hoseus, *Toyota culture: The heart and soul of the Toyota Way*, 2008, New York, NY: McGraw-Hill. Copyright © 1998 by McGraw-Hill. Reprinted with permission.

Library of Congress Cataloging-in-Publication Data

Jones, Alan C., associate professor.
  Becoming a strong instructional leader : saying no to business as usual / Alan C. Jones ; foreword by Robert V. Bullough Jr.
    p. cm.
  Includes bibliographical references and index.
    ISBN 978-0-8077-5338-5 (pbk. : alk. paper) — ISBN 978-0-8077-5339-2 (hardcover : alk. paper)
    1. School administrators—Professional relationships—United States. 2. Teacher-administrator relationships—United States. 3. School improvement programs—United States. I. Title.
    LB2831.82.J64 2012
    371.2'011–dc23

2012009457

ISBN 978-0-8077-5338-5 (paperback)
ISBN 978-0-8077-5339-2 (hardcover)

Printed on acid-free paper
Manufactured in the United States of America

19 18 17 16 15 14 13 12   8 7 6 5 4 3 2 1

For
Sebastian and Tyler.
May they attend schools led by Strong Instructional Leaders.

Contents

Foreword

What does one do as the new principal of an underperforming urban secondary school when facing a staff who is tired and frustrated by endless legislative mandates, each mandate tied to a set of assumptions about teaching and learning that promise only more failure? What does one do when neither teachers nor students are engaged in serious learning, and all that these mandates promise is a narrowing of the curriculum, a tightening of accountability measures, more and more student testing, and less and less trust of teachers and faith in their ability to learn on the job and to develop toward teaching excellence? And, what is one to do when the most institutionally rewarded activities of principals have to do with managing schooling—keeping things running smoothly—rather then leading schools and building faculty understanding and competence? *Becoming a Strong Instructional Leader* is Alan Jones's response to these questions.

As I read *Becoming a Strong Instructional Leader* I recalled being in the audience of a large gathering as Margaret Thatcher, former prime minister of England, spoke. With her usual forcefulness, she said, "Consensus is the abnegation of leadership." Like Alan Jones, she recognized the difference between the work of management, with all its seductive and self-serving pleasures for bureaucrats and their friends, and the calling of leadership. Also, like Jones, she warned of the danger that follows when too many "leaders" lack the courage to do what needs to be done, and who instead lick a finger and hold it to the wind to sense the direction of public opinion even as they struggle to get ahead of what they think is coming. One of my teachers, Harry Broudy, once quipped that behavior of this sort is what leads some people to proclaim themselves to be "progressive." "Leaders" of this sort seek and may even achieve moments of popularity and praise for themselves, but mostly they value quiet conformity in others and an illusive tidiness. What they most want is certainty and stability, the stuff of training but not of education. They are, of course, followers, and for such people—those who endlessly seek security and consensus but rarely tell the truth or reveal their motives—Alan Jones has only scorn, even as he offers a measure of understanding (particularly in Chapter 9).

Becoming a Strong Instructional Leader presents conclusions drawn from Jones's 35-year career as a teacher and school principal in and around Chicago, Illinois. Jones writes with the voice of experience and as a friend to young people.

He writes with urgency and passion, often rushing along impatiently. Along the way he makes accusations, offers some explanations, and consistently challenges what he sees as the "business as usual" of schooling, including the current dominant model of school reform—raise standards, test children, reward and punish teachers and principals.

The lessons offered clearly were hard won; the journey toward becoming a "strong" leader, as Jones describes it, is certainly not for the weak. There is no room on this journey for the unimaginative or the fearful, for those who are comfortable mostly following itineraries set by over-promising and tight-fisted tour guides and then sticking right with the tour. There is, however, plenty of room for those who have and can skillfully read maps but are willing to do some bushwhacking—to get off the beaten path in pursuit of deeper and richer learning experiences. Believing firmly in education and in the possibility of forming schools that encourage teacher and student learning and well-being and that foster richer, more interesting, engaged, and productive lives, such people—representing what Jones describes as a "fourth approach to school leadership"—are deeply suspicious of those who promise easy solutions to complex problems. They know there are no technical silver bullets to the problems of teaching and learning, and they are sensitive to how contextual differences require the alteration of all so-called best practices. They are idealists who inspire imagination but who, in Jones's terms, are also hardheaded "pragmatists," leaders who understand the "art of the eclectic" and get the job done. In addressing the too-often ignored but "fundamental questions of schooling," conversation leads to visions, a "strong instructional worldview"; visions lead to agendas; agendas lead to action; action, to "new instructional realities"; and these new realities, to greater and different forms of learning and nurturing. Along the way, research is involved, agency is exercised, trust builds, competence develops, and with greater competence comes greater confidence and power. In turn, confidence supports the development of the courage needed for "doing the right things" and doing them "well," as Jones suggests.

Chapters 7 through 13 of *Becoming a Strong Leader* describe some of the tools used by strong leaders when leading but focus, more broadly, on who strong leaders are. Passion for teaching and learning and clarity of vision are at the center of who a strong leader is and frame what a strong leader does. Getting purposes clear and keeping every aspect of schooling focused on achieving those purposes drives the strong leader's work.

> While policymakers express concern about quality teaching, they
> fail to see that managing instruction is a very different task from
> providing quality teaching by changing core teaching practices. . . . The
> essential difference between the two roles (manager/leader) rests with
> their primary focus—the means or the ends of an organization.

The purposes of education are not simple but are complex and evolving. Nor are they easily measured but they must be assessed. Hence, as Jones argues, strong leaders are "philosopher-educators." Philosopher-educators support ongoing "experiments in collective sensemaking" that result in the formation of new and resonant visions and instructional narratives that "'purpose' schooling, helping others to understand and communicate what is being done within a school and why it is being done.

In preparing for this role, strong leaders engage in a "private journey" of study and of deep thought, a "public journey," and a "situational journey," representing three "webs" of studying, planning, and doing. Described as more solitary than social (I would disagree with this assessment), the private journey, what I think of as the "inner drama" of leadership, is often missing in programs designed to educate (train) leaders and is seldom acknowledged in the wider published literature. Having long lived in schools, Jones well understands the importance of this journey, of how successful leaders know what they believe and where they stand, and so gives it a significant place in his thinking. The public journey involves the assumption of the "public responsibility for creating organizational configurations that permit school administrators and faculty to negotiate the meaning of a new instructional initiative." In this phase problems are framed and "teachers and administrators are positioned to deliberate over and practice unfamiliar theories, ideas, and practices." In this second journey, the strong leader is fully engaged with the faculty and wider community, "orchestrating an educative process that allocates time and expertise for conversations over dissatisfaction with current practices, presentations of alternative theories and practices, and opportunities to openly experiment with new pedagogies." The aim is to support and develop what Jones describes as "ambitious" teaching.

Jones understands change as an educational problem that involves a "process of making collective sense out of theories and practices that challenge firmly held views about the fundamental questions of schooling." In this process, research results play a significant role, although here I must admit I do not think research is as univocal as Jones suggests.

The third journey—the situational journey—seeks to develop within specific schools and classrooms cultures of professional growth. For principals this journey and challenge is daunting, again underscoring the importance of a clarity of vision

> Strong Instructional Leaders do not allow the external and internal constraints of institutional schooling to derail teachers from fully pursuing the goals, ideas, methods, and practices of a new [theory-based] instructional initiative. What keeps the situational journey moving forward is a commitment to valued ends of schooling—the moral purposes of schooling.

Fortunately, as Jones notes, there are abundant "master teachers . . . in universities and our schools" who model "ambitious teaching," and from these teachers, principals who are willing to listen can learn much. Rarer are "the instructional environments and training opportunities to develop master approaches to curriculum and instruction." *Becoming a Strong Instructional Leader* represents a strongly worded invitation to readers to leave the beaten path and to do the bushwhacking necessary to find their way toward the creation of these sorts of learning environments.

Robert V. Bullough Jr.

Preface

This book is the product of a career-long process of thinking about why schools fail to engage students. I have worked for more than 35 years as a teacher and school administrator in urban and suburban districts at all levels of schooling: elementary, secondary, and post-secondary institutions. In each of these venues, I have participated in numerous reform initiatives to improve student achievement and raise the level of engagement of students in academic learning. Throughout my years in education, whether as a teacher or school administrator, I had never felt good about my teaching or about my leadership. This is not to say that my superiors, the communities I worked in, or governmental agencies viewed me as a failure. During my career I received superior evaluations, was voted teacher of the year, and received a United States Department of Education Blue Ribbon Award. But as I drove home from school each day, I knew that most of the students in the classrooms of the schools I led were not engaged by or interested in academic learning and that those students were leaving our schools poorly prepared to compete in global economies, to be thoughtful citizens in a democracy, and to develop their communities.

In my career I did experience classrooms, curricula, and programs that generated the kinds of enthusiasm for learning that had originally drawn me to the profession of teaching and school administration. However, these rich learning experiences were few and far between and they proved difficult to sustain. Each glimpse of what a school could be pulled me further into the pursuit of instructional programs that engaged students socially, emotionally, and intellectually and that lifted instructional discourse above the mundane matters of institutional rules and routines.

My blurred vision of how to implement ambitious approaches to teaching and learning became clearer with Stein and Nelson's (2003) new construct of "leaders of content knowledge." Stein and Nelson found that school leaders who were well informed about the substance of an instructional initiative were more likely to see changes in core teaching practices than were school leaders who assumed the traditional role of instructional manager: dispenser of materials, scheduler of in-service days, employer of consultants, and author of grants. My personal experience with implementing instructional initiatives paralleled Stein and Nelson's finding that knowledge matters when it comes to asking teachers to change habitual approaches to teaching a subject. The more I knew about the theories, ideas, and practices that were driving a new pedagogy, the more I was able to assist teachers who were struggling with unfamiliar instructional strategies. What Stein and Nelson's new construct did not articulate was how school principals become leaders of content knowledge. In my journey to understand and practice the role of leader of content knowledge, I developed answers to seven questions that author a new construct in school administration—Strong Instructional Leadership.

1. Why do school administrators spend most of their days managing the routines of schooling rather than confronting the complexities of classroom instruction?
2. Why do efforts to implement ambitious approaches to curriculum and instruction result in incoherent mixtures of this theory and that technique?
3. What knowledge and skills must a school administrator acquire to effectively change core teaching strategies?
4. How do school administrators persuade skeptical (i.e., hostile) publics to adopt substantive changes in curriculum and instruction?
5. How do school administrators resist unschooled ideas in education that have the power to disrupt substantive improvements to curriculum and instruction?
6. How do school administrators work with teachers in classrooms to make collective sense of theory-based pedagogies?
7. What qualities of leadership are necessary to close the gap between what schools are and what they could be?

This book was written for busy school administrators who are willing to undertake the challenging work of becoming a strong instructional leaders. Each chapter in the book focuses on stages in a process for creating a school culture that persistently pursues a coherent response to the five fundamental questions of schooling:

1. How do children learn?
2. What knowledge is of greatest worth?
3. How should knowledge be organized?
4. How should students be assessed?
5. How should we teach?

Becoming a Strong Instructional Leader is a radical departure from what has been historically called developing "instructional leadership." The current literature on instructional leadership continues to promote the management function of instructional leadership. No book or study of instructional leadership explains the connection between the development of a strong instructional worldview and the implementation of coherent approaches to curriculum and instruction: Theories agree with ideas, ideas agree with actions, and actions agree with practice.

This book leads administrators on a journey that will be difficult for those instructional managers who historically have been rewarded for managing the forms of schooling. Administrators choosing to focus on the substance of schooling will enter classrooms and truly embark on a difficult path of discovering who they are educationally, what educational theories move faculty toward realizing valued ends of schooling, and how to build organizational capacity to support ambitious teaching. The pathways into classrooms are littered with decades of failed school reform initiatives. Entering the classroom—Becoming a Strong Instructional Leader—is our best hope to fully develop the creativity, intelligence, and competence of all children sitting in those classrooms.

Acknowledgments

For nearly 35 years, driving home from the schools I taught in and led as a principal, I was consumed with an ongoing conversation in my mind over this question: Why can't I make schooling more engaging for students? Contributing to the conversation were the voices of colleagues, family members, and students who helped me make sense out of my experiences in the classroom and main office and who shaped my journey toward becoming a strong instructional leader. My wife, Linda, deserves the credit for helping me understand that the lack of engagement of my students was actually a normal response of young people forced to attend institutions that paid little attention to their social and emotional needs.

My students at Du Sable Upper Grade School and Thornton Township High School taught me how difficult and complex a task it is to fully engage students socially, emotionally, and intellectually. Too often, I fell victim to the routines of moving a class through a lesson, but I did have those exceptional lessons that worked—when the bell rang and no student moved toward the door. These rare classroom situations sustained my belief in the vital role teachers could play in transforming the destinies of the students seated in front of them.

Early in my career as an administrator, I had the good fortune to work under four mentors who provided me with the knowledge and skills to become a Strong Instructional Leader. Maury Gladstone taught me how to teach; Steve Toth taught me how to control large populations of students; George Bieber taught me how to manage systems; and Richard Kamm taught me how to lead a school instructionally. Knowing how to teach, fostering safe school environments with buses that arrive on time, and supervising quality teaching are the fundamentals of strong instructional leadership.

Even with the fundamentals in place, I was continually pursuing organizational configurations that would transform a high school into an interesting place to learn. Again, I was fortunate to work with department chairpersons and administrators whose beliefs and knowledge about young people and teaching provided a template for transforming the constraints of institutional schooling. Gail Aronoff, Maura Bridges, John Highland, and Marianne Melvin helped me understand that instead of asking students to adjust to the routines of institutional schooling, I should make every effort to make the routines of institutional schooling work for students. Steven Arnold, Marjorie Appel, John Carter, Joe Crickard, Paul Junkroski, Tom McCann, and George Strecker provided me with the content and theoretical foundations for designing ambitious approaches to curriculum and instruction.

The lessons I learned from teaching and administering schools were reformulated and organized when I started teaching educational leadership courses at Saint Xavier University, Chicago. In my new role as a teacher and researcher, I was given the privilege of designing courses that provided the foundation for the principles of strong instructional leadership. The courage to believe that this new construct of school leadership had merit came from my graduate students who continually urged me "to write these ideas down someplace."

Writing the ideas down was the easy part. Formulating my experiences and ideas into a coherent guide for becoming a strong instructional leader can be largely attributed to Amy Daly. Amy played the vital role of editor-in-chief and a non-educator trying to make sense of how schools work from the inside out. Both roles were essential in formulating a logical argument for strong instructional leadership and making the argument readable for non-educators.

One message I hope to convey in this book is the importance of continually educating yourself in fields in which you have little knowledge. I learned this as a principal and have found that writing this book was no different. I was fortunate to be surrounded by colleagues at Saint Xavier University who provided technical assistance regarding topics in curriculum and instruction. I am particularly thankful to Jennifer Briody, Mary Campbell, Ann George, Michelle Sharpswain, and Maureen Spelman for taking time to critique my understandings of curriculum initiatives, described in this book, and to Mark Vargas and his library staff for patiently responding to every request for "just one more journal article." I would also like to acknowledge Maureen Sheehan for her expert attention to the details of preparing a manuscript for publication.

Finally, I deeply appreciate the editors of Teachers College Press for giving voice to ideas that challenge the current wave of accountability-driven reform initiatives. I am particularly grateful to Meg Hartmann, who patiently guided me through the long and often painful process of transforming many good ideas into a few well-argued ideas.

BECOMING A STRONG INSTRUCTIONAL LEADER

Introduction

Every school year begins with grand designs for reforming our nation's schools. National and state governmental leaders mandate new policies and goals for schools. National and state officials mandate new rules and regulations to enforce the new reform initiative of the day. Superintendents and principals vow to school communities that "no child [will be] left behind" in their school districts. The world of mandates, memos, and mission statements breeds a sense of optimism for finally raising the bar on student achievement.

There is another world of schooling far removed from the prescriptions of policy mandates and abstractions of mission statements. It is the world teachers occupy—the world of the classroom—a world that too few legislators and school administrators know enough about. While legislators and state education officers are busily sending out mandates, teachers are busy preparing their rooms for the coming school year. Teachers gather textbooks, copy worksheets and syllabi, and create seating charts—if the principal is nice, the first in-service day of the year allocates time for teachers to work on "getting to know you" activities in their classrooms. The freshly cleaned rooms, the new textbooks, and a new administrator in charge of discipline breed a sense of optimism that students will behave better and work harder when the school doors reopen.

Building administrators are also optimistic at the beginning of the school year. Newly designed systems appear to be working well, designated rooms were painted on schedule, and the addition of a reading coach should help test scores. There is little time, however, to think about how to raise test scores—after all, this is the beginning of the school year: We must assign lockers, process requisitions, assign rooms, and send out bus schedules.

Sometime in the early months of the school year, the sense of optimism filling legislative chambers, classrooms, and administrative offices begins to erode with a collision between the three realities of schooling in America: the reality of mandated instructional programs, the reality of classrooms filled with diverse learners, and the reality of administrative offices too busy with management tasks to pay any attention to the other two realities. The collision of these three realities of schooling sets off a chain reaction of dysfunctional behaviors: legislators frustrated with continuing low student achievement issue tougher sanctions for underperforming schools; local educational bureaucrats frustrated with continuing failed implementation of reforms issue rules and regulations mandating underperforming schools to reconstitute themselves or suffer the consequences (e.g., school closing, suspension of funding); and teachers frustrated with too few resources, too many kids, and too many theories engage in all manner of avoidance strategies to protect their classroom kingdoms from unwarranted and disruptive intrusions of yet another reform initiative.

Thrown into this perfect storm of low student achievement, tough accountability mandates, and tight budgets are school administrators charged with the responsibility of removing schools from watch lists, implementing ambitious reform initiatives, and accomplishing both goals with less money. Over the last 3 decades, legislators and educational bureaucrats have been calling for building administrators to assume control over their instructional programs. The reality of school administration, however, is quite different. School administrators are not paid to know a lot about curriculum and instruction; they are paid for timely buses, clean hallways, balanced budgets, accurate schedules, safe buildings, and contented parents.

The discrepancy between what school administrators are paid to do and what they ought to be doing is hidden from policymakers by superintendents, principals, department chairpersons, and all manner of educational specialists who "dance around the classroom." Administrators assume the role of instructional choreographers telling teachers to move here and there, to rehearse this and that, and making sure they see the latest dance move in the teachers' routines. Rarely do these directors of instruction partner with teachers on the classroom dance floor to make collective sense of contemporary theories and practices in the subjects they teach. School administrators readily admit they are spending too little time inside classrooms and too much time dancing around them. Administrators at every level of schooling want to become more involved in curriculum and instruction, but the demands of their positions allow them only a cursory view of what is happening on the dance floor.

There is some justification for the lack of instructional supervision in our schools. School administrators in today's schools are besieged by increased demands from public policymakers, special interest groups, teacher associations, and parents. At the same time, school administrators are working to resolve the larger problems of various school communities—they are expected to keep schools running smoothly and students under control, which means no lawsuits, no budget overruns, and no fights.

The mantras of "no time" and "no latitude" cover up two other realities of school administration that contribute to the lack of instructional supervision in our schools. First, solving management problems is satisfying. School administrators can feel a sense of accomplishment when they balance a budget, get the grades out on time, or complete a state report. Resolving a curriculum issue, working with problematic teachers, or implementing a theory-based instructional initiative is far less satisfying. *Instructional managers* oversee the certainties of budgets and boilers; *instructional leaders* oversee the uncertainties of curriculum and instruction.

Secondly, school administrators are woefully unprepared to understand, much less lead, reform initiatives in the complex and messy world of classroom instruction. University programs preparing future school administrators are dominated by "how to" approaches to managing boilers and budgets—paying scant attention to substantive understandings of curriculum and instruction (Levine, 2005). Given the uncertainties of supervising messy classrooms and the lack of academic preparation for understanding ambitious approaches to teaching and learning, it is no surprise that school administrators stay in their offices to deal with moving paper and materials and avoid changing beliefs and practices.

The inconvenient truth of school administration is that school personnel hired as instructional leaders are not students of curriculum and instruction. School administrators are employed because they manage school buildings well. This does not mean that school administrators have no knowledge of curriculum and instruction. They were teachers at one time and they attend conferences and workshops on instructional techniques and leadership. But do these prior experiences in the classroom and new instructional and leadership techniques actually provide them with the knowledge and skills to translate sophisticated educational theories into daily classroom practice?

Like the school administrators they charge with incompetence, policymakers also dance around the classroom. To use the metaphor originated by Larry Cuban (1984), mandates for school improvement have not disturbed the calm on the ocean floor (i.e., the classroom). Instead, policymakers spend a lot of time creating waves with new schedules, technologies, or programs, or by shouting from the shore that someone is drowning in a sea of low-performing schools. The beliefs, values, and practices controlling classrooms on the ocean floor remain untouched by those standing on the shore (i.e., lawmakers) and those churning water on the surface (i.e., school leaders).

Structure of the Book

Chapters 1 through 6 of *Becoming a Strong Instructional Leader* describe the internal realities of institutional schooling and the external realities of accountability-driven publics that prevent students from attaining authentic outcomes such as critical thinking, autonomous learning, and acquiring methods of inquiry for resolving problems. Few school administrators confront the aims of schooling. These aims are found by asking and answering philosophical questions: Why am I doing this? Instructional managers answer "how questions" well. Strong Instructional Leaders answer global questions well. The institutional schooling described in chapters 1 through 6 is a direct reflection of school systems consumed by implementing the technique or program of the day, with little or no reference to foundational questions in education. In schools without this foundation, there are no intellectual tools to critique a particular method or to gather together all the essentials of schooling (i.e., methods, routines, programs, and policies) into a coherent instructional worldview.

Chapters 5 and 6 provide a rationale for developing an educational philosophy—a strong instructional worldview—that provides a system of beliefs and vocabulary for a staff to make collective sense of substantial changes to the technical core of teaching and the daily routines of institutional schooling. Attending to the routines of institutional schooling keeps a school afloat but fails to steer the school in a particular direction. Chapters 1 through 3 analyze the failure of American schools to advance our students intellectually, socially, and emotionally.

Chapters 7 through 13 juxtapose two paradigms of instructional leadership. The widely accepted definition of instructional leadership, the one that policymakers promote and communities reward, equates school leadership to management: planning, directing, and monitoring, and improving the policies, procedures, and routines of institutional schooling—instructional managers handle these forms of schooling well. The other paradigm of instructional leadership, developed in chapters 7 through 13, views school leadership as an educational function: the ability to "purpose" schooling around a strong instructional worldview and to create the capacity, organizational configurations, and vocabulary for that worldview to be realized—performing the substance of schooling well. The process of becoming a Strong Instructional Leader is framed in a series of journeys: private, public, and situational.

The *private journey* requires a disciplined wandering back and forth between the fundamental questions of schooling (i.e., instructional worldview) and the theories and practices that govern instructional problems. Strong Instructional Leaders become experts in the art of weaving together loosely coupled systems of theories and practices into a recognizable mosaic of core teaching behaviors that make collective sense to a faculty and at the same time graduate students who possess the knowledge and skills to become productive workers and responsible citizens.

While developing an understanding of instructional problems is a private journey undertaken far from classrooms, the ultimate resolution of a particular problem occurs in classrooms. Before entering classrooms, Strong Instructional Leaders must persuade the school communities they serve of the worth and application of a theory-based instructional initiative. The *public journey* provides strategies (e.g., practical arguments, instructional narrative) for helping these communities to understand the rationale and implementation of a theory-based initiative. Embedded in these public presentations of ambitious approaches to curriculum and instruction are arguments countering unschooled beliefs about schooling that could impede or terminate the best thought-out plan for resolving an instructional problem.

The final destination of the private and public journeys of Strong Instructional Leaders is the classroom. The principle activity of the *situational journey* occurs when such leaders leave their offices and auditorium stages for locations where teachers practice their craft. Before entering teacher workspaces, Strong Instructional Leaders create environments where teachers have the resources, trust, and expertise to make sense of a theory-based instructional initiative. They initiate a series of conversations and educational moves to make sense out of theory-based pedagogies in workspaces inhabited by teachers who are at different places in their careers, coming from different experiences in classrooms, and working in particular school environments.

A Strong Instructional Leader must develop teachers who are masters. Master teachers are not artists or technocrats; they are individuals who engage in disciplined approaches to maximize their strengths in classrooms and who have a willingness to expand their teaching repertoire beyond comfortable habits of teaching. Cultivating master approaches to curriculum and instruction requires the skillful implementation of staff development programs that support teacher understandings and applications of a theory based reform initiative. By employing, training, and nurturing master teachers, administrators have the best part of the two paradigms of the teaching profession: the accurate representation of the form and substance of theory-based methods of instruction and the judgment to know when and how to pursue or discard a theory-based method.

The final chapter of *Becoming a Strong Instructional Leader* describes the qualities of leadership necessary to reignite the intellectual energies currently lying dormant in our schools. Being a Strong Instructional Leader is not about style, however, but substance: what you know, how you know it, how you communicate it, and how you execute it. The five qualities of leadership (passion, curiosity, discipline, entrepreneurship, and humility) generate the kind of focus, energy, and direction necessary for executing imaginative configurations of schooling—what schools *could* be.

A Conversation

A theme pursued in each chapter of this book is the underlying uncertainty governing reform initiatives and whole-school reform movements. The source of the uncertainty is the reality of agency in our schools: teachers, school administrators, educational researchers, and students all experience and act upon the world differently. Decades of reform initiatives flounder over the question of agency: how to develop common understandings and applications of instrumental (regarding techniques) and substantive (regarding valued ends of schooling) practices of teaching within school communities whose participants (school administrators, teachers, students, and parents) experience and act upon the world differently.

The last decade of school reform initiatives ignores the messy uncertainties of agents trying to make sense of the complex profession of teaching. These journeys into classrooms counter the uncertainties of educating a child with the certainties of policies, programs, and policing. Each "certainty" treats agency as a rational problem of declaring clear objectives (i.e., standards), applying scientific research methodologies (i.e., teaching scripts), and testing outcomes of applied scientific teaching models (i.e., standardized achievement scores). Rational reform initiatives transform intelligent subjects (i.e., administrators, teachers, and students) into passive objectives—to be managed, scripted, and tested.

Strong Instructional Leaders view agency very differently. Simply put, they acknowledge that fellow administrators, the teachers they supervise, and the students enrolled in their schools experience and act upon the world differently. Each chapter in this book describes the journey such leaders undertake to make sense of agency in our schools: a process for developing common understandings and practices among the different realities inhabiting our schools and, ultimately, pursuing an agreed upon instructional worldview.

The foundation for authoring a common purpose among individual agents in our schools is what I call the conversation. A good educational conversation is defined in this book as an exchange between practicing educators that

- interrogates current instructional methodologies in
  light of a perceived instructional problem;
- clarifies differing interpretations and resolutions
  of an instructional problem;
- establishes common instructional frameworks (e.g., vocabulary,
  metaphors, exemplars) for understanding a reform initiative;
- reflects on problems associated with implementing a reform initiative;
- responds to the moral question: Why should we care about this subject?

The conversation assumes that agents learn best in school environments where administrators and teachers regularly come together to author a new instructional reality. Authoring instructional realities cannot be mandated, regulated, or scripted. Common understandings and applications of ambitious approaches to teaching and learning only happen in workspaces where teachers and administrators talk over, act upon, and reflect about uncertain theories of teaching and learning.

Chapters 1 through 5 end with a series of prompts designed to draw teachers into conversations authoring new instructional realities. Embedded in these instructional conversations are discourse moves (i.e., listening, presenting, framing, responding, reframing) culminating in a message authoring a new instructional reality and defining a school's instructional worldview (see Figure I.1). Each conversation evokes an argument within oneself over the answers to the fundamental questions of schooling and, ultimately, transforms personal understandings of an instructional problem into public demonstrations of the form as well as the substance of a reform initiative. If done well, each conversation brings a measure of certainty to the uncertainties of classroom teaching. If done really well, the conversation infuses moral meaning (i.e., valued ends of schooling) into the daily routines and practices of classrooms brimming over with agency.

**Figure I.1. Authoring a New Instructional Reality:
Steps to Solving Instructional Problems**

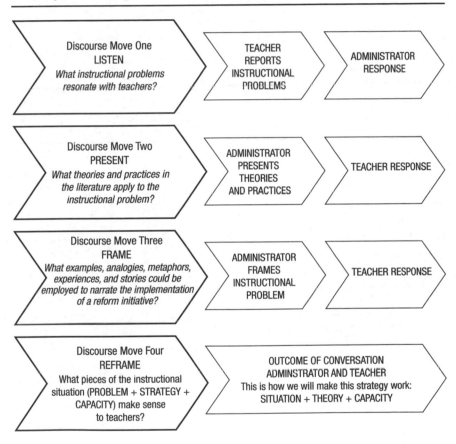

1

The Dance Around
the Classroom

School reformers agree on the vital role leadership plays in developing a quality instructional program. While acknowledging the importance of instructional leadership, school administrators continue to "dance around" the classroom. This chapter describes the dance moves made by four dance participants/participant-groups—a teacher, a department chairperson, a superintendent, and future school administrators—in the process of becoming "absentee landlords" to the classrooms they are supposed to supervise.

Where Is Alicia?

At the beginning of the school year, Alicia Lopez's principal asked her to become the bilingual coordinator for the elementary school in which she taught. Although Alicia had had no training in school administration, she was bright, energetic, and passionate about supporting students enrolled in her school's ESL (English as a second language) program. Alicia was conflicted about leaving the classroom. However, she felt that the role of bilingual coordinator offered her an opportunity to have a greater impact on second language learners in her school. To be effective in her new position, Alicia would have to spend most of her school day working in classrooms with teachers and students. From a research perspective and from a leadership perspective, Alicia's new position was, in administrative jargon, a "slam dunk."

While Alicia was busy enrolling second language learners, introducing herself to teachers, ordering appropriate materials, and designing workshops, the administrative team in Alicia's building was already overwhelmed by the managerial tasks required to get the school year off to a good start. There were not enough administrators to answer phones, talk to parents, direct secretaries, or take care of the crisis of the day. No matter how early or how late administrators in Alicia's building worked, they seemed to fall further and further behind. The customary response to chronic shortages of administrative staff is to look around the building for nonteaching personnel "who could probably handle a few more jobs."

Dance Move One: Other Assigned Duties

The duties nonteaching personnel ought to be doing are listed in job descriptions. What they really do on a daily basis is stated in the last sentence of their contracts: "other assigned duties."

Within a month of the school year starting, Alicia found herself supervising safety patrol officers, maintaining attendance rosters, and overseeing the state testing program. None of these functions was listed in her job description, but each consumed a significant portion of Alicia's time—time that she could have spent monitoring the placement of second language learners, working with teachers on instructional problems, talking with parents about their children's progress, and creating administrative policies and procedures responsive to the cultural backgrounds of Hispanic students.

By October of the school year, students in Alicia's program were floundering. Classroom teachers were frustrated with high failure rates. Administrators were concerned about high absenteeism rates. Teacher referrals were piling up on Alicia's desk. Few Hispanic parents attended the first open house. Where is Alicia? She is NOT in the classroom. She is NOT working with teachers or with the students in her program. If Alicia is not doing her job, what is she doing? Alicia is doing an excellent job of supervising the placement of safety patrol officers, maintaining attendance records, and preparing teachers for the upcoming state testing program. But her newly assigned responsibilities leave little time for supervising teachers and monitoring the progress of second language learners. In Alicia's own words, "It takes a lot of time making sure everyone is on the right corner."

Alicia learned that it was not a good idea to complain about the "other assigned duties." She also learned that her performance as bilingual coordinator had nothing to do with her knowledge of bilingual education. Alicia regretted her inability to see those kids, talk to parents, and help teachers. Alicia felt better about leaving the classroom behind when her principal assured her that newly assigned duties protected the school from lawsuits and brought in more funding for her program.

Dance Move Two: What Gets Managed Gets Done

Managerial tasks always assume priority over supervision of curriculum and instruction.

Alicia's initiation into the world of school administration is not unusual. A visit to any school finds nonteaching personnel spending significant time engaging in managerial duties having no direct relationship to classroom teaching. While still new to her position, Alicia learned an important lesson of school administration: Her bosses paid little attention to her supervisory functions; they paid a lot of attention to her ability to efficiently perform managerial tasks—what I have named the dance around the classroom (see Table 1.1).

Table 1.1. A Conversation: Dance Moves—*Where Is Alicia?*

	LISTEN	RESPONSE	LISTEN
Discourse Move One: LISTEN	"Our students cannot speak English. I thought our bilingual coordinator was going to help us with our ELL students?"	"I will direct Alicia to examine the data on ELL achievement scores."	"We know what the data say: Our ELL students cannot read or comprehend our textbooks or understand what we are saying in class."
	PRESENT	RESPONSE	PRESENT
Discourse Move Two: PRESENT	"Studies of ELL student performance do point to a body of literacy strategies assisting ELL students with comprehension."	"Oh please, no more one-day workshops on reading strategies. We need more Spanish-speaking aides."	"Studies find that smaller class sizes and a purposeful staff-development program are more effective than adding aides to classrooms."
	FRAME	RESPONSE	FRAME
Discourse Move Three: FRAME	(Instructional Narrative) "I decided to take away all of Alicia's administrative duties and assign her full time to assisting teachers in ELL classrooms. These duties will include spending specified times in classrooms and implementing an after-school staff-development program."	"What about reducing class sizes? Those after-school workshops are a waste of time. We are tired. Why can't we do more on our planning periods and work on strategies when we are fresh?"	"I just do not have the budget to reduce class sizes. However, I will look at the schedule for common planning times and talk to the district about late arrival times."

(continued)

11

Table 1.1. (continued)

Discourse Move Four: REFRAME	REFRAME	RESPONSE	REFRAME
	"After reviewing our staffing allocations, I am able to employ one additional teacher to help with the class-size problem, and beginning next month teachers will have common planning times. Alicia has designed a staff-development program that she believes can be implemented during common planning times."	"We appreciate reducing our class sizes and letting us work together in teams. But we need our planning periods to plan, not work with Alicia on ELL comprehension strategies."	"The schedule and instructional strategies Alicia designed spend little time on direct instruction during common planning periods. The focus of the professional-development program is coaching teachers in classrooms."

THIS CONVERSATION RESULTS IN THE FOLLOWING MESSAGE:

We recognize that recent demographic changes in our district are creating a need for significant changes in the way we teach reading and writing to ELL students (SITUATION). Alicia Lopez, our bilingual coordinator, has designed a staff-development program aimed at coaching teachers on reading strategies supporting ELL students' transition to English (THEORY). We plan to accomplish our goals by reducing class sizes at targeted grade levels, establishing common planning times for staff development, and freeing up Alicia's schedule so she can spend all of her time coaching teachers in their classrooms (CAPACITY). We believe in an inclusive school where the backgrounds of all students are respected and where we nurture the talents and abilities of all students (VALUED END OF SCHOOLING).

"Get My Daughter Out of That Class!"

Administrators, students, and parents all agreed that Joe Flynn was the best English teacher in the building. Not only could Joe talk at length about the theories and ideas informing his teaching, but more importantly, he brought these theories to life in his classroom. Joe began his classes with scenarios and problems teenagers cared about. Joe provided time and group structures for students to discuss possible strategies for resolving the problem posed at the beginning of class. Because the problem he posed was a common concern of the age group in his class, students were drawn into group deliberations. When Joe called a halt to group discussions, students were given ample opportunities to exchange solutions during whole-class discussions.

Joe's classes were not free-for-alls. Joe crafted discussion formats requiring students to adhere to certain rules of discourse: Students were expected to respond to different viewpoints in a respectful manner and provide evidence for claims stated in class. Joe's ultimate instructional goal was discovering pathways into works of literature eliciting the same themes found in a scenario or problem posed at the beginning of the week.

It was a joy to observe Joe's class. Students were intelligently talking to each other about themes in literature. Students in Joe's classes developed the habit of supporting their opinions with references to reputable sources. From a supervisory perspective, what made Joe's classes significant was observing how a teacher drew a group of teenagers into substantive discussions over interpretations of a piece of literature.

Although Joe readily admitted he still had a lot to learn about creating thoughtful discussions, he, like Alicia, felt passionately about helping other English teachers develop strategies for providing teenagers with opportunities to talk intelligently about enduring themes in literature. Apparently, Joe's experience in the classroom was very different from what was going on in the rooms of his colleagues. Few conversations with fellow English teachers ended without complaints about the symptoms (e.g., not doing homework, socializing at inappropriate times) of the traditional, and failed, stand-and-deliver teaching model.

It was inevitable that Joe's classroom teaching would come to the attention of his supervisors. Joe was young, but in the words of his immediate supervisor, he possessed all the tools to become a great department chairperson. At the end of the school year, Joe's dream was realized—he was named department chairperson for the English department.

Dance Move Three: Novice Supervision

Administrators with the least amount of experience are assigned the most responsibility for supervising classroom instruction.

Joe's first department meeting went well. His colleagues appeared receptive to his thoughts on thematic instruction, the selection of literature representing the cultural makeup of the student body, and problem-based learning. While Joe missed teaching full time, he felt good about how his colleagues were responding to his ideas about teaching literature.

The only troubling event in the first week of school was that the phone messages were piling up in Joe's mailbox. Most of the phone messages expressed a concern about Jeff Martin, one of the teachers in Joe's department. When Joe called parents back, he was subjected to a blistering critique of Mr. Martin's classroom performance. Each complaint contained the same comments about Mr. Martin's teaching: He is cruel, unfair, boring, and/or sarcastic. Each conversation ended with the same demand: Get my daughter out of Martin's class or I'm going to the superintendent. Joe decided that before returning any calls he would take a look at Mr. Martin's classes. Parents were not the best judges of quality instruction.

"Jeff, would it be okay if I sat in on one of your classes tomorrow?"

"So Joe, you are beginning to get the phone calls."

Joe was a bit startled by Mr. Martin's response.

"Yes, Jeff, I have."

Mr. Martin motioned Joe into his classroom.

"Joe, the first thing you need to understand is that this is a no-nonsense department. All of us maintain high standards. Just because students have gotten all A's in their other classes doesn't mean they automatically receive A's in my class. Students are expected to work in my class. Unlike in the rest of this school, in my class there is no free lunch. My past evaluations have commended me for maintaining rigor in my classrooms. Joe, if I could make a suggestion, call those parents back and tell them what I just told you, 'There is no free lunch.'"

Dance Move Four: No Trespassing

School administrators should stick to managing the building or whatever they do in their offices and leave classrooms alone. The classroom domain is considered a sacrosanct realm in schools: Teachers expect administrators to enter classrooms in short visits resulting in positive evaluations.

Joe stayed for 2 days in Mr. Martin's classes. It was a terrible experience. Joe's clinical experience left him unprepared for the lessons he observed. Mr. Martin was not cruel; he was boring and unfair. Honor students were being subjected to a teaching script placing strong emphasis on recitation, completion of worksheets, and questioning techniques asking students to guess what was on the mind of Mr. Martin. The real tragedy of Mr. Martin's classes was in the treatment of students attempting to change his teaching script. Mr. Martin turned away student questioning with the curt reminder: "We can't get bogged down here. Quarter exams are next week."

Joe needed help with Mr. Martin. It took several days for Joe to schedule a meeting with the principal. When Joe sat down with his principal, Joe was left with the distinct impression that the principal wanted neither to discuss Mr. Martin's classroom performance nor take action regarding it. As the conversation progressed, Joe received the subtle message that it would be in his best interest to quiet parents' complaints and leave Mr. Martin alone. Joe's meeting with the principal was a short one. Within minutes, the principal's secretary was knocking on the door. Joe, like Alicia, now understood that his performance was directly related to his ability to "dance around the classroom."

Dance Move Five: The Means Are the Ends
The goal of personnel in central offices is managing processes.

Mission Statements with No Mission

Karl Crawford was the superintendent that the Maplewood Board of Education was searching for. Dr. Crawford's vision for the district included all those qualities board members felt had been missing in the former superintendent. In his interviews, Dr. Crawford stated his strong belief in collaborative working environments where teams of administrators, teachers, parents, and students reached consensus over the challenges confronting schools in the 21st century.

Dr. Crawford hit the road running. Within a month of signing a contract, he initiated CATS—Community Action Teams for Strategic Planning. Letters of invitation to join a strategic planning exercise were sent to all stakeholders in the district.

After a 3-day retreat, the strategic planning committee developed a mission statement and 32 goals for Maplewood Community High School District. At the closing meeting of CATS, Dr. Crawford proudly introduced a PowerPoint presentation displaying the mission statement and the goals. Paw prints replaced bullets for each goal, and leaping out of each corner of the mission statement were animated cats. Stakeholders followed flickering paw tracks from one goal to the next. As the last paw track faded from the screen, lights were switched on. Dr. Crawford walked onto the stage wearing a construction helmet with a giant cat fastened to the front of it. He stepped forward and announced to the gathering, "We are on our way." Stakeholders seated in the auditorium began applauding. Members of the CATS team stood in unison repeating the slogan: "We are on our way."

Maplewood's new mission statement, like all school mission statements, is composed of a list of educational aims—what schools ought to be doing. Maplewood committed teachers and administrators to diversity; to foster lifelong learning, excellence, critical thinking, and technological literacy; to deliver a strong extracurricular program; and to promote continuous improvement and world-class standards. From a political perspective, which was Dr. Crawford's perspective, Maplewood's mission statement was a sure thing. The stakeholders felt good about the process of authoring the mission statement; they felt that a personal belief about schooling was mentioned in the mission statement. The problem with Maplewood's mission statement lay not in the agreed-upon aims, but in the inability of anyone, including Dr. Crawford, to articulate how agreed-upon aims are achieved in classrooms.

Dance Move Six: The Execution Gap

"Organizations don't fail when it comes to ideas, they fail when it comes to execution."

(Richard Wagoner, CEO, General Motors)

What Dr. Crawford used was an effective public relations tactic. But he failed to accomplish the construction of an instructional strategy for implementing agreed-upon tactics—what educators call a philosophy of education. A *tactic* is a process or a means. A *philosophy* formulates a coherent vision of teaching and learning—what happens in the classroom agrees with what is stated in the mission statement—aims agree with tactics.

Dance Move Seven: The Mission of Schools

The "dance around the classroom" is the mission of the school.

Unschooled Administrators

Midway through reviewing the syllabus for a course in curriculum and instruction, a student in a graduate program in school administration asked me the following question: "Dr. Jones, who is Ralph Tyler?" I turned to the rest of the class and asked, "Who is Ralph Tyler?" No one responded to my question. Instead, a student asked another question, "Who is Jerome Bruner?" The works of Jerome Bruner, along with Ralph Tyler, were required reading for the course.

The questions being posed by these students would be analogous to the question "Who is Plato?" being posed by students in a graduate philosophy class or to the question "Who is Einstein?" being posed by students in a graduate physics class. Professors in graduate programs in philosophy or physics would be alarmed if students were unfamiliar with seminal thinkers in their discipline. However, I was not shocked by the inability of students in my class to identify Tyler's or Bruner's contributions to the field of curriculum and instruction. After teaching for 5 years in the program, I rarely found students who knew these curriculum theorists or why they were important in educational pedagogy.

Dance Move Eight: Dancing in the Classroom

Administrators know little about the theories and practices serving as the foundation for the profession of teaching. Deficits in knowledge of curriculum and instruction are compensated for by perfunctory performance of instructional responsibilities: checking lists of observed/not observed teaching behaviors; inventorying and distributing instructional materials; and preparing agendas for half-day workshops.

The Bargain Struck Between Administrators and Teachers

The four vignettes introducing this chapter illustrate why school leaders dance around classrooms. Administrators may be too busy (Alicia), too timid (Joe), too politically motivated (Dr. Crawford), or too unschooled (graduate class in curriculum and instruction) to effectively engage in purposeful approaches to supervising classroom instruction. School years begin and end with administrators busily choreographing the *dance moves* described in this chapter. The goal of each dance move is what Seymour Sarason (2004) terms "the bargain" that school administrators strike with teachers: If you don't bother me, I won't bother you. The essence of the dance, Sarason observes, is that teachers really do not want school administrators who are instructional leaders—what teachers really want are good managers—and that good administrators don't interfere with daily classroom instruction; they spend their days keeping materials moving, parents at bay, kids in line, and services flowing for failing students.

The essential flaw of the dance is removing school administrators from the realities of classroom instruction. As the school year progresses, the distance between what teachers experience in classrooms and what busy managers think is happening in classrooms grows wider and wider. At some point during the school year, teachers become frustrated with administrative policies that bear little relationship to what is happening in classrooms, and school administrators become frustrated with teacher excuses for poor student achievement (Sarason, 2004). Administrators respond to their frustrations regarding student achievement by devising better supervisory mouse traps. Teachers respond to their frustrations with "absentee landlords" (p. 139) by performing dog-and-pony shows. The resulting dance around the classroom creates schools in which, in Sarason's words, "There is an appalling lack of anything resembling serious discussion of what is learning, the meaning of that word, or the concept that has formed them" (p. 139).

Becoming a Strong Instructional Leader

Today's schools are in trouble. Not the trouble the media report on or politicians tell their constituents (e.g., guns, drugs, gangs, low test scores). Focusing on these problems in our schools camouflages deep political, social, and economic forces that segregate our schools, our neighborhoods, and the future of our children behind the rhetoric of equal education opportunities for all children and the vocabulary of business accountability measures (i.e., test, inspect, and reconstitute).

But this book is not about the political, economic, and social forces that have given rise to our troubled schools. No matter how many different resources various communities pour into their schools, there is "little actual teaching" going on in American classrooms (Tharp, 1993). What is going on in American classrooms is a ritualistic dance between teachers, students, and school administrators. Teachers assume their positions on the dance floor by standing in front of classrooms and transmitting large amounts of information. Students partner up with teachers by sitting quietly at their desks completing large quantities of homework. The dance stops at the end of the week when students leave the dance floor to take a large test. The dance resumes early on Monday morning with teachers telling students that a large number of them failed Friday's test. The dance continues with teachers increasing the pace of the dance in order to cover large amounts of subject matter.

Administrators are rarely seen on the dance floor. After starting the dance, school administrators disappear behind office doors to manage the forms of schooling. The office doors remain closed until the end of the school year, when administrators re-emerge on the dance floor with grand moves for next year's dance.

What can change a system of teaching the goal of which is testing how much of the transmitted content can be regurgitated and a system of learning the goal of which is passing a test, obtaining a high grade, and earning a diploma—a school system designed more for "doing school" (Pope, 2001) than pursuing disciplined approaches for solving human and physical problems on our planet? The national debate on the "crisis in education" looks for answers in rigorous content, high professional standards, schoolwide reforms, and stiff accountability sanctions. By any measure, the last decade of rigor, silver-bullet reforms, and restructuring schools has failed to produce graduates, either at the high school or the university level, capable of solving the profound problems confronting an increasingly crowded world that is speedily competing for scarce resources and global markets. The remaining chapters in this book offer an alternative vision for our troubled school systems: a prescription for the development of Strong Instructional Leaders. What makes this new leadership construct distinctly different from traditional definitions of instructional leadership is a true commitment to building an instructional agenda devoted to generating the intellectual capacity to think well and dispositions to empathize with the pain and humiliation of others. These goals alone would satisfy most educators, but Strong Instructional Leaders go beyond the classrooms and schools they lead to deliver a message that deflates accepted ways of the seeing the world and have the courage to voice oppositional messages in an educational climate more attuned to examining test results than developing a passion for learning.

2

The Conflict Between Institutional Schooling and the Practice of Teaching

Administrators, teachers, and students spend their days in schools stuck between the uniformity of institutional schooling and the practice of teaching that requires flexibility and sensitivity to uniqueness. Administrators sitting in offices become focused on control and the management of the manifestations of schooling: schedules, grades, credits, and the awarding of diplomas. Teachers standing in classrooms designed to efficiently deliver large amounts of information in short periods of time carry out school routines. Students completely drained of emotion and meaning, seated in classrooms, respond to the daily routines of sitting, listening, and taking tests by doing school. Working in schools designed to only produce manifestations of schooling creates a daily struggle to personalize the daily grind of teaching.

Welcome Back to School

Sometime in early July, our nation's teachers open up a letter from their school districts with the heading "Welcome Back." Teachers refer to the "Welcome Back" letter as "the letter." The letter always begins with the same theme: "Change is in the air" or some other metaphor signifying a "new beginning." Teachers skip over the new beginnings of the letter—too much educational terminology saying little about the classrooms they teach in. Teachers' eyes focus on the last sentence of the last paragraph of the letter—it is in this sentence that the starting date of school is stated. After noting the starting date on their calendar, the letter is thrown on the top of a desk filled with textbooks and planning guides. Time still remains to get to that desk—it's only the first week in July.

The thoughts running through a teacher's mind in those remaining weeks of summer have nothing to do with new beginnings. Teachers are weary and wary, as they have already experienced many new beginnings. School administrators hope that a new discipline program, a new strategic plan, a new consultant, a new schedule, and/or a new grading system will somehow transform the "daily grind" (Jackson, 1968) of teaching into the kind of profession they expected when they entered student teaching: a profession in which their intellectual growth would be fostered and students would leave their classrooms with an enthusiasm for learning and a desire to know more about the subject they taught. The reality of the classrooms they teach in, however, quickly displaces the aims of intellectual and professional growth with routines and techniques designed to control the behavior of large groups of students. The school districts employing them talk a lot about innovative teaching techniques and developing 21st-century thinkers. Yet performance is judged on teachers' ability to efficiently carry out myriad accountability mandates.

The irony invoked by the new beginnings listed in the letter (and now published in several glossy pamphlets found in the opening-day packet) becomes stark in auditoriums on opening day. Teachers sit with their colleagues studying class lists while administrators stand on stage quoting John Dewey. On the first day of school, teachers do not want to hear about new beginnings—those preservice ideals have long since faded. Teachers want to know about the particulars: what students are assigned to their classrooms, what subjects they will be teaching, and what textbooks they will be using. Opening day for teachers is all about particular policies and procedures to help them keep order and cover subject matter—it is nothing about presentations promoting the initiative of the day.

The divergence between what administrators proclaim on opening day and what teachers experience in their classrooms lies with the professional aim of developing an instructional program sensitive to the individual personalities and abilities of children and, at the same time, executing the institutional functions that ensure all individual personalities sit quietly in classrooms conforming to a uniform model of learning. Each decade, teachers and school administrators adopt a variety of instructional strategies and configurations designed to solve the problem of accommodating the individual dreams, interests, and capacities of children within institutional arrangements valuing measurement, documentation, and standardization. The inherent conflict between the practice of teaching and the institutional goals of schooling becomes even more precarious when educational goals (the ability to analyze, synthesize, evaluate, and communicate knowledge) are usurped by institutional requirements to grant a credential, report high test scores, and ensure admission to well-respected colleges.

All teachers are left with in schools that are designed for students to succeed without really learning (Labaree, 1997) are techniques founded on carrot-and-stick approaches to learning. "Do what I say, or I will hurt you" works well in instructional environments where personal understanding and meaning are beside the point. Institutional settings reduce teaching to a ceremonial function: Teachers tell students to sit down, be quiet, and listen to lesson presentations; students take notes, directions, and tests. There is no place in this ceremony for the nuances of a profession founded on subtle deciphering of human intentions, feelings, and emotions. In essence, teaching in an institution is not an art; it is not a science; it is merely accounting.

The Futility of Discipline Codes

My first job in a school was as a middle school–study-hall monitor. I thought the part-time–study-hall position advertised by the local middle school would be a valuable learning experience for someone enrolled in a teacher training program.

My interview with Mr. Schmidt, the middle school principal, was brief. He was not interested in seeing my transcripts or my application. He asked only two questions: first, "Where are you from?" (I am positive the first question originated from a Midwesterner's difficulty in understanding my Long Island accent) and second, "Did you wrestle in high school?" (A friend of mine, who also worked in the school, recommended me to Mr. Schmidt. My friend confused high school track with high school wrestling.)

My responses to the questions seemed to satisfy Mr. Schmidt and he gave me a tour of the study hall and an orientation. The orientation, like the interview, was a short one. I was given the rules of the study hall and the following directive from Mr. Schmidt: There were NO exceptions to the rules. "Young man, there is a saying around this school, 'control with Schmidt.' The teachers know that if they follow the rules, I will enforce them. I control this building and I expect you to control this study hall. Never forget that your job is to keep these students quiet in their seats doing school work. Do you understand?"

Before walking me to the entrance of the building, Mr. Schmidt stopped by his office and picked up a referral pad. "I developed these forms last year. The teachers love them. They're easy to fill out. All you have to do is carry around these pads, not a lot of papers in a folder. Just check the right boxes, drop the referrals off in my office, and I will deal with the student that day."

Admittedly, even for the 1960s, Mr. Schmidt was a little rough around the edges. His fixation on student discipline, however, remains an obsession among school administrators. From their very first pep rally, school administrators learn the importance of keeping student populations under control. Parents, board members, superintendents, teachers, and students judge a school leader by how safe and orderly the building feels. Nothing is more threatening to a building administrator than the perception by a superintendent, the staff, or parents that students are out of control.

When a school community believes students are out of control, a call goes out for stricter rules and stronger punishments—a discipline code that students will take seriously. School conduct codes are designed to gain compliance with the purposes and routines of institutional schooling—not to enhance the social, emotional, and intellectual development of young people.

The fixation on controlling student populations is founded on the belief that students are not to be trusted to do the right thing, behaviorally or academically. To combat the behaviors associated with the natural dispositions of young people, school administrations formulate long lists of rules and consequences managed by administrative personnel. Efficiently managing a school discipline program not only becomes a preoccupation of school administrators, but also the sole topic of conversation among the teaching staff. In the eyes of teachers, effective administrators are managers who run a tight ship. Administrators who run a tight ship deal quickly with student referrals, strictly follow the discipline code, and remove repeat offenders from classrooms—forever. Mr. Schmidt was not much of an instructional leader, but in the words of a lead teacher in the building, "He is the best principal in the county."

Student discipline concerns do not diminish because school communities view student discipline as a management problem, not an instructional problem. School administrators who manage student discipline generally resort to two strategies for resolving discipline problems. The first strategy is founded on the belief that discipline problems are caused by deviant personality traits. Students disciplined in this model are turned over to an educational specialist who "cures" abnormal personality traits. In clinical schools, teachers become diagnosticians; administrators become coordinators of support services.

The second strategy does not focus on the cause of discipline problems, but rather on the impact they have on institutional measures of school performance: dropout rates, test scores, or absentee rates. Students disciplined in this model are subjected to programs that market the school's ability to move one of these data points up or down. In these data-driven schools, teachers become accountants and administrators become instructional managers.

Most school administrators have not been trained nor have they acquired the academic background to critically examine the structural, curricular, or pedagogical conditions causing children to resist the institutional goals and routines of formal schooling in the United States. Instead, school administrators and teachers continue to search for the sources of misbehavior in the individual pathologies of students or *quantifiable* outcomes of institutional schooling. Both perspectives completely leave out the personal beliefs, personal goals, and personal satisfactions (Olson, 2003) of students. In an era preoccupied with managing abstract measures of schooling or developing efficient ways of diagnosing and placing students in special programs, administrators find little time to talk to students about their day-to-day experiences in schools, to write curricula designed to achieve the instructional goals articulated in "the letter," or to develop pedagogies designed to stimulate the interest and curiosity children bring to classrooms from outside the walls of schools (Csikszentmihalyi, 1997).

The reality of discipline codes is played out every day in various administrative offices. Sitting in the principal's office, students offer three explanations for violating the discipline code: (1) they sincerely did not know they were violating the code; (2) they feel the disciplinary process is unfair; or (3) they had a good reason for committing the infraction. No matter how well defined the discipline code is, each response (1, 2, or 3) throws the situation into gray areas between the institutional tendency to suppress individuality and the normal developmental needs of young people to express individuality. Administrators spend enormous amounts of time splitting the difference between kids being kids and institutions being institutions.

"Doing School"

Throughout my career as a high school principal, every dinner conversation was consumed with discussions about the problems I was encountering leading a large comprehensive high school. My wife, who was also a school administrator, was the perfect person to bounce ideas off of. She helped me see connections between the theories of schooling I felt passionate about and how they might work in the real world of schooling. While my wife and I talked, my two children sat in quiet boredom listening to "more school talk."

In the midst of one of these dinner conversations, my son made a comment crystallizing for me how students view schools in the United States. I cannot remember what I was saying about schools, but I do recall my son saying in exasperation, "Hey Dad, it's high school." If I could paraphrase my son's succinct analysis of secondary education in America, it would go something like this:

> Dad, relax. Stop getting so upset with student apathy toward learning, teacher indifference towards professional growth, the misplaced priorities of parents, the political moves of superintendents and Boards of Education, and all the athletic events you have to attend. High school is all about what happens before and after school, during lunch time, and between periods and on weekends. It has nothing to do with what happens in classrooms. Students understand this; teachers understand this; parents understand this. The only one that doesn't seem to get it is you—so lighten up, it's only high school.

My son's glib analysis of schooling in America masks a deep divide between the realities of contemporary classroom learning and the kinds of schools students would like to attend. Rarely does the literature on school reform examine the divide between adult and student perceptions of what a good school looks and feels like. In the eyes of students, schools designed for success employ "teachers who care" (Phelan, 1992, p. 698) about them and behave in ways that "acknowledged" them as "worthwhile individuals" (Phelan, 1992, p. 698). Students say they learn best in classrooms where teachers allow them to work in groups and openly discuss their feelings and perceptions; students express dissatisfaction with classrooms where they sit all day and "simply read from textbooks" (Phelan, 1992, p. 699). Students look for teachers who are patient and willing to provide additional explanations and help for the rough patches in class. Most importantly, students want adults throughout the school to respect and empower their individual talents, abilities, personalities, and cultural backgrounds (Phelan, 1992).

The list of qualities students would like to see in the schools they attend can be reduced to one recommendation: We learn best when our emotions and affiliations are considered to be as important as our intellectual development (Phelan, 1992). There were moments in the history of U.S. schooling when educators made valiant efforts to formulate curricula and school configurations accommodating the social and emotional as well as the intellectual development of the child. These educators, however, were unable to stand up to the vocational and social mobility goals of schooling. Not only were these brief interludes into educating the whole child quickly discarded by efficiency-minded administrators, but the theories and practices associated with progressive approaches to schooling received the unshakable label of being too soft to produce graduates who could compete in a global economy (Cremin, 1961; Kliebard, 1987). Instead of John Dewey's hope for democracy in education, policymakers and school administrators opted for a configuration of schooling more conducive to producing a compliant workforce and avid consumers.

How do young people survive in the barren wastelands of schooling in America? They "do school" (Pope, 2001). Returning to my son's experience in high school, he astutely figured out how the school system worked and played it well. The system works something like this: attend class; figure out what the teacher wants from you; smile at the teacher; take notes; hand in homework; participate in after-school activities, and always remember—adults are never wrong. In my son's mind, it would be naïve to enter school systems anticipating interesting classes, passionate teachers, thought-provoking assignments, and preparation for the real world of work (see Table 2.1).

Forms Versus the Substance of Schooling

Parents legitimize institutionalized schooling by paying little attention to the substance of schooling (can my child read, write, and think well) and a lot of attention to the manifestations of schooling (grades, credits, diplomas, and placement in high-status programs). When parents call principals about their child, the topic of conversation is about a manifestation of schooling (e.g., my child's placement in the gifted program). Most parents don't ask questions about the substance of schooling (e.g., what goes on in the gifted class). Daily conversations carried on by parents and children about schooling reinforce the emphasis on the manifestations rather than the substance of schooling. Children know their parents seldom ask questions about what content they were working on in class that day or about what teaching practices were used to work on the content, and they rarely look at actual work samples brought home from school.

Conversations about school turn serious when a child is not "doing well" in school—is getting low grades, isn't handing in assignments, has missed criteria for admission into an advanced program, or has failed to earn enough points to receive a specified grade in an advanced class. The intention of these conversations is

Table 2.1. A Conversation: "Doing School"—Students Are Not Listening to Us

	LISTEN / PRESENT / FRAME	RESPONSE	LISTEN / PRESENT / FRAME
Discourse Move One: LISTEN	**LISTEN** "Students today are not listening to us. All they listen to are their cell phones and iPods. They don't do their homework, don't take notes, and don't attend regularly. We need rules that will begin to hold students accountable for paying attention in class and completing school work."	**RESPONSE** "We are educating a generation more attuned to a media environment. I am concerned about our failure rates and the general lack of engagement of our student body. We have a cell phone policy and our deans have become more aggressive with students who disrupt class."	**LISTEN** "Well, the deans and the cell phone policy have helped, but students are not paying attention in class and just don't read or complete assigned work."
Discourse Move Two: PRESENT	**PRESENT** "What you are experiencing in your classrooms is not abnormal. Studies of student engagement throughout the country are discouraging. The question becomes: Will more policies and sanctions work? Every year we try a new discipline policy, but by November we are overwhelmed with referrals. Should we continue down the policy/punishment road or should we begin looking at our instructional program?"	**RESPONSE** "It's always our fault, never the students' fault. Students need to be held responsible for completing work and coming to class prepared. We need rules and consequences that have some teeth in them."	**PRESENT** "Individuals become responsible when they are provided meaningful options. Studies of schooling in the United States document schedules, course sequences, and instructional methodologies that provide students with no options except to sit quietly for 6 hours a day, take notes, and take tests. The way we do schooling is a recipe for the oppositional behaviors you are experiencing in your classrooms."
Discourse Move Three: FRAME	**FRAME** (Instructional Narrative) "During the summer I brought in our Pupil Personal Services (PPS) team and department chairpersons to discuss our instructional program. Two outcomes of these meetings were (1) we need a purposeful approach to working with students who are chronically causing problems in your classes and (2) we need to look honestly at the way we organize, present, and assess the subjects we teach."	**RESPONSE** "Finally, something is going to be done about chronic behavior problems. We need more than just some 'problem solving approach' to student discipline. We need to get tough. There is too much to cover and kids are overwhelmed, but with all these state standards and testing, what else do you expect?"	**FRAME** "Our PPS team developed an intervention approach that will be more user friendly for you and hold students and parents more accountable for behavior plans we draw up. I have always stated that we should not allow state mandates to control our instructional program. As professional educators, we need to reflect on how we organize and deliver subject matter and begin a process of designing curricula that are meaningful to students."

(continued)

Table 2.1. (continued)

	REFRAME	RESPONSE	REFRAME
Discourse Move Four: REFRAME	"In addition to changes to our approach to chronic offenders of school policies, I asked the district to devote the remainder of our in-service days, and I allocated 3 more half-days to departmental assessment of our instructional programs. I have already received funding for summer curriculum writing projects aimed at increasing student engagement."	"We are always the ones that have to make changes. What about parents and students?"	"All of us agree: Our students are different today. We can continue down the discipline road with more rules and consequences or we can travel a different road where we do school differently. The first approach is not working; you and I know that. Administratively we need to provide you with the capacity to organize and deliver instruction that draws students into our classrooms rather than spending all of our energy trying to prevent students from escaping from our school."

THIS CONVERSATIONS RESULT IN THE FOLLOWING MESSAGE:

We recognize that students entering our schools today are products of an entertainment culture containing and presenting messages more meaningful than the world we work in (SITUATION). We work in a world of symbol systems, theories, and concepts that are abstract and difficult to acquire. The goal of education is to make us more thoughtful, more responsible, and more human (VALUED END OF SCHOOLING). Our problem is how to make this abstract symbol world we inhabit more meaningful for our students. We know enough now about how to organize and deliver instruction in more meaningful ways (THEORY). Our plan for the coming years at our school is to provide you with the time, materials, expertise, and organizational configurations to draw students into our classrooms, rather than push them out (CAPACITY).

not to find out whether their child is receiving a quality education but rather how to comply with the institutional forms of schooling in order to make their child more competitive. A quality education, for consumers of schooling, is defined as obtaining high grades in the right programs. Good schools, according to consumers, prepare their students for the right colleges. Administrators are in the difficult position of resolving the discrepancy between mission statements promoting responsible citizenship and productive workers and schools organized to prepare students to compete for grades and diplomas.

When schooling becomes a commodity, the two most important people in a school become the dean, whose role is to keep the losers (i.e., those who do not cooperate with their assigned social status in school) in line, and the registrar, whose role is to accurately record how much of a commodity the winners earned (i.e., credits, grade points). Both of these roles become less important in schools where school leaders and teachers routinely interrogate their practices: "What should be the substance of classroom events that could be categorized as education?" This question, however, is seldom asked in a school system designed to certify the future movers and shakers in our society.

How do school administrators lead in schools where parents value the management of the forms of schooling over the supervision of the substance of schooling? In the words of a colleague of mine, "Feed them well and show up to all the games." This comment reveals a reality of school administration: Administrators are never fired because they know little about curriculum and instruction; administrators are fired if they do not perform the forms of schooling efficiently—getting grades out on time, organizing the open house well, and attending *all* extracurricular activities. Parents repeatedly reminded me of this reality of schooling when I arrived at a game or school event: "Dr. Jones, so good to see you. You know, Dr. Baker (principal from another high school) attends every game—even away games." That was the community's reminder of where I should be spending my time. The official reminder came from the superintendent's evaluation of my performance: "Al, the board likes your academic orientation, but would like to see you become more involved with our extracurricular program."

At the extremes, parents care most about a principal who knows the latest award their son won, knows how their daughter's team is performing, and speaks knowledgeably about a sport's offenses and defenses. Superintendents care most about a principal who runs a tight ship and can effectively mediate parents seeking favored status in schools organized to award privileged positions to a limited number of students. Parents pay little attention to what a principal knows about the substance of schooling—what goes on in classrooms; they pay a lot of attention to how well a principal helps their child with the forms of schooling—securing admission to the gifted program.

In fact, the safest career move for school administrators is managing the forms of schooling. Supervising the substance of schooling is risky for administrators in commodity-driven school systems. Putting aside the risks of developing meaningful pedagogies and curricula, school administrators pay a heavy price emotionally and professionally for challenging the institutional, cultural, and political norms of schools designed to pick winners and losers in the academic race. School administrators secure their jobs by standing on stages bestowing awards on the winners. Administrators place themselves in less secure positions when they stand in front of boards of education proposing a fairer playing field for the losers.

Failed Approaches to School Leadership

School administrators work in school landscapes populated with teachers constrained by accountability-driven schools, students bored by the daily grind of schooling; and parents valuing facades of schooling. They experience firsthand what I call the No Man's Land of school administration: the social, emotional, and intellectual fallout from teachers sitting in auditoriums checking class lists, students "doing school," and parents striving to be winners in an academic arms race. The boundary lines of the No Man's Land of school administration are drawn around the minute-by-minute conflict between teachers' and students' expressions of individuality (i.e., feelings, values, and behaviors) and control mechanisms designed to ensure conformity with institutional goals of schooling (i.e., high grades, diplomas, and orderly schools). School administrators understand that any decision made in No Man's Land, no matter how well reasoned, will be looked upon by some group as wrong. If administrators side with the institution, teachers consider them to be ineffective. If administrators side with teachers, superiors consider them to be ineffective. If administrators side with the students, teachers and superiors consider them to be ineffective.

School administrators survive in No Man's Land by adopting one of four approaches to instructional leadership. In the first scenario, they become an "absentee landlord" (Sarason, 2004): You don't bother me and I won't bother you. Absentee landlords spend their days dancing around classrooms. Teachers in schools led by absentee landlords exert a tremendous amount of intellectual and physical energy trying to make sense of goals, programs, and ideas that are vague, conflicting, and poorly implemented.

In the second scenario, they adopt the belief that bureaucratic approaches to schooling will increase student achievement. Instructional technocrats take this approach and fill their days viewing student data, managing the efficient administration of the state testing program, reviewing scripted lesson plans, and implementing the latest state mandate. Teachers in schools led by instructional technocrats spend countless hours mapping curricula, aligning lesson plans with state standards, staring at hundreds of data points, and making sure their rooms and lessons compare favorably with checklists carried into classrooms by visiting administrators.

In the third scenario, they split the difference. The literature on organizational behavior names this strategy "situational leadership" (Hersey, Blanchard, & Johnson, 1996). At the end of the school day, some administrative decisions benefit the institution and some decisions benefit learning. Teachers working in schools led by situational leaders see issues bargained, compromised, or, in some instances, swept under the rug.

Strong Instructional Leadership, the fourth scenario, is not satisfied with merely surviving No Man's Land, but in transforming the No Man's Land of school administration into intellectually engaging places to learn and manage. Such leaders believe that employees and students achieve optimal performance pursuing an instructional narrative that is compelling and nurtures individual talent. To "purpose" (Sergiovanni, 1996) a school means to restore meaning to what teachers and students do in classrooms. A school is purposed when valued ends of schooling (i.e., why teachers entered the profession of teaching) are embedded in valued means of schooling (i.e., the intersection of materials, subject matter, and pedagogy). The development and substance of this new construct of instructional leadership is the subject of chapters 7 through 13. What should be noted at this point about Strong Instructional Leadership is its dramatic contrast to the other leadership approaches described in this chapter. It is not a leadership tactic (e.g., hiding, enforcing, or bargaining), but a leadership strategy designed to optimize the individualities of teachers and students within the confines of institutional environments and to continually move the instructional conversation from a focus on the little problems of schooling to the big problems of schooling.

Big-Picture Thinking

Administrators, by their very position in the organization, are driven into "big-picture" thinking about teaching, learning, and organizational behavior. While administrative thinking may not be sophisticated in these realms, school administrators intuitively know that controlling student populations is a myth.

The No Man's Land of school administration, in reality, is the space in schools between what Quay (2004) describes as the big problems and little problems of life. Little problems in life are solved by using routines, practices, or techniques that worked in the past. Big problems in life and in school demand rethinking beliefs, values, and assumptions that proved effective in the past but have stopped working now. The cultural tools most amendable to answering big questions in life and in schools do not emanate from habitual ways of knowing the world but from employing abstract theories and principles to solve real-world problems.

Teachers frustrated with student absenteeism demand action from administrators, not theory talk. Action in schools translates into the implementation of techniques, programs, or sanctions to solve little problems in classrooms. The bigger problem lies in the question why are students cutting classes. Teachers have been heard to attribute class cutting to faulty adolescent personality (i.e., irrespon-sibility), biological traits (i.e., raging hormones), or social pathologies (i.e., unsup-portive home environment). From that quick diagnosis, faculties offer answers founded on causal relationships between desirable institutional traits (e.g., po-liteness and obedience) and the institutional goals of schooling (i.e., attendance, grades, and credits). Faculty meetings are testaments to the continuous transfor-mation of big problems into little problems, which in turn results in little answers: techniques, routines, or punishments.

As a matter of course, the technique of the day fails to stop class cutting (or other institutional violations such as inappropriate talking in class) and faculty members fault administrators who are too political, incompetent, or overwhelmed to rein in undisciplined students. The endless failure of routines and techniques to solve student disciplinary or achievement problems cannot be blamed on faulty implementation or weak administrators. The blame rests with an institutional culture that responds to big problems in teaching, learning, and our society with cursory bureaucratic responses: rules, routines, or processes.

School administrators know from experience that they are pawns in institu-tions designed for processing students rather than educating them. They know that stronger penalties and other little solutions offered by faculties won't work. In fact, they know from experience that the answers offered by faculty will, at best, have some short-term impact and, at worst, have a detrimental effect—the rule or procedure will further alienate students from school. What administrators do not know is why these bad things are happening to them—after all, they are nice people, they were classroom teachers, and they like kids. The little answer embed-ded in the occupational culture of administrators is to fault teachers—they are too experienced, inexperienced, cynical, selfish, or uncaring.

The big answer to "Why is this happening to me?" begins with a weak under-standing (Who is Ralph Tyler?) of disciplined ways of thinking about big problems of schooling—why are students cutting classes? Without theory, without academic understanding of an instructional problem, school administrators are unable to put into words and action the resolutions to big problems of schooling. Without theory, school administrators are reduced to implementing one technique of the day after another.

Strong Instructional Leaders possess a passionate desire to understand the big problems of institutional schooling and the courage to question the purposes and methods employed by school bureaucracies. They are not revolutionaries. They are pragmatists in the tradition of John Dewey. They understand very well that institutional schooling conforms to powerful social and cultural norms that his-torically have proven impervious to progressive reform initiatives. Such leaders develop the capability to nibble away at goals, pedagogical practices, and curricula that are antithetical to the ways children learn. At some juncture in the journey, this persistent nibbling away uncovers the original purposes of education and the organizational capacity to accomplish these purposes. The journey out of the No Man's Land of school administration rests with the answers to the large questions of schooling that I name "The Fundamental Questions of Schooling."

- How do children learn?
- What knowledge is of greatest worth?
- How should knowledge be organized?
- How should we assess what students know?
- How should we teach?

Working with faculty to develop common responses to the fundamental questions of schooling requires knowledge and skills that are rarely taught in educational administration programs and that are set aside in order to attend to the managerial tasks of school administration. Even if a practicing school administrator were inclined to follow the path of Strong Instructional Leadership, the beliefs and practices of bureaucratic schooling are formidable obstacles to resolving the big problems of schooling.

The Failure of Bureaucratic Schooling

At the turn of the century, John Dewey could not understand why his progressive approaches to teaching were not catching on in schools. Dewey believed he had made a compelling case for inserting the child back into the curriculum and the school back into the society. While some of Dewey's ideas found their way into schools, a survey of the educational landscape found most children seated in rows of desks listening to teachers talk at them about academic subjects that were far removed from the problems they experienced at home and in their neighborhoods.

Dewey's thoughts on the removal of the child from the curriculum and the isolation of the school from society appeared in a series of essays titled *The Educational Situation* (1906/1969). Each essay elaborates on Dewey's long-standing contention that the historical oppositions established between child and curriculum or school and society are false ones. Dewey attributed the artificial separation of children and schools from curriculum and society to the way schools in America were organized—what he termed the "machinery" of schooling (p. 24).

For Dewey, the machinery of schooling—the way schools organized themselves to deliver instruction—trumped all theories and practices working to make schools more human, more interesting, and more thoughtful. What Dewey came to understand, and what contemporary school reformers often forget, is that the Dance Floor matters. The machinery of schooling described in this chapter establishes a set of beliefs and practices valuing the efficient management of large groups of students and questioning the rigor of child-centered programs. An occupational culture and public worldview founded on theories and practices designed to manage students and manage instruction supports a paradigm of schooling characteristic of schools that educators currently teach and supervise in and that parents send their children to. A different occupational culture and public worldview of schooling evolves from schools in which the child is welcomed back into the curriculum and recognizes that schools are located in neighborhoods.

Reform initiatives designed to transform the symbols of institutional schooling (e.g., grades, subjects, and tests) have not fared well in the United States. In fact, just the opposite has occurred. Present state and national policy initiatives direct school administrators and teachers to enforce practices designed to grease the gears of the school machine. Dewey's lament about the form of schooling determining the function of schooling appears to be as true today as it was when he wrote *The Educational Situation* (1906/1969).

But what Dewey did not write about, and what today's school reformers pay little attention to, is the role school administrators who are Strong Instructional Leaders can play in transforming the symbols and practices of institutional schooling. Instead of thinking of school transformation as an outside job—to be handled by legislators, board members, and superintendents—educators must accept the charge that making our schools more human, more interesting, and more thoughtful will always be an inside job.

The key to successfully orchestrating the inside job of school reform does not lie in the knowledge and skills employed to manage the forms of schooling—what the literature calls instructional leadership (and what I call instructional management). Becoming a Strong Instructional Leader requires a wholly different regime of knowledge, skills, and approaches to leadership. The learning and leadership regime of Strong Instructional Leadership is the subject of chapters 7 through 13. Before leaving the calm of managing outside jobs for the turbulence of leading inside jobs, educators should fully understand what they are getting themselves into: that learning begins with finding out why teachers so dread receiving "the letter" announcing the beginning of the school year and why students "do school."

3

The Classroom

Larry Cuban uses the metaphor "calm on the ocean floor" to represent an established system of teaching in the United States—teachers talk a lot, students listen a lot—that has remained undisturbed by turbulent decades of school reform. The constancy of frontal teaching in U.S. classrooms is supported by definitions of rigor that promote a one-size-fits-all approach to curriculum and instruction. Administrators and teachers trapped on the ocean floor resort to classroom routines and the technique of the day to achieve some semblance of order in classrooms. Instructional managers are quite comfortable enforcing the routines of institutional schooling and implementing the technique of the day—their recipe for calm schools. Strong Instructional Leaders, on the other hand, believe that only by disturbing the ocean floor can we bring purpose and meaning to our nation's classrooms.

What does this "calm at the ocean floor" (Cuban, 1984, p. 2) look like? Goodlad's (1984) study of the instructional programs of 13 high schools remains, after 30 years, the best account of what Sarason (1982) terms the "regularities" (p. 96) of schooling in the United States. Goodlad's team of researchers found that the calm in Texas was the same calm observed in New York. The calm described in Goodlad's study of high school classrooms is a highly scripted performance that includes

> the teacher explaining or lecturing to the total class or a single student, occasionally asking questions requiring factual answers; the teacher, when not lecturing, observing or monitoring students working individually at their desks; students listening or appearing to listen to the teacher and occasionally responding to the teacher's questions; students working individually at their desks on reading or writing assignments; and all with little emotion, from interpersonal warmth to expressions of hostility. (Goodlad, 1984, p. 230)

The calm of the teaching script described by Goodlad reflects a larger system of teaching (Stigler & Hiebert, 1999), within which students and teachers play out highly prescribed roles: Students are expected to sit quietly and learn facts and conventional problem-solving procedures; teachers are expected to talk most of the time and distribute a lot of practice exercises and worksheets; and schools are expected to test often. The goal of "assign and assess" (Tharp, 1993, p. 230) teaching systems is to cover large amounts of subject matter in the shortest amount of time. Efficient content delivery systems deprive teachers of the time and activity settings for establishing emotional and intellectual connections with disciplined ways of knowing the world. Personal dispositions and inclinations of young people (i.e., beliefs, dreams, personalities, cultural understandings, and passions) are often disregarded in a crude calculus requiring schools to efficiently execute inputs (i.e., information, rewards, and punishments) in order to maximize outputs (i.e., test scores, graduation rates, college admissions). Teaching systems in accountability-driven schools draw upon a set of beliefs about learning that systematically remove the social and emotional components of learning from the intellectual—in effect, children vanish before the eyes of teachers and school administrators. When students vanish in classrooms, so do passions that teachers bring to the subjects they teach and the personal give-and-take necessary for translating passion into disciplined ways of thinking about the world. Here are short versions of the educational beliefs that support the separation of the child from the curriculum:

- Learning takes place in the mind, not in the body.
- Everyone learns, or should learn, in the same way.
- Children are deficient and specialists should provide remedies.
- Everyone should learn the same subject matter.
- Learning takes place in the classroom, not in the world.
- Knowledge is inherently fragmented.
- Knowledge exists outside of the child.
- Schools communicate the truth.
- Learning is primarily individualistic.
- Competition accelerates learning.
- Paper and pencil tests are the fairest way to assess
  what has been learned.

The Daily Grind of Schooling

How do students respond to the "relentless monotony" (Goodlad, 1984, p. 335) and enforced conformity of crowded classrooms? One does not have to be an educational psychologist to see the disconnect between "the daily grind" of schooling (Jackson, 1968, p. 50) and the normal developmental needs of children and adolescents. Few children or adolescents become excited about learning in an environment that requires them to sit quietly in small desks and listen to teachers talk *at* them for 6 hours, requires them to complete highly uniform assignments, and subjects them frequently to judgment based on continuous testing (Jackson, 1968). In an organizational environment designed to control young people and accomplish institutional goals (i.e., grades, diplomas, high test scores), children and adolescents have three choices: They can conform, rebel, or "do" school.

Students who conform are rewarded handsomely by schools. Institutional schooling likes students who complete assignments on time, hand in homework, do not speak unless spoken to, and participate in extracurricular activities. Conforming students behave in ways (i.e., are quiet and obedient) that align perfectly with how formal schooling defines success (good grades) and defines deportment (good behavior).

Students who do school develop strategies for physically or mentally escaping from the daily grind of schooling. Students who do school view school as a game: figure out the rules and reward structures and then play the system. Showing enthusiasm for a class, developing a repertoire of plausible excuses, knowing the how and when of plagiarism, and understanding that teachers have too many students to thoroughly evaluate most assignments and that absences from classes must always be excused are all part of succeeding in school without really learning (Labaree, 1997). Administrators and teachers are blind to the difference between students who are doing school and students who are conforming. However, students who do school are known for skillfully manipulating a system that long ago displaced the ideal of becoming educated with the reality of earning a credential. The collateral damage of institutional schooling is the social, emotional, and intellectual detachment of large segments of our student populations from school environments designed to control them rather than educate them. Students who do school turn the tables on institutional schooling by controlling administrators and teachers and educating their peers on how to work the system.

Students who rebel suffer the wrath of the institution. Subtle forms of institutional wrath consist of bureaucratic processes and categories (e.g., ability grouping, remedial programs, classroom seating arrangements) that isolate and marginalize the talents, beliefs, and values of students who voice opposition to the routines and boredom of institutional schooling. The not-so-subtle expressions of institutional wrath are codified as policies and procedures removing students (either temporarily or permanently) from the student body. Each expression of institutional wrath is designed to prevent the behaviors and values of rebellious students from infecting the rest of the student body. More sophisticated expressions of institutional wrath find the rebellious child referred to a school psychologist for testing of personality traits that correspond well to sitting quietly, waiting in line, taking notes, and taking tests—the daily grind of schooling.

Ironically, behaving "normally" in school (i.e., sitting quietly, listening to the teacher talk, working individually at desks, taking tests) contradicts goals often expressed in a school's mission statement—lifelong learning, creativity, critical thinking, and passion for learning. While mission statements posted on walls call for innovative thinkers, the classrooms behind the walls call for obedience. Teachers and school administrators intuitively know that institutional definitions of normality correlate poorly with the personality traits, dispositions, and abilities children bring to school. The only value one could ascribe to institutionally sanctioned personality traits is preparation for the next institution in schooling and the rigors of contemporary schooling.

Standardizing Classrooms

The ideology of contemporary schooling is founded on toughness—good schools (really good schools) are rigorous ones. A rigorous curriculum is standardized and skill based. Rigorous teaching is about achieving control over student behavior and transmitting large amounts of factual knowledge through processes (drill and kill) that expect students to mimic (on a test) what their teachers said during the week. Rigorous administrators maintain high standards (dictated by the state or textbook manufacturer), run a tight ship, develop competitive extracurricular programs, and apply management techniques acquired from the private sector. Rigorous schools are highly stratified fortresses with plenty of levels, academic courses, grading, competition, and rules. Theories and practices challenging the norms of institutional schooling are not welcomed into rigorous schools.

While the public supports the idea of rigor and legislators pass mandates requiring more rigorous schools, few parents, policymakers, or educators question the prevailing definition of rigor or the consequences of pursuing the current definition of rigorous schooling. Rigor, as currently defined by legislative bodies, is reflected in the forms of schooling: graduation requirements, number of advanced placement courses, standardized-achievement-test scores, graduation rates, and dropout rates. The institutional definition of rigor is silent on centuries-old questions of the substance and the value of education: What does it mean to be educated? What knowledge is of greatest worth? What does an examined life look like? What habits of thinking mature social, emotional, and intellectual behaviors?

Defining rigor in terms of quantifiable forms of schooling makes sense to a public and policymakers schooled in systems within which the number of graduation requirements, the number of students admitted to college, and the scores on standardized achievement tests serve as the gold standard for measuring the quality of a school. Defining rigor by a publishable number mistakenly equates a means of schooling with an end of schooling. The transformation of a data point of schooling into a valued end of education inexorably reduces the complexities of teaching and learning to mechanical and routine practices that are easily observed and measured. None of these data tell us much about qualities of teaching that foster students who are more humane, more thoughtful, and more curious about the world they encounter each day.

Teachers are the natural casualties of the current definition of rigor and concomitant calls for higher test scores, higher academic standards, and higher standards of behavior. Data-driven schools demand data-driven teachers. Teaching to the test transforms a profession guided by intuition and inspiration into teaching guided by strict adherence to routines and aimed at achieving quantifiable outcomes. Artful teaching values idiosyncrasy, creativity, and unexpected outcomes. Scientific teaching values objectivity, predictability, and prescribed outcomes. Artistic teachers know they have done their job well when the diverse talents of the students seated in front of them have been optimized. Data-driven teachers know they have done their job well when the diverse talents of the students seated in front of them are reduced to predictable measures on common standards.

One cannot walk through the halls of a school today, read a popular educational journal, or attend a well-liked staff-development program without acknowledging which paradigm of teaching dominates contemporary schooling in the United States. The ideology of standards, summarized in the following text box, commands the hearts and minds of those who lead and teach in our schools. The demand for objectivity, measurement, and conformity permeates a discipline historically founded on a tradition of Socratic questioning, developing individual talents of children, inculcating a sense of civic responsibility, and the capacity to develop I-thou relationships in a global society.

The Ideology of Standards
- Goals of schooling are technical questions: how best to deliver a service or implement a program.
- Education is training.
- Knowledge is scientifically proven.
- Learning occurs when all students complete the same assignments at the same time with the same outcomes.
- Teaching and learning can be measured, predicted, and controlled.
- Teaching is management of children and curriculum.
- Curriculum development aligns course content with state standards and state testing instruments.
- A test measures knowledge.

When teachers express frustration with their profession, they evoke a crude causality between a particular measurable outcome of schooling (e.g., low reading score) and the failure of families, students, school administrators, or a particular technique to assist them with raising whatever number the school administration talks about on opening day. Teachers do not blame low reading scores on substantive matters of schooling: how children employ different reading strategies when they read and how children are attracted to different kinds of reading material. Teachers and school administrators assume the ideology of standards already answered these questions—which they have. No Child Left Behind translates the ideology of standards into a policy mandate requiring all children to achieve the same outcomes on common subject matter (state standards). Absent from this legislation is the recognition that children are different, determining what should be studied is a matter of interpretation, and the aims of schooling are contentious. Teaching in a system within which questions of purpose and meaning are rarely asked, and where the imposition of order on teaching and learning becomes the sole goal of schooling, reduces instruction to the proper selection of techniques that convince students that they are no different from their peers; that what they study is interesting; and that earning a credit or a place on the honor roll is a worthwhile goal.

When Students Vanish Before the Eyes of Teachers

In classrooms that have standardized the meaning and purpose of schooling, teachers are left with little else than techniques or management routines to control their learning environments. The popularity of make-and-take workshops and canned programs on behavior management, character development, or whatever we want kids to be hooked on, illustrates the illusive search by educators for the one best technique.

The ultimate fate of the technique of the day rests in the closets and storerooms of schools—the graveyards of techniques past and techniques present. What custodians and school administrators discover in these graveyards is a trail of boxes documenting programs that never delivered on advertised results. In the midst of expressing frustration with the latest failed technique of the day, teachers and school administrators habitually return to their mailboxes looking for pamphlets marketing the newest technique of the day—which leads to the most frequently asked question on opening day, "Didn't we try this before?"

The recycling of one technique after another is rooted in behaviors and methods that are disconnected from their theoretical ancestry. For example, researchers correlate wait time with the amount and quality of student responses; more wait time results in more responses. Teachers readily admit that increasing wait time does increase student responses. At the same time, these teachers quickly admit that the level of discourse in their classrooms remains quite low. The perceived failure of wait time to raise the level of thinking and discourse in classrooms cannot, however, be attributed to a technique. Wait time fails to raise classroom discourse because teachers fail to incorporate the technique of increasing wait time into a larger repertoire of teaching strategies grounded in a theory of learning: how children learn to read, write, ask higher-order questions, and understand the cognitive importance of classroom conversation (Richardson, 1990). What remains of pedagogy removed from theory is myriad techniques—or variables—floating around classrooms doing some of this and doing some of that but never really doing much of anything.

Without a learning theory, teachers develop routines imposing order on the mass of techniques flying around their classrooms, which is better than capricious implementation of one activity and technique after another. The imposition of a routine on a confused mass of techniques, however, is not a theory of instruction—it is merely a collection of methods. A theory of instruction, on the other hand explains the why of methods: What is an appropriate technique? In what situations should the technique be applied? What is the relationship between one technique and another technique? When is the technique not working? Why is the technique not working? The fundamental flaw in reform initiatives is fiddling around with workshops on the proper implementation of the technique of the day (e.g., learning centers, cooperative learning) rather than grounding a set of techniques in a larger theoretical framework (Richardson, 1990). The former approach aims at changing teaching behaviors; the latter approach aims at changing teachers' personal theories, beliefs, and attitudes about teaching and learning (see Table 3.1).

School administrators are as susceptible as teachers to adopting silver-bullet nostrums to remedy complex organizational and instructional problems. Central and building offices house similar graveyards of failed management techniques of the day: Total Quality Management; data-driven instruction; outcomes-based instruction. Some of these techniques contain processes and ways of thinking that could prove helpful for developing a quality instructional program. School administrators, like their peers in the classroom, however, proceed with one management technique after another without understanding the theoretical justifications supporting the technique and failing to incorporate the technique into a larger repertoire of management strategies.

Gang activity, bullying, or drugs, for example, are dangers to students and teachers and gravely threaten any instructional environment. Routinely, administrators confront such threats with a program (e.g., Character Counts), additional personnel (e.g., add a dean), or a gadget (e.g., surveillance cameras). When these techniques fail, school administrators routinely begin the cycle anew with requests for another program, additional staff, or a new gadget.

Research in social psychology, however, would offer a more inexpensive and effective strategy for reducing school violence. The theory of "unowned places" (Astor, Meyer, & Behre, 1999) found that adolescents will refrain from antisocial activities in locations owned by adults in the building (administrators and teachers). Administrators adopting the theory of unowned places design supervisory schedules transforming unowned places of a school building into owned places. Without theory, an explanation for why social phenomena happen, administrators wander with their counterparts in the classroom through a labyrinth of discarded programs, techniques, and gadgets.

Conventional understandings of instructional leadership view capable school leaders as individuals who gain control over teachers and students by the proper management of rewards and punishments and the efficient selection and implementation of instructional techniques. There is little room in established understandings of instructional leadership for school administrators who pursue purposeful approaches to problem-solving or adopting instructional systems connecting theories with everyday classroom practices.

Instructional leaders, or what I term instructional managers, along with their colleagues teaching on the "ocean floor," are uncomfortable with modes of inquiry requiring quantifiable and experimentally derived knowledge. A conscientious

Table 3.1. A Conversation: The Technique of the Day—We Have Tried Character Counts and Assertive Discipline but Nothing Seems to Work

	LISTEN	RESPONSE	LISTEN
Discourse Move One: LISTEN	"We need a behavior plan that works. Teachers throughout the building are experiencing more and more students who engage in disruptive behaviors. We have tried Character Counts and Assertive Discipline but nothing seems to work."	"We are experiencing more referrals to the principal's office for inappropriate behavior. As you point out, our discipline code and other programs we have initiated are not reducing disruptive classroom behavior. We are observing dramatic changes in behavior with our new alternative program and at certain grade levels that are experimenting with a more student-centered curriculum."	"Why can't we refer more students to the alternative program? It only takes one or two students to destroy a lesson. We have tried cooperative learning and several projects, but these approaches really take a lot of time. There is just too much to cover for the state exam."

	PRESENT	RESPONSE	PRESENT
Discourse Move Two: PRESENT	"We are all wrestling with the age-old problem of how to motivate young people in an institutional setting. For decades, schools have continued to employ discipline codes and behavior programs to control student populations. As you point out, discipline plans and the technique of the day do not work. What do work are school environments where students feel included, respected, and engaged in meaningful learning activities. All three qualities are present in our alternative program."	"The alternative program has only 16 kids enrolled with one assigned teacher's aide. We don't have the luxury of allowing students to study what they want at the pace they want. We need a room where we can send disruptive students so we can get on with our lessons."	"What we are all experiencing are students who see little meaning in what they are doing and feeling that the talents they bring to school are not valued. Many of our students consider our school a hostile environment. Our emphasis on high standards, coverage of subject matter, and elimination of elective offerings has turned students against us. Why come to a place where you are expected to sit and listen for 6 hours a day and where no one seems to care much about what interests you or what is going on in your life?"

	FRAME	RESPONSE	FRAME
Discourse Move Three: FRAME	(Instructional Narrative) "Last year I asked a team of consultants to conduct an audit of our instructional program and overall school environment. At the exit interview, the team made three recommendations: (1) Administratively we should include more students in our extracurricular program; (2) we need to reexamine a curriculum that is a mile wide and an inch deep, and (3) the configuration and instructional strategies developed in our alternative programs should be expanded to include other struggling populations in our building."	"We have been asking for the expansion of our alternative program. More kids are looking for something to do after school. With the amount of information called for on the state exam, how can we possibly cut topics out of our curriculum?"	"Our assistant principal has researched different approaches to including more students in the life of our school. At our next faculty meeting, I will present our program for welcoming the multiple talents of our student body. Beginning in the spring, I will organize teacher teams to reexamine the breadth and depth of our curriculum in each subject area. This summer I have asked two subject-matter teams to participate in a workshop on problem-based learning. The goal of these workshops is the implementation of several problem-based instructional units for the coming school year."
	REFRAME	RESPONSE	REFRAME
Discourse Move Four: REFRAME	"All of us in this room are worried about state test scores and subject matter that is not engaging our students. We also admit that the same old approaches to discipline and trying to trick kids into learning is not working. I believe that by providing a more participative environment for our students and a curriculum that is engaging, we will achieve the goal of high test scores and, at the same time, create a school environment where students feel they personally belong."	"This seems like a lot of work. Our entire curriculum is built around the content on the state test. We do not have the materials or school schedule to accommodate problem-based learning. All this talk of depth and breadth is nice in theory, but where do we find the time to design these units? We still have those few disruptive kids in our classes."	"I would agree with you that what I am proposing is ambitious and requires a lot of hard work. But what we are doing is not working, and doing it harder will continue to aggravate our situation. In the short term, I will pursue additional alternative classrooms to help you with those students who are interfering with classroom instruction. In the long term, our goals are to involve more students in the life of our school and to make our curriculum more meaningful to them."

THIS CONVERSATION RESULTS IN THE FOLLOWING MESSAGE:

Our focus on test scores and the technique of the day have created an instructional program that alienates our students. Each day you face students who see little meaning in what they do in classrooms and experience no outlet for the talents they bring to school (SITUATION). We work in an institutional environment valuing compliance and ability rather than thoughtfulness and effort (VALUED END OF SCHOOLING). Our problem is how to transform a system of schooling based on rules and routines into an instructional system based on personal meaning and interpersonal relationships (THEORY). Our plan for the coming years at our school is to provide you with the time, materials, and expertise to develop curricula that are more engaging and with organizational configurations that value the diverse talents students bring to our school.

effort to think and work scientifically in schools continually collides with the "daily grind" of schooling where actions always speak louder than words. Science and practice are shaped by different worlds: the scientific world of observed regularities and natural laws and the practical world of the vagaries of human conduct. The disjuncture between these two worlds becomes personal when teachers try to apply a generalized theory of instruction to particular children in particular classes. Understandably, school administrators and teachers rely on past experience and routines to make sense of events and behaviors that defy quantification.

However, without a conceptual explanation of how a specific combination of people (teachers, students, administrators, and parents), materials, methods, and environment (classroom and community) come together to form a learning organization, school administrators are left with no intellectual tools to restore meaning and purpose to the schools they lead. Without theory, school administrators remain managers of the daily grind of schooling.

Creating Schools with a Purpose

From a leadership perspective, it would appear we have reached an impasse. On one side of the schooling divide we have bureaucratic schooling founded on an ideology of control and accountability valuing compliance, prescribed routines, measurable outcomes, and a business discourse of inputs, outputs, and efficient resource management. On the other side of the schooling divide we have learning organizations founded on an ideology of reflection and continuous improvement valuing innovation, purpose, thoughtfulness, inquiry, and an educational discourse of development, interest, and joy.

The resolution of this division between bureaucratic schooling and the human side of schooling lies with how administrators and teachers think about their actions in schools. Reflection, the core value of a learning organization, is not the kind of thinking you find in bureaucratic schooling. Managerial approaches to reflection merely require some process and venue to determine if a technique, a policy, or a procedure is working. In a learning organization, reflection is the ability to differentiate between the real world and what one believes about the real world. Reflective managers focus on how a technique, policy, or procedure is achieving a predetermined (unquestioned) goal of the organization. Reflective practitioners (Schön, 1983), which include what I call Strong Instructional Leaders, possess the capacity (dispositions, ways of thinking, and proficiency in a variety of disciplined ways of thinking) to see how others in their organization view the world and orchestrate common understandings of the meaning and purpose of that world. They view schooling from the bridge of the ship rather than the ocean floor. Reflective managers treat students, teachers, parents, and curriculum and instruction as objects that must be manipulated to achieve the forms of schooling (grades, diplomas, etc.). Reflective practitioners treat students, teachers, and parents as individuals—subjects—who enter schools with individual interpretations of the meaning and purpose of education. Leadership in schools where meaning and purpose (subjectivities) replace order (objectivities) requires intellectual tools and interpersonal skills to develop common understandings (as opposed to consensus) around the "Fundamental Questions of Schooling."

School administrators who decide to become Strong Instructional Leaders acquire a distinctly different set of intellectual tools from those who choose to remain instructional managers. Managing curriculum and instruction and controlling large groups of students demands organizational and interpersonal skills that efficiently implement routines and procedures. Great managers are rewarded for directing and monitoring what is already in place. By knowing the rules, attending to detail, reducing tasks to procedures, persevering, and negotiating, an instructional manager "gets things right." They may, however, not be the right things to get right.

Strong Instructional Leaders, on the other hand, assume responsibility for "purposing" a school (Sergiovanni, 1996). Doing the right things in schools (purposing) requires the ability to create the capacity, the vocabulary, and the organizational configuration for the aims of the organization to be realized in the daily functions of employees and the student body. In addition to developing common understandings of the meaning and purpose of schooling, such leaders replace habitual ways of responding to instructional problems with thoughtful methods of inquiry and disciplined ways of knowing the world.

What the leader must know and how this knowledge looks in action are subjects described in chapters 7 through 13 of this book. Suffice it to say that Strong Instructional Leaders become expert at what Joseph Schwab called the "arts of eclectic" (1978, p. 328). What Schwab meant by this term lies in his proposition that the possessor of only one theory or a series of similar theories (the ideology of standards, the machinery of schooling) experiences tunnel vision in a world of radical pluralism. Thus, he and other contemporary organizational theorists call for practitioners with knowledge and skills to wisely select fragments of theories, methods of inquiry, and practices from a wide array of disciplines to solve the evolving problems accompanying the growth of complex organizations and societies.

4

The Diversions of School Administration

Rather than confront the complexities of improving classroom instruction, often administrators choose to spend their days on the diversions of schooling (e.g., paperwork, public relations, bents, parents, student discipline, personnel, central office, mandates, and violence). In an educational system that values form over substance, the choice is not a difficult one to make: Doing diversions is valued by school communities; doing curriculum and instruction is viewed as a sideshow.

While teachers are busily applying the technique of the day, school administrators spend their days moving from meeting to meeting, solving crisis after crisis, taking phone call after phone call, and attending one school event after another. Even teachers, who often question administrative decisions, honestly admit they are very busy people. Behind the meetings, the phone calls, the crisis of the day, however, is a pattern of behavior adopted by administrators that results in avoidance of curriculum and instruction. The avoidance of instructional supervision leads to a focus on the diversions of school administration. The following is a list of tasks that divert administrators from the role they were ostensibly hired for—that of instructional leader.

Public Relations

The literature on school administration in general would vehemently disagree with listing public relations as a diversion. Researchers and the administrative community have a mythic belief in the power of newsletters, supervision of extracurricular activities, and open houses to energize the school communities they serve and to symbolize all that is good about the schools they lead. In reality, standing at athletic games, sending out professional-looking newsletters, and putting on a welcoming open house has nothing to do with developing instructional programs that foster students who read better, write better, or think better. In the words of a former colleague of mine, public relations is nothing but "smoke and mirrors." School administrators learn early in their careers that parents equate public images of good schools (winning teams, honor rolls, a student going to Harvard, new computer lab, number of AP classes) with quality instructional programs. This belief is reinforced by the fact that the movers and shakers in the community (a small percentage), including school board members, have children who are involved in one or more of these activities. The preoccupation with public relations is codified in the criteria listed in administrator-performance documents and routinely appears as one of the top three goals established by boards of education for the superintendents they employ.

This is the dilemma of the public relations diversion. If school administrators pursue public relations with the dedication expected by the communities they serve and the supervisors evaluating them, they have less time to engage in the kinds of reading, writing, thinking, and supervising necessary for developing a quality instructional program. Strong Instructional Leaders find ways to minimize the time they spend on public relations and transform public events and pronouncements into opportunities to communicate a narrative that contains a compelling instructional message.

Systems Problems

No school runs well if buses are late and hallways are dirty. Administrators are never fired for not knowing a lot about curriculum and instruction. Administrators are fired when grades do not go out on time or students regularly find themselves in the wrong classes. Grades go out on time and hallways are kept clean through systems (schedules, procedures, and technologies) designed to accomplish routine organizational functions efficiently. It would appear that the management of systems is a fairly straightforward affair requiring little attention from school administrators. If systems were only about schedules, procedures, and technologies, they could be left alone. But no system runs by itself. Systems require humans to set the wheels in motion and make sure the wheels are greased and stay pointed in the right direction. No matter how clearly tasks are defined by a system, personnel in charge of the system will understand the goals and the functions of the system differently from what was originally determined. There is nothing bad about this reality—it is just humans being humans. In fact, most of the time the efficiency of the system is enhanced by modifications initiated by personnel whose proximity to the system provides them with unique insights into how to make the system run better.

Even in the best circumstances, however, systems lose their effectiveness at the hands of the most well-intentioned employee. The typical system malfunction originates with an employee whose "better way of doing things" serves his or her needs better than the aims of the school. It is normal behavior to lose sight of the big problems when working all day on little problems.

Closely supervising the little problems that keep the buses running on time is a consuming task but a gratifying one. In the uncertain environments of schools, it feels good at the end of the day to point to some tangible process that is working well—"Yes, Dr. Smith, the grades went out on time." Systems management, however, becomes a diversion when school administrators become enchanted with the details of each system—tweaking details here and there. "Not only did the grades go out on time, but I negotiated a great deal on the grading forms we are us-ing." Tweaking the details of a system not only consumes a lot of administrative time, but removes school administrators from classrooms and positions them in offices, storerooms, central offices, and vendor sites. In places far from classrooms, school administrators spend their time talking to clerks, custodians, business managers, and salespersons. Little time is left to talk to teachers in places where teaching occurs.

Strong Instructional Leaders view systems management as an opportunity to further the instructional aims of their schools. They purpose systems in two ways. First, they understand that no system is neutral—a system can either work for or against teachers and students. They tailor all systems to support student learning. Designing systems for teaching and learning is no easy matter in schools configured to further institutional goals rather than create inviting learning en-vironments. Buses, for example, can arrive at the cost-effective time of 6:30 a.m. (another district offers to share the cost resulting in early pick-ups), or they can arrive later in the morning when students are conscious.

Second, such leaders employ every venue in a school, including systems, to communicate their instructional agenda. The principal's secretary, as well as the night custodian, can embody the educational goals of a school or sabotage the best intentions of a mission statement. This is especially true of clerical staff whose appearance, manner, and way of handling problems communicate seriousness about teaching and learning. Listening to clerical personnel interrupt classes to announce the fall homecoming schedule would not occur in schools where in-structional time is considered sacrosanct. Well-performing systems are vital to supporting a quality instructional environment. More importantly, however, all systems serve teaching and learning.

"Bents"

School administrators are born and raised with interests and aptitudes (bents) that they pursue over a lifetime. Some excel at academic work, some at athletics, and some at music. Schools are fertile grounds for the development and expres-sion of bents. When school administrators enter school buildings in the morning, they can choose to walk to the athletic director's office, design a newsletter on their computer, or talk with the maintenance foreman. School administrators quickly justify these wanderings by pointing to the need for a new football coach, a new newsletter format, or a new tractor. There is no end to the number and variety of bents school administrators think are important to managing a school well. Bents satisfy two longings of school administrators. First, they serve as a respite from what they see as the daily grind of schooling. Second, they allow administrators the satisfaction of skillfully performing a task well. Both longings can easily lure school administrators away from the uncertain world of classrooms into the cer-tain worlds of locker rooms and maintenance garages.

The bent of Strong Instructional Leaders is curriculum and instruction. They understand that culturing a school building begins and ends with where and how they spend their time. They spend their time around classrooms talking to teachers about what they are most passionate about—teaching and learning. If a teacher in a building was asked by a stranger what the principal cares most about, such leaders would expect the following response: "Teaching is all this principal cares about."

Parents

In my first position as a school administrator, my mentor took me into his office and stated the first rule of school administration, "Whatever you do in this school, never leave the building without returning parent phone calls." No school administrator would disagree with my mentor's first rule of administration.

Parent phone calls fall into two categories: (1) Your institution is hurting my child—do something about it and (2) my child needs a favor from the institution—please do something about it. Administrators expend enormous amounts of time fixing systems that are not working for students, talking to personnel who are not working for students, or negotiating special adjustments for a student in special circumstances. In fact, typical administrators feel a sense of meaning and accomplishment when they end the day knowing they had a hand in making the institution work for kids and their parents. Good fixers, however, can become parachute administrators—"Give me a parent request and I will jump in and solve it."

Although an administrator may become very good at parachuting, his or her actions can undermine two fundamental principles of a learning organization. The first principle of knowledge organizations assumes that the personnel closest to an organizational problem (teachers) are in the best position to understand and fix a problem. Teachers who see parachutes in the air stop taking responsibility for resolving classroom problems. In buildings led by Strong Instructional Leaders teachers do not look up in the air for help but to themselves and their colleagues for solving problems in their classrooms.

The second principle of knowledge organizations views parachutes in the air as a symptom of a weak organizational culture. Employees in weak cultures are unsure about the goals of the organization. Teachers in weak cultures react to the problem of the day with the solution of the day. Strong Instructional Leaders develop cultures in which teachers and support staff are clear about what is important in their school (e.g., teaching, learning, treating staff and students as intentional agents) and how these priorities look in hallways, classrooms, and administrative offices. They are rarely diverted by parent phone calls because a staff member closest to the situation assumed responsibility for the problem and made the right decision.

Personnel

Teaching is a relatively isolated activity. Once the classroom door shuts, teachers are left alone to ply their trade. Despite little hints of teacher incompetence, for the most part, teachers believe that all their colleagues are doing a great job in the classroom. New administrators are quickly disabused of this perception in their first disciplinary meeting with a former colleague. No program in school administration prepares future administrators for face-to-face encounters with the consequences of poor health, poor lifestyle decisions, or poor professional decision-making.

Unlike the other diversions on the list, there is no strategy for minimizing the time devoted to personnel problems. Humans will be humans—they require attention. The emotional turmoil accompanying the efforts of school administrators to resolve a human misfortune often masks a dilemma peculiar to personnel problems in schools. At some juncture in working with a personnel problem, school administrators are confronted with the question: Do I act in the best interest of kids in this matter or do I act in the best interest of the teacher? Non-educators would view this question as a no-brainer—of course you act in the best interest of students. Inside schools, however, the obvious answer to the question is obscured by a culture expecting school administrators to employ extraordinary efforts to save a teaching career—even if that means sacrificing a couple of weeks (months or a year) of classroom instruction. Teachers feel good about administrators who save teaching careers. Teachers do not feel good about administrators who end teaching careers.

Administrators are inclined, especially in cases in which teachers have no control over what is happening to them, to piece together a course of action moving a teacher through a rough patch in their life. In the process of determining a course of action in personnel matters, Strong Instructional Leaders are vigilant in protecting the sanctity of classroom instruction. A day with a substitute teacher is not the same as a day with their regular teacher. A day with a teacher whose pedagogy is compromised by a personal problem is never recovered. A day during which a teacher endangers the well-being of the students in her class is unacceptable. Strong Instructional Leaders are intent on making sure that the misfortunes of personnel in their buildings do not become the misfortunes of the students in their classrooms.

Mandates

In the last decade, politicians from all parties and ideological stripes have placed their solution to the problem of low student achievement in their arsenal of talking points. Politicians know that comments on education are low risk (who could disagree with another test) and high value (who does not want to outscore Japan on mathematics). The weapon of choice for state and national policymakers is the mandate. Every year, policymakers require school administrators to divert their attention from the classroom and focus on their pet peeve of the day: drugs, water safety, obesity, abstinence education, or flag etiquette. Tacked on to the mandate of choice for the new school year is always a new test to be taken, collected, boxed, and sent to some multimillion-dollar–testing conglomerate.

State and national mandates assume a high position on the list of diversions because attached to each mandate are sanctions (loss of funding or loss of accreditation) for noncompliance. Sanctions can never be taken lightly by school administrators. When a new mandate arrives, all administrators snap into their compliance mode—"What do I need to do to keep the state out of my school?"

The decisive advantage schools have over state educational agencies is the fact these agencies are, after all, bureaucracies. The only thing that state officials want from schools is a response that fits into a box. School administrators who have spent their careers skillfully navigating the diversions explained in this chapter are more than capable of checking the yes box.

Strong Instructional Leaders adopt a love-hate relationship with legislative mandates. They hate those mandates that impose goals or methods of institutional schooling on their faculties (e.g., state-mandated-testing programs). They employ all the administrative tools at their disposal to protect their instructional program from unwelcome legislative mandates. On the first day of school, should teachers be permitted to prepare their classrooms for the first day of school or should they be required to attend an all-day workshop on the new state standards? Should teachers be permitted to work with colleagues on designing an interdisciplinary program or participate in state-mandated school improvement programs? Should a school adopt the state model for teacher evaluation or engage in a process of developing a teacher-evaluation process that reflects a school's instructional worldview? Instructional managers see only one answer to these questions: Teachers will comply with the state guidelines. Strong Instructional Leaders author an instructional response to these questions: Teachers will participate in programs and processes that advance a school's instructional worldview and expand the professional knowledge of teachers.

There are those mandates, however, that put the full weight of state or national government behind a good instructional idea (school improvement plans fall into this category). Strong Instructional Leaders are quick to build on mandates legitimizing, and even enhancing, a worthwhile educational goal. As with any legislative mandate, they interpret friendly mandates in ways that fit into a school's instructional worldview and purposefully decouple unfriendly mandates from a school's instructional program.

Violence

Nothing is more threatening to school administrators than violence in their schools. To be told by a dean that there might be a gun in the building strikes fear in the hearts of even the most seasoned administrators. What is most threatening about fights, weapons, drugs, or bullying is not the fear of losing control of the building, but knowing intuitively that such antisocial behaviors tear at the very fabric of an instructional program. No matter how far school administrators may be from the classroom, they know learning cannot take place in a fearful school environment. The obvious responses to school violence look to *little answers* to stop particular acts of violence: increasing security in the building (e.g., adding cameras, security personnel), aggressively pursuing perpetrators of violence, and providing harsh consequences for those who would hurt students or staff members.

While Strong Instructional Leaders would not disagree with the implementation of little answers, they view school violence as a symptom of large problems caused by institutional approaches to schooling. Granted, school administrators do not have the tools to predict or prevent outbreaks of occasional acts of violence in their building. What they do possess is a large body of literature on the effects that institutional structures have on the emotional, social, and intellectual development of young people. Although school administrators may be unaware of this body of literature, they see firsthand the effects of the daily grind of schooling. Spending all day sitting, being talked at, completing worksheets, and being tested completely disregards, or "subtracts," the social, emotional, and intellectual attributes young people bring to school. But only certain groups of students become the victims of subtractive schooling (Valenzuela, 1999). There are those students who possess the talents and abilities to fit neatly into the institutionally defined roles of smart and well-behaved student or good athlete. The students in this small group find themselves in an additive school environment—whatever they do is rewarded (or forgiven).

Strong Instructional Leaders simultaneously pursue the little answers to school violence and the larger answers to student disenchantment with institutional schooling. Depending on the culture of the school communities that such leaders serve, they might pursue polices eliminating reward structures honoring a narrow band of talents and abilities; expand opportunities for students to exhibit talents and abilities left behind in a rush to raise test scores; look inside the school for service opportunities fitting unique talents and abilities; or work with teachers to create pedagogical approaches, curricular structures, and assessment strategies that are friendly to a broad range of talents, abilities, and styles of learning.

Each of these strategies for creating an additive, rather than a subtractive, school environment evolves out of theories and philosophies of education that are very different from the ones presently embedded in the practices of institutional schooling. Any one of these strategies will raise the ire of some favored group in a school system and disturb the quiet of the central office. Strong Instructional Leaders consider these disturbances worthwhile diversions.

Doing the Right Things Well

The late W. Edwards Deming, the father of Total Quality Management, reminded CEOs throughout the world that when a company fails, it is never due to lack of effort or a lack of intelligence. Companies fail when they lose purpose—what Deming (1986) termed constancy of purpose. Companies that succeed, according to Deming, clearly understand the purpose of their organizations. CEOs of successful organizations never permit lesser goals, new opportunities (no matter how inviting), or business fads to divert attention from what a company does best. Fragmentation—loss of purpose—was, for Deming, the single factor that separated great companies from failed companies—great companies never lose focus.

Strong Instructional Leaders view the "diversions of school administration" as a loss of purpose—the purpose of schooling is quality instruction. At the same time, however, anyone reading the list of diversions in this chapter would be hard pressed to deny that someone, somewhere, in schools should be handling these diversions. Herein lies the dilemma of institutional schooling. Each day, school administrators are called upon to make the difficult choice between attending to a diversion deemed important by the school community they serve and focusing on the core purposes of their industry: curriculum and instruction (see Table 4.1).

This choice becomes even more difficult because each diversion listed in this chapter offers the possibility of knowing that you did something well. The same cannot be said about the messy world of classroom supervision. The complexities of classroom teaching create emotional and intellectual problems that are never entirely resolved and always seem to leave teachers and administrators unsettled at the end of an instructional conversation.

On the surface, this dilemma looks much like the distinction Bennis (1989) makes between "doing things right" (diversions) and "doing the right things" (curriculum and instruction). In an educational system valuing form over substance, the answer for administrators is an easy one: Doing diversions well will keep you employed; doing curriculum and instruction garners a lot of grief. In an effort to resolve this dilemma of school administration, policymakers mistakenly pass accountability legislation that is intended to focus school administrators on teaching and learning—doing the right things. The unintended consequence of these accountability mandates is that they focus administrators on merely managing mandates well—efficiently administering tests, accurately reporting data, and aligning curriculum with state standards. Administrators find themselves back where they started: "What diversion do I take care of today?"

Table 4.1. A Conversation: Diversions of Schooling—I Supervise Transportation and Building Operations

	LISTEN	RESPONSE	LISTEN
Discourse Move One: LISTEN	"Yesterday at our first team meeting, all of you shared with me the administrative functions consuming your time during the school day. When I toured the building during my interviews for principal, I found that all of you are doing a superb job making this building safe, clean, personable, and efficient. At the end of yesterday's meeting, I noted that little time appears to be left over for supervision of teaching and learning in the building."	"Dr. Jones, as you noted, this building runs well. But running a building of this size, with over 2,500 students, is time-consuming. We pay attention to the details, and details take time. As we admitted to you yesterday, all of us lack the kind of experience required to supervise teaching effectively."	"I appreciate your honesty on this issue. My experience in schools and my research on programs preparing future administrators reflect the viewpoints expressed yesterday. It is true that your training focused on the management of systems rather than instructional leadership. Again, all of you demonstrate superior competence in running a safe, clean, and orderly building."
Discourse Move Two: PRESENT	**PRESENT** "Our job, our primary responsibility, is continually improving the instructional program in this building. That goal can only be accomplished if all us seated around this table become instructional leaders."	**RESPONSE** "Dr. Jones, we all agree with the goal of improving our school's instructional program. We also respect your passion for curriculum and instruction. As some of us have said, we barely have any time in the day left over for supervision. Our bigger concern is our lack of training in curriculum and instruction. As you know, all of our teachers are content specialists. For us to come up to speed in these subject areas seems an impossible undertaking."	**PRESENT** "I don't disagree with any of your points. Managing a high school is a full-time job and, you are correct, high school faculty have little respect for supervisors with little knowledge of their content areas. I do not intend to compromise the efficient running of this building nor place you in an awkward situation with faculty. Having said that, I also cannot compromise the core function of our organization, which is instruction."

	FRAME	RESPONSE	FRAME
Discourse Move Three: FRAME	(Instructional Narrative) "As an administrative team, we must send a message to the faculty that we are serious about instruction. That will mean that each of you sitting around this table will take responsibility for some aspect of our instructional program. I will meet with each of you to determine what that role might look like. Most of the supervision will become the responsibility of our department chairpersons, but each of you will be assigned to a department to assist with curriculum, instruction, and staff development."	"Dr. Jones, we appreciate your understanding of our situation and will fully support your focus on curriculum and instruction. We are willing to learn and find ways to work more efficiently with our management duties. But all of us are a bit nervous with our new instructional leadership roles. It is one thing to purchase materials and design a schedule for an in-service day and quite another to sit in a math classroom and provide the teacher with meaningful feedback on our observations."	"No one in this room will be placed in a supervisory role they are unprepared for; that would be a worse situation than having no supervision at all. Everyone sitting in this room was a teacher at one time and I know from reading your personnel files that you were outstanding in the classroom. I am asking each one of you to do the kind of reading that will bring you up to speed in your content area and to spend a greater share of your day helping teachers become the kind of teachers you were."
Discourse Move Four: REFRAME	"I know this will not strike anyone in this room as revolutionary, but research study after research study is screaming at us that quality teaching matters. We now have in place the supervisory tools we need to develop quality teaching in every classroom in this building. We have a moral and professional obligation to provide our students with a quality instructional program."	"Dr. Jones, this is an entirely new direction for us as an administrative team. Principals that came before you expected us to manage the building, not supervise teachers. We agree with your focus, but are uneasy about your expectations for us and whether there are enough hours in the day to both manage a building and supervise classrooms."	"I understand your concerns about lack of time and expertise to assume responsibility for our instructional program. As we start this journey together, I can assure you that I will make every effort to optimize your individual strengths and will never leave you without the resources and training you need to do your job well."

THIS CONVERSATION RESULTS IN THE FOLLOWING MESSAGE:

The truth in plain sight is that quality teaching matters. The unfortunate truth in plain sight is that most classrooms are subject to passive or nonexistent supervision (SITUATION). Every student in this school deserves quality teaching and an engaging curriculum (VALUED END OF SCHOOLING). Only Strong Instructional Leaders can guarantee high levels of teacher performance and the development of meaningful subject matter (THEORY). We will organize the functions of our administrative team around the development of a quality instructional program.

Strong Instructional Leaders think about this dilemma very differently than do policymakers or their administrative peers. They understand that the quality of an educational experience, whether in schools, life, or work, requires the seamless weaving of courses of action with the valued ends of the organization—graduating lifelong learners, for example. When framed this way, the dilemma of school administration is resolved. Yes, diversions are important and must be attended to, but they are only a means (one among many) of accomplishing a valued aim of schooling. Each diversion of school administration listed in this chapter possesses no power to enlarge a school socially, emotionally, or intellectually. At best, diversions create routines to "do school" well. At their worst, diversions of schooling reduce the emotional and intellectual energy necessary to expand the tools of inquiry that inform us what things to do well. The ultimate resolution of the dilemma over doing things right and doing the right things in schools lies with that age-old question of schooling: What are the aims of education?

5

Aims Talk: Schools with Purpose

School systems consumed with implementing the technique or program of the day pay little attention to foundational questions in education. Administrators in these schools, unsure of who they are educationally, adopt and discard one program after another and become frustrated with trying to implement mandates and methods from widely differing philosophical orientations. The aims of schooling are found by asking and answering philosophical questions such as "Why am I doing this?" Without this foundation, there are no intellectual tools to critique a particular method or to gather together all the essentials of schooling (methods, routines, programs, and policies) into a coherent instructional worldview.

Why Am I Doing This?

School administrators organize their calendars—usually in half-hour intervals—around daily functions that must be completed by the end of the day. A close inspection of these functions finds the administrator's entire day consumed by managing or resolving diversions described in Chapter 4—a grant form was completed, a parent went home happy, a teacher received her textbooks, and the superintendent received a photograph for the newsletter. Managing diversions is no easy task, especially when you are resolving them in half-hour intervals. School administrators feel a sense of accomplishment when they finish the day with no diversions lying in the inbox. Of course there are those odds and ends that do not fit neatly into half-hour time slots—Mr. Smith continues to refer a lot of students to the dean's office; the failure rate among Hispanic students seems awfully high; teachers are not using the new lab equipment purchased over the summer; and a group of freshman students are not coming to school on a regular basis. But these odds and ends never seem to make the calendar that week or of the coming weeks or the remainder of the school year; there are just too many pressing diversions to be checked off.

The daily diversions scheduled in administrator calendars leave little time for thinking about or confronting the aims of schooling. A school administrator should be working toward the aims of the organization, for example, by sitting in Mr. Smith's class, by getting involved in some form of problem-solving dialogue with staff about failure rates among Hispanic students, by talking to someone in the field about lab-based science programs, or by talking to counselors and truant officers about freshman students not coming to school. Instead, the administrator is checking off diversions on the daily calendar—the diversions of the day become the aims of schooling.

Table 5.1 provides an overview of the questions, policies, and practices fueling the dilemma between what educators should be doing (aims of schooling), what others want them to do (diversions), and what they actually do on a daily basis (functions). The aims of schooling are found by asking and answering philosophical questions, such as, "Why am I doing this?" The diversions of schooling are found by asking and answering political questions, such as, "How do I comply with policies and requests of external interest groups?" The functions of schooling are what administrators and teachers really do—answering the question "How do I make it through the day?" Instructional managers do the "how" questions well: The diversions of schooling become the functions of schooling. Strong Instructional Leaders do the "why" questions well: The aims of schooling become the functions of schooling.

In today's schools, the dilemma between doing things right (the diversions of schooling) and doing the right things (the aims of schooling) is resolved in favor of getting through the day. Administrators dance around classrooms, teachers implement the technique of the day, and students do school. The daily grind of schooling is a direct reflection of school systems consumed with implementing the diversions of schooling at the expense of what really matters in educating young people—how young people read, write, and talk with each other; how they discover and wrestle with ideas; how they strengthen, broaden, and deepen their literacy; and how they critique and understand social, economic, and political forces in our society.

Rarely in this frenetic pursuit of one diversion after another is there a purposeful approach to thinking, discussing, and experimenting with the theories and practices embedded in the aims of schooling. With no inner compass for what schools should be doing, school administrators and teachers find themselves reacting to the diversion of the day or adopting the program of the day.

What is the source of this great omission in contemporary schooling? It originates with school administrators who are unsure about who they are educationally—they have not authored a personal philosophy of education. School administrators speak passionately about why they entered the field of education (love of some area of study), what they like about education (being around kids), and what they like about school administration (helping people). While these dispositions are not a bad start, they do little to bring coherence to the aims, diversions, and functions of schooling.

A philosophy of education serves three vital functions for school administrators. First, from a philosophy of education one can evaluate the causes and consequences of the educational values articulated in district mission state-

Table 5.1. Aims, Diversions, and Functions

Aims of Schooling (What Administrators and Teachers Should Be Doing)	Diversions (Things That Govern What Administrators and Teachers Do)	Functions of Schooling (What Administrators and Teachers Do on a Daily Basis)
Societal • Instill in our students the values and worldviews of a particular group in society. • Teach forms of knowledge that give students a rational view of reality. • Develop the natural abilities and talents of students. • Teach methods of inquiry and levels of thinking that question the economic, political, and social structures of a society. *Institutional* • Begin with a child's interests and proclivities. • Translate interests and proclivities into social applications. • Participate in democratic communities governed by deliberate discourse. • Translate subjects into tools for examining and ultimately solving societal problems. • Believe that truth is never found in textbooks but is discovered by disciplined methods of inquiry. *Ideological* • Believe that great disparities in income result in political and social inequality. • Believe that either-or thinking finds "right answers" instead of "right solutions."	*National and state mandates* • No child left behind • Special education • Standardized testing • Drug education • Drivers' education • Sex education • Parenting • Reading & mathematics *Programs* • Model reform programs • Differentiated instruction • Character education • Assertive discipline • Institutional requirements • Safety • Attendance • Balanced budgets • Transportation • Grants • Accountability mandates *Special interest groups* • Booster clubs • Extracurricular programs • Advanced academic programs	*Daily routines of schooling* • Establishing schedules • Recording attendance • Enforcing discipline procedures • Organizing breakfast & lunch programs • Ensuring reliable transportation *Daily routines of the classroom* • Taking attendance • Presenting information • Assigning tasks • Grading papers • Organizing activities • Disciplining students *Curriculum expectations* • Align curriculum with standards • Analyze data • Write lesson plans • Teach scripted lessons • Allocate time for test-prep exercises

ments, national and state policy mandates, and professional associations in teaching, curriculum, and administration. Second, a philosophy of education dissolves the distinction between aims, diversions, and functions of schooling—the diversions and functions of schooling are entrenched in the aims of schooling. Third, educational philosophies incorporate the broad aims of schooling—what knowledge, habits of thought, and dispositions should young people possess at the end of 12 years of education?

The aims of education listed in Table 5.1 represent John Dewey's philosophy of education. Dewey begins describing his philosophy by identifying the type of society that does the best job in providing opportunities for each individual "to escape from the limitations of the social group into which he was born, and to come into living contact with a broader environment" (Dewey, 1916/1966, p. 20). Next, Dewey describes the forms of teaching and curricula that are conducive to graduating students with the intellectual tools and dispositions to realize the aims of a democratic society. Additionally, Dewey identifies the social, economic, and political conditions in a society that serve as obstacles to providing individuals with the opportunity to optimize their talents and abilities. Finally, Dewey's philosophy of education incorporates in the aims of schooling the kinds of knowledge and skills required to solve the societal problems of economic inequality, social injustice, and political partisanship. Dewey's philosophy of education is one among many philosophical systems educators reference when talking about developing ideal societies. While each philosophical system promotes different ideal societies, all philosophical systems require societies and their institutions to act out their ideals—the aims of a democracy ought to preside over the everyday functions of school administrators and teachers.

In the busy school world of diversions, a reference to a philosophy of education brings about confused looks from fellow school administrators. Yes, they remember taking a course in the philosophy of education and reading excerpts from Plato, Aristotle, Whitehead, and Dewey. Rarely are the abstract thoughts of these philosophers connected to the real world of institutional schooling. What makes more sense to school administrators and teachers is the concrete world of methods and techniques of teaching and school administration. Courses dealing with the latter are popular because of their immediate applicability to real-world administrative or classroom problems. The detachment of methods (means) from valued ends (aims) invites an endless cascade of ideologies, special interest requests, and information.

Without a philosophy of education, school administrators allow their schools to drift among the turbulent waves of state and national policy initiatives and the diversions of schooling. The daily functions of schooling are always perceived through the eyes and ears of the diversion of the day. Each school day is marked by the daily march of one diversion after another and one technique after another. In schools without philosophies, there are no intellectual tools or ideological frameworks to critique a particular method in relationship to a valued end of schooling or to gather together all the particulars of schooling (methods, routines, programs, and policies) into a coherent instructional program in which the particulars serve the general aims of schooling. Trapped in school environments without an overarching purpose, school administrators may make it through the day, but the schools they lead never possess the constancy of purpose necessary to achieve the educational values listed in school mission statements.

Philosopher-Educators

At first glance, most administrators would look upon becoming a philosopher-educator as unnecessary—aims talk belongs at the university; function talk belongs in schools. At the same time school administrators are expressing skepticism about philosophies of education, they understand, at least intuitively, that coherence and quality are fundamental attributes of an effective instructional program. Then how does a school administrator become a philosopher-educator? The preparation of Strong Instructional Leaders is taken up in chapters 7 through 13. At this juncture it is appropriate to point out where school administrators do *not* find help in becoming philosopher-educators.

The logical starting point for developing a personal philosophy would be a school mission statement. Although school districts spend a great deal of time developing mission statements, these proclamations are merely a list of values in education (e.g., critical thinking, child-centered curriculum). While few in the school community would disagree with these values, many would define each one quite differently. From a political perspective, this is the strength of school mission statements—they are large on intention and short on explanations.

What is missing from school mission statements is the means of accomplishing educational goals. A casual walk through any school in the United States will find: children receiving F's in child-centered schools, the elimination of recess in developmentally appropriate environments, and students becoming technologically literate on 10-year-old computers. When declared outcomes in a philosophy are removed from the process for attaining them, school administrators become utopian philosopher-educators (having a commitment to a declared outcome with no idea how to achieve it). Superintendents fill this role in schools.

Other logical settings for developing a philosophy of education are undergraduate and graduate programs in teaching and school administration. Aims talk in teacher education programs, however, is crowded out by methods talk. Preservice programs in education are designed to train future teachers to convince or compel students to conform to the institutional goals of schooling (grades, diplomas, high test scores). Since institutional goals take priority over educational goals, teachers look to classroom routines and teaching methods to maintain control over students who see little meaning in a test score. When valued ends in a philosophy are replaced by the one best method, educators become partisan philosopher-educators (having a commitment to a method with no regard for a valued end of schooling). Consultants fill this role in schools.

Building-level administrators' general distrust of philosophies of education is founded on experiences with superintendents who arrive on their doorsteps with the latest valued end of schooling or high-priced gurus who take over their staff-development program with the latest method of the day. To survive in an environment where the coherence and permanence of ends and means are problematic, building administrators develop a philosophy of education based on diversions. When philosophy is removed from valued ends and the means to achieve them, educators become opportunists (having a commitment to what works today, with little thought of tomorrow). Principals and teachers fill this role in schools.

In school systems where the inputs (students), processes (curriculum and instruction), and outputs (goals) are uncertain, it is easy to see why participants in the system are attracted to philosophies that are overly idealistic, overly dogmatic, or overly expedient. Strong Instructional Leaders, however, are not guilty of these philosophical vices. They see no value in searching for ultimate truths in education or imposing ultimate pedagogies on school faculties. What they do focus on, and how they define a philosophy of education, are methods of inquiry that bring coherence to an instructional program. In hallways, classrooms, and boardrooms, such leaders continually ask two questions: How do the theories, programs, standards, and techniques fit together? How do the consequences of a school practice help reach a valued aim of schooling?

The whole point of developing a philosophy of education is acquiring habits of thought that continually assess how the valued outcomes of schooling expressed in mission statements are actually played out in classrooms and hallways. Policies, procedures, discipline codes, curriculum handbooks, and classroom teaching ought to be expressions of the valued ends of schooling. When a policy, procedure, or method deviates from the norms of a school's instructional worldview, teachers and administrators possess tools of inquiry and modes of discourse to reconnect a school practice with a valued end of schooling. A school culture that values questioning the economic, political, and social structures of society (see Table 5.2) would oppose forms of pedagogy inducing passivity and conformity in their students. The same disconnect between the means and ends of schooling occurs when boards of education eliminate recess, students are instructed on 10-year-old computers, and a test score becomes the arbiter of quality schooling. A strong instructional worldview sees each of these instructional means as disconnected from valued ends of schooling. Embedded in a strong, philosophically based worldview is a process for evaluating the consequences of a school practice in relationship to an aim of schooling—what are the social, emotional, and intellectual consequences of eliminating recess for students in elementary schools?

On the surface, the philosophy of Strong Instructional Leaders appears to be a version of programs designed to support increased collaboration in schools (e.g., learning communities, mentor programs). Programs designed to increase dialogue between administrators, teachers, and students can function as forums for discussing the relationship between aims, diversions, and functions of schooling. Too often, however, aims talk is quickly displaced by function talk, i.e., how best to implement a managerial goal. The absence of aims talk in school discourse communities is the Achilles heel of any philosophy of education. Without valued ends of schooling, administrators and teachers are reduced to discussing the best

Table 5.2. Philosophical Questions About Schooling

Goal	Question
Clarifying Purposes	What is a desirable outcome of schooling?
Assessing Consequences of Instructional Decisions	What is the relationship between a lesson objective, materials, activities, selected pedagogies, and a goal of education?
Questioning Assumptions and Beliefs	What theory or method of inquiry supports that practice?
Constructing Frameworks for Making Sense of Instructional Problems	• How do students learn? • What knowledge is of greatest worth? • How should knowledge be organized? • How should we assess what students know? • How should we teach?
Creating Instructional Discourse Communities	What does a balanced reading program look like in a 3rd-grade classroom?
Distinguishing between "big problems" and "little problems" of schooling	Are we addressing a symptom of a problem (change in policy or procedures) or the cause of the problem (change in goals and configuration of organization)?
Questioning the institutional goals of schooling	• How can we design this schedule to accommodate team planning times? • Why should buses arrive at 6:30 in the morning? • What is the purpose of an honor roll?

way to implement a diversion of schooling. Discussions involving valued ends rejuvenate the dilemma of school administration—resolving the conflict between the diversions of schooling and valued ends of education.

How does a school administrator move an instructional conversation from how to raise a test score to how to raise student engagement? This question goes to the very heart of Strong Instructional Leadership. Throughout the school day, week, and year, administrators are placed in myriad formal and information situations in which they are able to articulate an instructional agenda. In each of these conversations, Strong Instructional Leaders seize the opportunity to further an instructional worldview constructed from responses to the kinds of questions educational philosophers ask about schooling (see Table 5.3).

Table 5.3. A Conversation: Instructional Worldviews—
We Need More Media and Real-World Experiences in Our Curriculum

	LISTEN	RESPONSE	LISTEN
Discourse Move One: LISTEN	"Dr. Jones, the English and social studies departments are enthusiastic about introducing Channel One into our program. We believe that the introduction of more media and current events in our curriculum is motivating for students and would complement our focus on interdisciplinary topics."	"Bill, I have read a lot about Channel One and have gone through the information you sent me. To begin with, you should understand that I value what teachers do in classrooms. My primary role in this school is optimizing instructional time in classrooms and providing students with a meaningful curriculum."	"Dr. Jones, Channel One's main focus is the same as yours: increasing instructional time. While students are listening to the morning announcements they also view an informative video on current topics of the day. I feel certain that we can integrate these current event topics in the themes you have asked us to develop in our daily lessons."
Discourse Move Two: PRESENT	**PRESENT** "Bill, it is my understanding that Channel One's presentation consumes approximately 10 minutes of instructional time each day and that included in Channel One presentations are advertisements that have no relationship to the educational goals in our curriculum. It is also my understanding that Channel One's informative videos amount to random current happenings in the world. In our last cabinet meeting we had a lengthy discussion of the importance of developing a coherent approach to selecting themes and concepts in English and social studies. From reading the literature from Channel One I see no purposeful approach assisting your teachers with developing deep understandings of concepts in English or social studies."	**RESPONSE** "Dr. Jones, I respect your position on instructional time. I can also assure you that our monthly department chair meetings have opened our eyes to the importance of developing coherent approaches to curriculum and instruction. But you also have put an emphasis on relating subject-matter concepts and principles to the everyday lives of students. The Channel One videos we have viewed are professionally produced and will keep our students current on topics that directly affect their lives. I can provide you with testimonials from department chairs in the area on the instructional worth of these videos. You should know that every high school in this conference has signed with Channel One."	**PRESENT** "Bill, my objection to Channel One is that it uses 10 minutes of instructional time to show commercials and superficial treatments of wars, crimes, and celebrities. Our students are better served by lessons that have enough time to develop purposeful approaches to thinking about, as you put it, 'topics that directly affect their lives.'"

	FRAME	RESPONSE	FRAMING
Discourse Move Three: **FRAME**	(Instructional Narrative) "Bill, while I appreciate your exploration of media sources and meaningful approaches to curriculum and instruction, Channel One introduces an approach to teaching and representation of subject matter that does not fit into our aims of optimizing instructional time and designing coherent approaches to curriculum and instruction."	"I am surprised by your response, Dr. Jones. I felt that you would be enthusiastic about introducing more media and real-world experiences into our classrooms."	"Bill, I do believe that we need more media in our classrooms and certainly more connections to the real world. Having said that, my larger concern with Channel One is bringing into classrooms the kinds of images and thinking that do not reflect disciplined ways of understanding the world."
	REFRAMING	RESPONSE	REFRAMING
Discourse Move Four: **REFRAME**	"Bill, I think it is safe to say that the introduction of more technology in our schools is the wave of the future. So, I understand your puzzlement over my response today. I am not opposed to the hardware offered by Channel One. I am opposed to how that hardware would be applied in our classrooms. I cannot permit any technique, program, or technology to compromise our aim of teaching young people to become thoughtful citizens, workers, and consumers."	"Dr. Jones, I must admit that I did not think this conversation would go like this. I disagree with your assessment of Channel One, but respect a single-minded focus on developing coherent and meaningful approaches to representing subject matter. You probably know that Channel One offers some leeway on programming; the amount of minutes committed to commercial time and current events topics. Would you be interested in exploring those options?"	"Bill, I did review the packages offered by Channel One, but the content is in fundamental opposition with how I believe children learn disciplined ways of knowing the world. At the very heart of how children learn is the choice and organization of subject matter and how teachers allocate time in their classrooms. Channel One's format would compromise our core beliefs in quality teaching and quality curriculum."

THIS CONVERSATION RESULTS IN THE FOLLOWING MESSAGE:

Schools are continually under pressure to find silver bullets to increase student achievement. The purchase and dissemination of technology in all classrooms is the newest and most powerful silver bullet present in our schools. Every day in schools, computers are installed, libraries are converted into media centers, and centralized distribution centers permit access to endless sources of information (SITUATION). The question that educators must ask of all this hardware and software: What instructional purposes do all these boxes, wires, and databases serve? Will our curriculum become more meaningful and our teaching more engaging in environments dominated by videos and databases? Our problem is how to transform vast reservoirs of information into knowledge (VALUED END OF SCHOOLING). Information-based learning aligns well with frontal teaching models and textbook-driven curriculum. Knowledge-based learning aligns well with problem-based curricula requiring the flexibility to access information quickly and the model of teaching promoting inquiry and discussion (THEORY). The problem we are confronting is implementing a knowledge-based instructional program within an information-based school program. Our aim is to continually pursue curricular and instructional approaches that optimize the skills necessary to succeed in a 21st-century knowledge-based society.

The resolution to this dilemma lies with school leaders who insert themselves into public and situational venues where a philosophy of education guides discussions of school practices and valued ends of schooling. However, before inserting themselves into public and situational venues, school administrators must first be confident with who they are educationally. When, where, and how a Strong Instructional Leader employs one or more of these opportunities depends on the local context of the school they lead. Given the great variation in the demographics of schools throughout the country, what remains constant is the ability of the Strong Instructional Leader to exercise his or her role as a philosopher-educator—a role demanding that no practice in their school goes unexamined.

6

Overcoming the Barriers
to School Reform

While doing diversions well garners accolades from their communities and their superiors, school administrators intuitively know that their schools are adrift morally and intellectually. Without an instructional anchor, a sea of legislative mandates, board initiatives, model programs, and the demands of special interest groups batter the school. Doing diversions well keeps the school afloat, but fails to navigate the school in any particular direction. A philosophy of education provides a blueprint for the what and the how of schooling.

Chapters 1 through 6 present an overview of why and how school administrators "dance around the classroom." No matter how well school administrators orchestrate this dance, they often find themselves caught between superiors who value order and conformity and teachers and students who value individuality and autonomy. To resolve the tension between managing the diversions of schooling and developing the individualities of teachers and students, school administrators look for guidance in district mission statements and in their former coursework. Instead of finding an instructional bearing in a mission statement or university course work, administrators find themselves tossed about by waves of educational platitudes, programs, and techniques of the day. Their only alternative in this hurricane of visions and nostrums is returning to the helm where, at a minimum, they can keep the school afloat. But as they right their school vessels, they remain unclear where the ship is headed.

In their quests for instructional direction, school administrators are missing a philosophy of education that restores value to classroom activities and provides tools of inquiry that examine the consequences of school practices designed for institutional outcomes. Many philosophers of education, including John Dewey, have a philosophy of education that places methods of problem-solving at the center of the curriculum. Dewey's conception of curriculum and instruction required children and teachers to step out of the confines of their culture and personal self-interest to resolve the real social, economic, and political problems confronting their communities. Dewey went on to describe in great detail the kind of pedagogy and curricula that matures a child from the purposeful resolution of personal needs and desires to the purposeful resolution of public needs and desires.

A philosophy of education, whether it is Dewey's or some other philosopher-educator's, offers school administrators a blueprint for the what and the how of schooling—valued outcomes of schooling interpenetrate the practices of schooling. School administrators and teachers who work in school cultures that are woven together with a common philosophy of education are able to discern what theories, programs, and mandates will improve or disrupt a school's instructional program.

Problem-Based School Leadership

Even with an instructional worldview that is well thought out, school administrators and teachers still work in institutions that value conformity over creativity, passivity over engagement, and credentialing over understanding. A philosophy of education must be comprehensive and strong enough to resolve the tension between honoring and developing the individualities of teachers and students in schools designed to standardize talent and performance. It must find pathways between the theories and ideas informing teaching, learning, and organizational behavior and the practical world of classroom teaching. It must also understand and address in purposeful ways the five problems of schooling that cut instructional anchors from schools and sink most instructional reform initiatives.

The problem of institutions. The history of schooling in America is the story of the movement from teaching the child (one-room schoolhouse) to processing large populations of students (the comprehensive high school). The steady march toward more efficiency and greater capacity gradually replaced the debate over what it means to be educated with instructions on how best to perform the institutional functions of certification, preparation, and custodial care. The "machinery of school-work" (Dewey, 1906/1969, p. 24) places teachers in schools where the aims of schooling (high test scores, admission to college, preparation for the workforce) and the means of schooling (large classes, standardized curriculum, large quantities of testing) are antithetical to a profession requiring creativity, flexibility, and sensitivity to uniqueness. Children find themselves in classrooms where the aims of schooling (promotion, good grades, following rules) and the means of schooling (sitting quietly, listening, completing worksheets) are hostile to their social need to be known, their emotional need to be interested, and their intellectual need to make sense of their experiences.

Dewey largely blamed the failure of schools to educate on school administrators who are more concerned with rules, procedures, and documentation than with creating environments where children could explore individual interests in socially constructive ways. Studies that have documented the endurance of the assign and assess model of teaching (Cuban, 1984; Goodlad, 1984) confirm Dewey's belief that institutional requirements of efficiency and conformity induce school administrators to focus on the diversions of schooling while turning away from what is happening in classrooms and induce teachers to focus on proper implementation of routines and techniques, while turning away from the interests and curiosity of the children seated in front of them.

Table 6.1 summarizes the attributes of "Bureaucratic Organizations" and "Knowledge Organizations." Contemporary organizational theorists (Deming, 1986; Senge, 1990) recommend that CEOs competing in global business environments look for employees who are better at breaking the rules than following the rules. Flexibility, creativity, and innovativeness are essential attributes of organizations that will prosper in a "flat world" of no borders, no rules, and no lifelong careers (Friedman, 2005). School mission statements calling for lifelong learners, critical-thinkers, and knowledge workers for the 21st century make little sense to teachers in classrooms designed for taking orders and recalling information. Strong Instructional Leaders recognize that the schools they lead are preparing students for the 19th century instead of the 21st century.

Strong Instructional Leader's Instructional Worldview 1

An essential component of a Strong Instructional Leader's instructional worldview is the commitment to developing curricular offerings, pedagogical practices, and organizational configurations that advance the goals, values, and practices of knowledge organizations.

The problem of goals. The knowledge and skills taught to students in our schools originate from an age-old struggle between four competing conceptions of what students should know and understand upon graduation from high school. Two conceptions of schooling—civic (Dewey, 1916/1966) and vocational (Bobbitt, 1915)—view school as the principal organization for preparing youth for an occupation and democratic habits of mind. The other two conceptions of schooling—cultivation of humanity (Nussbaum, 1997) and creation of an authentic self (Morris, 1966) view schooling as a place where young people learn love and imagination (Nussbaum, 1997) and become authors of "one's own values" (Morris, 1996, p. 41). In the ideal republic, the community supports a way of life (the civic and instrumental goals) that gives full expression to an individual's search for meaning and a greater understanding of the world around them (the goals of cultivating humanity and the authentic self).

Underlying the "struggle for the American curriculum" are two views of knowledge that support the pursuit of each aim of education (Kliebard, 1987). Educators who view schooling as a process of socialization see knowledge as the acquisition of power to control the environment, society, and one's self (knowledge as power). Educators who view schooling as a process of cultivating humanity and authenticity see knowledge as a process of understanding (knowledge as interpretation).

Table 6.1. Bureaucratic Organizations Versus Knowledge Organizations

Attributes	Bureaucratic Organizations	Knowledge Organizations
Goals	• Efficiency • Certainty • Conformity	• Creativity • Innovation • Flexibility
Culture	• Hierarchy: top-down decision-making	• Flat structure & egalitarian culture
Occupational roles	• Position in a hierarchy • Prescribed responsibilities & functions (job descriptions)	• Expertise • Particular requirements to complete a task (task specifications)
Organizational environments	• Impersonal • Roles & position in chain of command • Discourse focused on efficiently implementing rules & procedures	• Interpersonal • Professionalism & autonomy • Discourse focused on solving problems
Personnel evaluation	• Prescribed criteria listed in job descriptions • Rating on performance of criteria	• Completion of tasks • Furthering knowledge in organization
Documentation	• A priority • Codification of rules, procedures, & institutional decision-making	• A nuisance • Journals, notebooks, scraps of paper, chalkboards documenting relationships between theories and practices
Accountability	• Analysis of data • Sanctions for noncompliance • Benchmarks • Alignment with rules & procedures • Standardized measures of achievement	• Observation of intentional states (beliefs, satisfactions, feelings, judgments) • Reflection on practice • Level of thinking • Methods of inquiry • Performance on real-world tasks

Mixed into the traditional struggles over what sort of student the public wants schools to graduate are the institutional goals of schooling (e.g., credentialing, documenting) and myriad legislative mandates that require schools to fix the latest social ill. The easiest solution to the problem of goals is to pursue outcomes most favored by the public and policymakers. In today's society, policymakers and parents judge schools by how well they pursue the vocational goals of schooling: preparing students for a job or for college. Schools have translated the vocational goals of schooling into the college-bound curriculum: All students are required to complete 4 years of science, social studies, mathematics, and English.

With the added requirement of foreign language to the college-bound curriculum and courses devoted to preparing students for the SAT/ACT test, students have little opportunity to pursue courses that would cultivate humanity or create an authentic self. The most complex curriculum to apply in schools is to adopt the view that the four goals of schooling (vocational, civic, liberal, and creative) are mutually enforcing rather than mutually exclusive. This is the view Dewey expressed in his writings and one that is lost in the political determinations of what knowledge is of greatest worth. For Dewey, and other contemporary curricular theorists (Greene, 1995; Katz, 1988), the optimum curricular configuration is one in which a child's personal ways of developing meaning find expression and full realization in vocational and civic undertakings. The meaning of life in such a curriculum is employing private interests and talents in public ways of making a living and contributing to the common good.

How do Strong Instructional Leaders approach the struggle for the goals of schooling? First, they accept the reality that their beliefs about what it means to be educated will have to take into account what curriculum goals legislators and parents believe schools should be pursuing. Second, they understand that the schools they inherit are burdened with decisions made by past school leaders who favored one goal of schooling over another or who tried to make peace by evenly dividing resources between each goal. Third, they know from firsthand experience that credentialing one school goal over all others disenfranchises the interests, talents, and abilities of large groups of students. Finally, they know that creating a shopping mall curriculum violates the first law of curriculum and instruction: Deep understanding of subject matter is wholly dependent on continuity and coherence.

Strong Instructional Leader's Instructional Worldview 2

An essential component of a Strong Instructional Leader's instructional worldview is a commitment to developing curricular offerings, pedagogical practices, and organizational configurations that synchronize public ways of knowing the world with personal ways of knowing the world.

The problem of the self. Schools are designed by societies to purposefully influence "the attitudes and dispositions necessary for the continuous and progressive life of a society" (Dewey, 1916/1966, p. 22). The pedagogy endorsed by schools of education for socializing the young into the life of society originates in Rousseau's dictum that educators should follow the path traced by nature (Rousseau, 1762/1979). The problem that teachers confront when applying a pedagogy devoted to developing the nature of the child is the inherent conflict between a child's private ways of knowing the world (language, culture, personal interests, experiences, etc.) and institutional ways of knowing the world (the methods, structure, and content of a discipline).

Schools are institutions. To achieve the recognition and funding necessary to preserve their governmental status, education leaders displace pedagogies devoted to developing the child with pedagogies enforcing institutional categories—certifications, grade levels, ability groups, subjects. To be an expert in today's educational environment, one must know the vocabulary, the processes, and the methods of accountability that normalize a child's private ways of knowing. Schools as institutions are not designed to develop a love of learning. They are designed to determine where a child fits within the results of some standardized achievement measure—along the bell-shaped curve.

This normalization process is most apparent in the field of special education where administrators, teachers, and all manner of specialists create labels (L.D., B.D.) for pathologies that explain why a child is unable to conform to the routines of institutional schooling or reach a cut-score on a state test. This search for pathology concludes with a prescription (intervention) for curing the diagnosed deviant behavior. Strong Instructional Leaders recognize that the schools they lead are institutions designed to normalize the unique beliefs, desires, and intentions of the children entering their schools each day.

Strong Instructional Leader's Instructional Worldview 3

An essential component of a Strong Instructional Leader's worldview is a commitment to developing curricular offerings, pedagogical practices, and organizational configurations that respect and give voice to "abnormal" talents, interests, and abilities.

The problem of experience. Not knowing what counts as an educational experience causes great confusion in schooling. School administrators, teachers, policymakers, parents, and students see no confusion; everything that happens in school is a bona fide educational experience. Sitting in classrooms all day, students experience definitions of terms, demonstrations of procedures, notetaking, recitations, and tests. All of us who have gone to school would nod our heads in agreement—yes, these are legitimate educational experiences. Pursuing this definition further, educators would offer a learning theory that explains how the foregoing list of educational experiences constitutes learning.

The theory of choice for institutional schooling is behaviorism. School administrators and teachers are drawn to those definitions of educational experience and those learning theories that impose neatness and order on teaching and learning—the alignment of state standards with behavioral objectives. The institutionalized curricula found in state standards, textbooks, and achievement testing fit well with theories of learning that define a child as a blank slate on which you list facts and procedures; repeat facts and procedures; and reward recall of facts and procedures.

Classrooms organized around learning theories that impose order become data-driven and reduce a thriving but uncertain world to a one-dimensional but certain world of definitions, lists, and multiple-choice tests. This definition omits the obvious: No child, no adolescent, no adult comes from nowhere—all humans look at the world from some place in the world. No definition of educational experience or supporting theory of learning is complete without finding room in the definition for the messy particulars of the world that a child, an adolescent, or an adult lives in. Our purposes in the world and how we make sense of what happens to us *in* the world depend on where we stand in the world. Whatever individuals look *at* will always be reconstituted in systems of beliefs, understandings, meanings, and practices *from* where a child, adolescent, or adult stands in the world.

Good schools house a vast array of intellectual tools to help students make sense of the world they come from, and imagine the world they would like to arrive at. When educational experience is defined in this way, curriculum and instruction begin with where an individual comes from not with what an individual should be looking at. Learning theories that take into account how a child talks about and feels about what they are looking at promote messy pedagogies that disrupt the certainties of institutional schooling. Messy learning theories focus on how children construct meaning rather than how they mirror objective knowledge. Children in messy classrooms are presented with a situation, a case, or a scenario that draws them into a problem for a particular group of students. Teachers in messy classrooms provide students with modes of inquiry and activity structures that permit them to discuss possible solutions for the problem. Messy classroom experiences become messier when students are given the time, space, and materials to experiment with courses of action that they believe will resolve a problem they are interested in. The true educational value of messy classroom experiences occurs when teachers guide students into a purposeful process of examining the consequences of their courses of action and what other courses of action might better achieve a valued common good.

Creating educational experiences that give equal attention to both where a child is standing and what a child is looking at leads to curricular structures and pedagogies that are difficult to design, difficult to observe, and difficult to assess. It is easy to see why the certainties of institutional schooling (e.g., standards, scripted lesson plans, objective tests) historically overwhelm the uncertainties or progressive approaches to schooling (e.g., themes, discussions, performances). Strong Instructional Leaders recognize that the schools they lead are institutions designed for looking *at* the world and not looking from the world.

Strong Instructional Leader's Instructional Worldview 4

An essential component of a Strong Instructional Leader's worldview is a commitment to developing curricular offerings, pedagogical practices, and organizational configurations through which all students fully undergo educational experiences *from where they stand.*

The problem of pedagogy. Schools as institutions require administrators and teachers to design efficient instructional programs. Efficiency in the context of institutional schooling is defined as transmitting large quantities of information to large groups of students with the minimum expenditure of time, money, and effort. Studies of the social context of schooling (Jackson, 1968; Lortie, 2002) describe how institutional approaches to schooling influence how teachers think about pedagogy and how those beliefs are realized in classrooms. The normal pedagogy of institutional schooling expects teachers to cover objects of knowledge so students can possess the knowledge for final transfer to a test. Opposed to this assign and assess model of instruction is John Dewey's portrayal of a teacher creating situations requiring students to interact with their environments to discover possible solutions to problematic situations that arise in a society with scarce resources and different identities.

Boards of education and state legislative bodies largely ignore the other problems of schooling (e.g., institutions, goals, the self, and experience). They want educators to use research agendas and policy initiatives to identify methods that support the efficient transmission and testing of information. Educational researchers spend their days searching for causal relationships between effective methods of transmitting information and test scores. Legislative bodies find the quantifiable relationships that are established between effective methods of teaching and student achievement are a powerful tool, for holding teachers and school administrators accountable for the effective implementation of scientific approaches to teaching and learning. The scientific turn in education has displaced the philosophical inquiries into what it means to be educated and reduced the complex practice of teaching into the proper implementation of techniques.

Table 6.2 represents the two traditions of pedagogy that have clashed in schools for the last century. The organizational structure of institutional schooling, public perceptions of what schools should look like, and accountability mandates favor the employment of mimetic tradition of pedagogy in our nation's schools. There have been brief periods in the history of U.S. schooling where transformative traditions of pedagogy bubbled to the surface in particular schools (Kridel & Bullough, 2007). These experiments in progressive pedagogy were quickly silenced by scientific management strategies (raise productivity by standardizing outputs) that viewed progressive teaching as too costly and too idiosyncratic for the efficient operation of schools (Tyack & Hansot, 1982). Strong Instructional Leaders recognize that the schools they lead are subject to legislative mandates, community expectations, and institutional structures that promote a pedagogy suited for imposing order and accountability on large groups of students.

Strong Instructional Leader's Instructional Worldview 5

An essential component of a Strong Instructional Leader's worldview is a commitment to developing curricular offerings, pedagogical practices, and organizational configurations expanding theories and practices of transformative pedagogies.

Table 6.2. The Two Traditions of Pedagogy

Fundamental Question of Schooling	Mimetic	Transformative
How do children learn?	• Imitate • Possess	• Discover • Acquire
What knowledge is of greatest worth?	• Factual • Procedural	• Conceptual • Interpretive
How should subject matter be organized?	• Textbook	• Thematic units • Interdisciplinary units
How should we assess what students understand?	• Summative assessments • Achievement tests	• Formative assessments • Authentic assessments
How should we teach?	• Tell • Demonstrate • Recite • Practice • Assess • Reinforce • Remediate	• Pose a problem • Investigate the problem • Formulate alternative solutions • Substantiate claims • Offer a plan of action • Evaluate consequences of action plan • Revise action plan

Adapted from Jackson, 1986.

The Functions of Strong Instructional Leadership

Worldviews, conceptual frameworks, big pictures, or philosophies of education provide a way of thinking about the problems of schooling—making sense out of how schools work and how they ought to work. The terminology one adopts for big-picture thinking is unimportant. It is vital to Strong Instructional Leadership to formulate a framework (or worldview, or philosophy, or big picture) of how their schools work politically, socially, economically, and intellectually (the reality of the schools they stand in) and how their schools *ought* to work politically, socially, economically, and intellectually. Embedded in this worldview should be a range of intellectual tools—habits of thought—to examine the gaps that exist between the reality and ideal of their schools.

Why should Strong Instructional Leaders preoccupy themselves with philosophies, frameworks, worldviews, or big pictures? First, when school administrators walk into a school, they can be assured that staff and faculty are looking *at* them *from* someplace. That someplace is a system of theories and practices gathered in their lives and careers. This system of beliefs is their worldview, which makes sense of their private and public experiences. School administrators ignore the private beliefs and understandings of teachers when they assume that the function of instructional leader is announcing an instructional initiative, providing the appropriate materials to teachers, and managing the logistics of a new program. This is the same mistake teachers make when they think that students learn by looking *at* subject-matter content. Students and teachers will always interpret authoritative messages in the context of where they come from.

Second, the normative theories and practices that shape school cultures originate from daily interactions between faculty members over problematic situations in their schools. After a time, a dominant worldview emerges around a problematic situation in a school. This dominant worldview becomes the foundation for diagnosing the causes and solutions for a school's instructional problems—what collective action researchers term "diagnostic framing" and "prognostic framing" (Benford & Snow, 2000). A faculty could, for example, diagnose the problem of low reading achievement as a lack of parental support and prescribe an after-school program to teach parents how to support their children's progress in reading. Another diagnosis of low reading achievement might lie in classrooms in which teachers do not know how to teach reading. One frame moves the problem of poor reading achievement outside the classroom. The other frame moves the problem of poor reading achievement inside the classroom.

Third, curricular and instructional reforms, especially those designed to change the assign and assess model of classroom instruction, are not brought into a school building in a format that is readily understood by school administrators and teachers. All curricular and instructional reforms originate with theories and practices woven together by professionals with their own worldviews of how reading, math, social studies, or science should be organized, taught, and assessed. The diverse experiences of teachers in any school building prevent replication of reforms—foreign instructional worldviews—introduced at the beginning of the school year. In the process of trying to make sense of instructional reforms, school administrators and teachers will construct an interpretation of a pedagogy through the lens of how they were taught to teach mathematics, what works for them in the classroom, and how their school buildings work. Ultimately, some teachers will reject the reform, some will modify it to fit what they are already doing, some will run parallel programs, and some will revise their underlying beliefs and practices about how to teach a subject or skill (Coburn, 2004). Most instructional reforms are designed to achieve the last goal. For most teachers, however, much gets lost in translation.

For the last 2 decades, instructional reforms were implemented as a regulative (Scott, 2008) activity. School administrators in a regulative environment manage a reform initiative by inspecting the surface details of a mandated way to teach, to present materials, and to organize classrooms. When you see a school administrator "walking through" (a supervisory strategy employed in the Chicago public schools) a classroom with a clipboard filled with lists, you are in a regulative environment. Checking off the presence of word walls, "I can" statements, and plan books displayed on a teacher's desk requires little knowledge of curriculum and instruction or the kinds of instructional discourses that influence faculties to change worldviews of teaching and learning. School administrators in regulative schools get by quite well with managing the diversions of schooling and periodically "walking through" with a clipboard.

School administrators who desire to substantially change the technical core of teaching must acquire an entirely different set of knowledge and skills to facilitate the collective sensemaking of their faculties (Coburn, 2001). Collective sensemaking requires a public explanation of a worldview or philosophy of education in a way that makes sense to faculties and the publics served by a school. More than that, it is a deeply complex process of working with teachers in a variety of environments to change personal and professional beliefs about teaching and learning. School administrators perform the functions of Strong Instructional Leadership in these environments.

Functions of Strong Instructional Leadership

1. **Develop** an instructional discourse and organizational capacity that help teachers make collective sense of the theories and practices of an instructional reform initiative.
2. **Make irrelevant** the reasons teachers give for not implementing an instructional reform initiative (Coburn, 2001, pp. 154–155):
   - Does not apply to their grade level
   - Too difficult for students
   - Does not align with philosophy of education
   - Completely outside the bounds of comprehension
   - Doesn't "fit"
   - Unmanageable
   - Not understandable
3. **Assist** teachers with understanding the theory and practice of teaching a new pedagogy.
4. **Provide** the time, materials, and expertise for teachers to learn, converse, experiment, and receive feedback on a new instructional reform initiative.

Expertly performing the functions of Strong Instructional Leadership requires a very different form of leadership in schools. Coming up through the ranks of school administration (or attending a graduate program in school administration) falls short of providing the knowledge and skills one needs to change the normative and cognitive structures of an organization and to frame a worldview of a school community. Those who decide to leave the diversions of schooling for the complex task of changing the worldviews of the schools they lead, at least for the time being, will engage in a highly personalized journey. The remainder of this book provides a guide for the private, public, and situational journeys that school administrators will take as they become Strong Instructional Leaders.

7

The Private Journey:
Discovering a Unique Instructional Voice

The most misunderstood part of school reform is the role of instructional leaders. Policymakers view the role of instructional leaders as a management function: planning, directing, monitoring, and improving what is already in place. The transformation of core teaching practices in today's schools, however, calls for Strong Instructional Leaders—school administrators who "purpose" schooling around a strong instructional worldview and the capacity for that worldview to be realized in the daily functions of teachers.

In chapters 1 through 6, I listed the characteristics of school administrators I refer to as Strong Instructional Leaders. For the last decade, policymakers and boards of education have been mandating the hiring of leaders who possess these qualities. The name often given to these school administrators is instructional leaders. Policymakers largely view the role of an instructional leader as a school administrator who effectively manages test-driven curricular and instructional programs—what I call instructional management.

While policymakers express concern about quality teaching, they fail to see that managing instruction is a very different task from providing quality teaching by changing core teaching practices (how subject matter is organized, presented, and assessed). The essential difference between the two roles rests with their primary focus—the means and ends of providing instruction. Instructional managers are rewarded for focusing on the means: planning, directing, and improving what is already in place. Instructional leaders, on the other hand, focus on the ends and assume responsibility for "purposing" (Sergiovanni, 1996) the organization. Leaders who purpose well create the capacity, the vocabulary, and the organizational configuration for the aims of the organization to be realized in the daily functions of employees. The literature on school reform continually points to the vital role instructional leaders play in improving student achievement. States have followed the recommendations in these studies with legislative mandates requiring administrators to allocate a majority of their time to supervising classrooms. Yet, the diversions of schooling continue to overwhelm the supervisory functions of school administration. The question remains, "Why do schools continue to be," in the words of Sergiovanni (2005), "overmanaged and underled" (p. 4)?

School administrators who venture into the realm of curriculum and instruction face a formidable set of institutional, cultural, and political obstacles that are never fully overcome, are messy to mediate, and exert a heavy emotional toll on those who challenge the prevailing norms of institutional schooling in the United States. Not only must instructional leaders confront public and institutional norms that are hostile to changing how we all experienced school, but they face hostile publics with little or no training in the knowledge and skills necessary to assume the role of instructional leader. A recent study (Levine, 2005) of programs in educational leadership concluded that the design and implementation of the curriculum for most educational leadership programs continues to support the role of manager. Little content in these university programs is devoted to the kinds of knowledge and skills necessary to lead a school instructionally (Levine, 2005). The conclusions in this study imply that the process of becoming an instructional leader will be a highly personal affair with little assistance from formal institutions of learning.

Having said that, the literature on organizational leadership is replete with examples of women and men who have orchestrated fundamental changes in the direction and the day-to-day operations of the organizations they lead. Herb Kelleher, CEO of Southwest Airlines, started up a new model for airline travel in an era when the "majors" thought that serving peanuts and not assigning seats bordered on the bizarre. Alan Mullaly, CEO of Ford Motor Company, transformed the culture of an auto company known more for recalls than reliability. Lou Gerstner, CEO of IBM, refocused a technology giant on what it did best rather than on what it could acquire. Although the portraits of these individuals exhibit a wide range of personality types, working styles, and experiences, one common attribute of these leaders is the ability to transform the *ought* of the organization into the everyday functions of their employees (Drucker, 2006).

Another quality that sets these leaders apart is their personal commitment to becoming students of their industry. This quality contrasts dramatically in that literature with portrayals of the ideal CEO as one who possesses a set of generic management skills with regard to, for example, staffing, budgeting, goal-setting.

In emerging global economies, doing the right things is as important as doing things right. Generic management skills might make your organization good, but it will not make it great (Collins, 2001). Good organizations manage information and people well; great organizations transform information into knowledge and manage talent well. The latter qualities of great organizations are enlarged by leaders who select the right information from the environment, employ the right people, establish the right systems for effective execution of great ideas, and maintain focus on the aims of the organization. Few organizations have the kind of leaders who select well, employ well, execute well, and purpose well. Leaders who do this, however, understand their organizations well enough to act like a hedgehog while those in the same industry who don't do these things well act like foxes. Table 7.1 summarizes the distinction between how great leaders (hedgehogs) think about organizations and how good leaders (foxes) think about organizations (Collins, 2001). Hedgehog leaders burrow deep into an organization to see what he or she is best at in the world and allow no distractions to divert attention from the goal of being great at what he or she does best. Fox leaders are always scanning the business environment for the latest business platform, technique, or acquisition to achieve fast growth and advance their careers. Great leaders possess the knowledge and skills to simplify a complex message so that it becomes a single worldview, discard messages that do not support that worldview, and focus all resources on executing the worldview. Simply put, great leaders implement aims; good leaders implement diversions. Chapters 1 through 6 described the thinking, activities, and outcomes prevalent in schools governed by a fox-like mentality in a world requiring hedgehog-like leadership.

In the field of education, the qualities of hedgehog-like leadership find parallels in a new construct called "Leadership Content Knowledge" (Stein & Nelson, 2003, p. 423). This model asserts that implementing an instructional initiative demands that school administrators understand the theories and practices embedded in new pedagogies. Stein and Nelson's (2003) new definition of instructional leadership says school administrators simultaneously carry on the management function of instructional improvement (the traditional definition of instructional leadership) and the teaching function of instructional improvement (leader of content knowledge). The latter role requires school administrators to enter classrooms and assist teachers with resolving the fundamental questions of schooling. Like a hedgehog, leaders of content knowledge carry the aims of schooling into the functions of schooling.

Table 7.1. Implementing Aims Versus Implementing Diversions

Implementing Aims	Implementing Diversions
Simplified	Diffused
Reduce the complexities of an industry into a single organizing idea, basic principles, or a concept that unifies and guides all decisions.	Pursue many ends at the same time with no one end serving to guide decision-making or the direction of the organization (the diversions of school administration).
Integrated	Disjointed
Reduce everything to simple hedgehog ideas. Any idea that does not relate to the hedgehog idea is discarded.	Treat all ideas equally and pursue them with equal energy on many different levels of the organization (the dance floor).
Focused	Distracted
Concentrate on carrying out one idea or concept with excellence and imagination.	Complete as many tasks as possible before the day ends ("the classroom").

Note: The hedgehog and fox idea were inspired by Collins, 2001.

.Missing from this new construct of "administrators-as-teachers" (Stein & Nelson, 2003, p. 426) are concrete examples of how you transform yourself from a traditional instructional manager to a leader of content knowledge—what I have named Strong Instructional Leadership. Chapters 7 through 13 describe a model for becoming a Strong Instructional Leader. The model is framed as a series of three journeys. The journeys are presented in a learn-plan-do sequence. In the real world of schooling, however, the journeys collapse into seamless webs of studying (private journey), planning (public journey), and doing (situational journey). Each journey undergoes modifications from its outset as a result of the vagaries of resolving particular instructional problems in particular settings. However, along their journeys, these leaders never lose sight of the instructional worldview developed during their private journeys.

Authoring Instructional Worldviews

The foundation of Strong Instructional Leadership is the development of an instructional worldview (a philosophy or explanatory framework) for thinking about emerging or persistent instructional problems. An instructional worldview is a conceptual understanding of how curriculum, instruction, assessment, and organizational environments are brought together to resolve particular instructional problems. In the classroom, a school's instructional worldview results in a pattern of teaching that originates with a consistent response to the five fundamental questions of schooling:

1. How do children learn?
2. What knowledge is of greatest worth?
3. How should knowledge be organized?
4. How should we assess what students understand?
5. How should we teach?

The formulation of a coherent instructional worldview is particularly important for school administrators who work in organizations with little control over inputs, who supervise a profession with little understanding of what constitutes quality teaching, and who are unable to standardize the processes and outcomes of their organization. In such an uncertain organizational environment, Strong Instructional Leaders always begin a school reform journey with an instructional worldview that provides teachers with an instructional framework to make sense of the storm of mandates, learning theories, instructional programs, teaching techniques, and the daily crises swirling around their schools. The process for developing an instructional worldview is an eclectic one; they search for the right combination of terminology, metaphors, and analogies to connect the theory and practice of a teacher with a theory and valued end of schooling.

The first journey of three undertaken by such a leader is a private one that requires disciplined wandering back and forth between the fundamental questions of schooling (see Table 7.2) and the theories and practices governing an instructional problem. Throughout this mental wandering between the world of theory and the world of practice, Strong Instructional Leaders read pertinent research, talk with experts in the field, and conduct conversations with teachers who are most affected by an instructional problem. Emerging from these intellectual wanderings, these leaders author coherent instructional solutions for messy classroom problems. They become experts in the art of piecing together loosely coupled systems of theories and practices into a recognizable mosaic of core teaching behaviors that make collective sense to a faculty and clarify a valued end of schooling— what kind of person do we want our students to become?

Coherent expressions of theory, practice, and valued ends of schooling alone, however, will not influence a faculty to embark on a new instructional journey. The final piece in the instructional tapestry crafted by a Strong Instructional Leader is a plan of action that sounds feasible to a staff. No matter how clear an instructional worldview might be, in the practical world of schooling, teachers want to know how school administrators intend to make school practices consistent with a school's response to the fundamental questions of schooling. It is at this juncture in constructing an instructional worldview that Strong Instructional Leaders become specific about the amount and kind of time, materials, training, and changes in organizational structure that they are capable of committing to move teachers from an old pedagogical worldview to a new pedagogical worldview.

Effective instructional worldviews accomplish four goals. First, they establish a link between valued ends of schooling and particularities of pedagogical practice. The emotional draw of educational goals cited in school mission statements (e.g., critical thinking, child-centeredness, excellence) needs a vehicle for translating a valued end of schooling into the practical realities of classroom teaching. Good instructional worldviews provide connections between vague educational ideals and specific classroom practices.

Second, instructional worldviews are composed of vocabularies, analogies, metaphors, exemplars, and stories that help teachers translate prior understandings of teaching and learning into contemporary understandings of how subject matter should be taught. New pedagogies evolving out of state and professional content standards clearly reflect an instructional ideology that favors constructivist approaches to developing curriculum and teaching subject matter. While these new ambitious standards for teaching reflect the best theoretical thinking in curriculum and instruction, they fall short in clearly articulating what these theories look like in classrooms. Wide gaps now exist between adopting constructivist theories of curriculum and instruction and actual classroom teaching (Windschitl, 2002). Policymakers are calling upon school administrators to become the lead interpreters in erasing the gap between pedagogical theory and practice. Bridging

Table 7.2. Framework for Constructing an Instructional Worldview

Fundamental Questions of Schooling	Educational Beliefs		
How do children learn?	Mimic	←→	Construct
What knowledge is of greatest worth?	Instrumental Outcomes	←→	Intellectual Growth
How should we organize subject matter?	Cover	←→	Understand
How should we assess what students understand?	Evaluate	←→	Assess
How should we treat children?	Objects	←→	Subjects
How should we teach?	Tell	←→	Facilitate

gaps between theory and practice requires scaffolding, an instructional worldview, that supports the development of new pedagogies from old understandings of how to organize and teach subject matter.

Third, instructional worldviews provide school administrators with a framework for developing priorities and focusing resources. The history of failed school reform initiatives begins and ends with school administrators trying to implement ambitious pedagogical initiatives with too few resources. For any ambitious pedagogy to have a fighting chance, school administrators must make strategic decisions on how many reforms they are able to undertake (breadth) in a school year and on the complexity of the theories and practices associated with a new pedagogy (depth). Instructional worldviews provide school administrators with a framework for understanding the relationship between the breadth and depth of new instructional initiatives.

Fourth, and most importantly, instructional worldviews provide an interpretative framework for teachers to notice what is important in their classrooms, to place what is important within a theoretical framework, and to translate theory into teaching practice. It makes more sense to teachers to implement an instructional initiative that is framed with a coherent worldview of teaching and learning than it does to implement a little of this theory, some of those ideas, and a few of these practices. Teachers are more willing to make fundamental changes in pedagogy when school leadership helps them connect the dots—theories agree with ideas, ideas agree with actions, and actions agree with practices. The most pervasive impediment to instructional improvement is the failure on the part of teachers and school administrators to know how and what to discard, modify, or fully embrace in the vast world of educational theory and practice. Coherent instructional worldviews provide boundaries between theories and practices that are welcomed into a school and theories and practices that are left at the entrance door.

Constructing a coherent response to an instructional problem is the most difficult component of the school improvement process because the abstractions of educational theory do not easily apply to the messy world of classroom practice. Not only is theory talk usually far removed from practice talk, but the range of theories and ideas in education is wide and often contentious. The last century of public schooling placed administrators and teachers onto school battlefields where a diverse array of theories and practices in curriculum and instruction struggled (Kliebard, 1987) for dominance in classroom teaching. Each decade witnessed the comings and goings of one underdeveloped instructional worldview after another. School administrators adopted whatever instructional worldview aligned with the most recent perfect storm of national priorities (e.g., the launch of Sputnik), public mood swings ("Why can't Johnny read?"), and the ideology of the day (e.g., data-driven schools). Fox-like responses to instructional problems, however, do not provide the continuity and coherence for establishing a purpose (a philosophy) for accommodating a new pedagogy.

The ability to simplify, integrate, and implement an ambitious pedagogy in education requires leaders who know who they are educationally. School administrators who begin a school improvement process with strong understandings of theories and practices that govern a particular instructional initiative are able to frame instructional problems in ways that continually establish connections between a particular instructional worldview and a particular theory or practice in education. Table 7.2 shows the components of one version of a framework for constructing an instructional worldview. The left column identifies six fundamental questions of schooling that educators have asked for centuries about teaching and learning. The right column represents a continuum of theories and practices that offers answers to the fundamental questions of schooling.

The literature on organizational behavior looks upon teaching as a coping profession governed by unclear goals, unsure definitions of good teaching, and an inability to measure outcomes (Wilson, 1989). Given the uncertainties surrounding schooling in the United States, Strong Instructional Leaders come to believe that no single pattern of theories or practices could possibly resolve a complex instructional or curricular problem. They are not dogmatists captured by the ideology of the day or opportunists implementing the technique of the day. They are pragmatists who continually evaluate the combined abilities of their choices of theories and practices to develop a child intellectually, socially, and emotionally.

Admitting to the uncertainties associated with teaching and learning is not a rationale for discordant combinations of theories and practices. The overarching goal of an instructional worldview is to bring sense to the uncertainties, dichotomies, and dilemmas embedded in the messy worlds of classrooms. The ultimate outcome of the private journey is the construction of an instructional worldview that imposes order on unclear goals, uncertain characteristics of good teaching, and immeasurable outcomes.

Bringing clarity, coherence, and continuity to an instructional problem requires an elaboration of the broad categories represented in Table 7.2 followed by the placement of these elaborated responses into a system of theories and practices. The resulting resolution to an instructional problem establishes, albeit imperfectly, cause-and-effect relationships, expectations for certain desirable outcomes, and acceptable patterns of behavior. Table 7.3 summarizes three instructional worldviews that have dominated schooling in the past century. Depending on the political, economic, and social circumstances of a particular period in our history, each worldview has assumed a privileged place in our nation's schools. For the purposes of this book, it is not important to recount the historical influence of each instructional worldview on schooling in the last century. The goal of Table 7.3 is to represent systems of theories and practices that could serve as a starting point for the development of a private instructional worldview.

Table 7.3. Historical Instructional Worldviews

Fundamental Questions of Schooling	Instructional Worldviews		
	Humanism	Behaviorism	Progressivism
What are the aims of schooling?	Truth and rationality	Training	Critical thinking
What is the nature of the self?	Humans are pre-wired	Humans are blank slates	Humans are social beings
How do students learn?	Imitation	Association	Social interaction
What knowledge is of greatest worth?	Classical texts	Cultural reproduction	Problems of society
How should knowledge be organized?	Structure of the disciplines	Task analysis of predetermined knowledge and skills	Inquiry-based learning
How should we assess what students understand?	Essays & tests	Achievement scores	Authentic performances
How should we teach?	Didactic	Technologists	Facilitator

The focus of Strong Instructional Leaders is influence—finding opportunities to help teachers understand the why and how of a new instructional initiative. While the particularities of an instructional problem call for emphasis on different questions and different theories and practices composing an instructional worldview, what holds the problem-solving process together is an unyielding adherence to a valued end of schooling and a pedagogical worldview supporting those ends.

More will be said about the problem-solving process in Chapter 8. Before leaving the subject, however, I do not want to leave the impression that Strong Instructional Leaders are educator-philosopher-kings who spend their days spreading pedagogical wisdom among their faculties. On the contrary, learning, both in adults and in children, is a highly social process involving thought and language (Vygotsky, 1962). Teachers do not change core teaching practices by looking at the principal talking about a new idea. Teachers make significant changes in core teaching practices through ongoing conversations with the principal, with other teachers, and with consultants about their understandings of unfamiliar theories and by experimenting with a new pedagogy. Problem-solving is less about promoting the one best instructional worldview and more about the ability to create school cultures in which teachers have time to collaborate, venues in which to observe and experiment with a new pedagogical skill, and a trusted process for receiving feedback from experts. Throughout the problem-solving process, Strong Instructional Leaders are strong narrators of a new pedagogy and strong choreographers of social contexts in which teachers work at and talk about a new way of teaching.

School administrators who are comfortable with solving the diversions of the day are uncomfortable with hedgehog-like processes that require study, deliberation, and negotiation to link particular instructional problems with a larger worldview of schooling. Some might view the entire framing process as a huge waste of time. An administrator with a fox-like mentality is more comfortable making rapid-fire decisions based on instinct and what worked in the past. While fox-like approaches may solve little problems and check off diversions, they do not result in fundamental changes to the technical core of teaching.

The profound insight of Stein and Nelson's (2003) construct of leadership content knowledge is the essential role that knowledge of subject matter and pedagogy plays in the ongoing dialogue between instructional leaders and their staff about instructional problems. Instructional leaders gain legitimacy in the eyes of teachers and are more likely to be invited into discussions about instructional problems when they connect theory to practice—not the practices recommended by the theory, but what teachers are actually practicing in the classroom. An invitation to discuss an instructional problem provides the leader of content knowledge (Strong Instructional Leader) with opportunities to formulate, along with teachers, a coherent approach to understanding and acting upon an instructional problem. Common responses to the big and little problems that grow out of any instructional change effort are part of the process for solving an instructional problem. The challenge is to weave into every conversation a blend of theories and practices that reflect a coherent response to the fundamental questions of schooling and a pedagogical framework that builds bridges between the remote world of theory and the immediate world of the classroom.

These instructional discourses include healthy disagreements over proposed systems of theories and practices that are a natural result of teachers and administrators coming to instructional problems from different worlds. School administrators who are not properly prepared for these healthy disagreements (they have skipped the private journey) are uncomfortable with instructional conversations. Strong Instructional Leaders, however, view instructional conversations as opportunities to influence the direction and thinking about a pedagogical worldview. Influencing worldviews requires strong preparation. Long before formal announcements of a new instructional initiative, such leaders spend their time out of the view of their faculty engaged in a learning process through which they acquire a personal understanding of the theories and practices supporting a new pedagogical approach, develop an understanding of how a pedagogical theory works in real classrooms, and then author a narrative weaving together theory, practice, and the school's worldview. One cannot teach or coach teachers through the collective sensemaking process without a thorough grasp of the theories and ideas controlling a new pedagogical practice. Simply put, Strong Instructional Leaders do their homework.

As pointed out in earlier chapters, no program in educational administration provides a purposeful path for learning the necessary knowledge to move from the role of instructional manager to instructional leader (Levine, 2005). Even if there were such a path, authoring instructional worldviews, practical arguments, and coaching conversations is a private undertaking. Each instructional worldview, practical argument, and coaching conversation bears the stamp of a unique perspective on teaching and learning that, if communicated well by Strong Instructional Leaders, permeates the conversations and practices of teachers in their buildings.

Where do these unique perspectives on teaching and learning come from? Table 7.4 outlines one version of a course of study that school administrators could pursue to prepare for authoring instructional worldviews, practical arguments, and artful coaching sessions. The bold text represents the normal discourses of schooling. For more than a century, discourses over schooling originate from one or more of the theories, practices, and questions listed beneath the discourse. School administrators who choose to become Strong Instructional Leaders must privately become fluent with the foundational theories and practices in education. Fluency in the private journey means developing different levels of understanding for each normal discourse of schooling. The social context of a school determines what discourses become operative in a given instructional situation and what level of understanding of each discourse is necessary to intelligently solve an instructional problem. The normal discourses are not intended to be a list of required topics for all school administrators to know and understand. Leaders who earnestly engage in these discourses construct a personal instructional worldview that makes sense to them—a worldview that they are willing to publicly promote.

Although normal discourses in education provide a historical account of how educators settled the problems of schooling in their time, the theories, ideas, and practices listed in the chart may or may not hold answers to contemporary problems of schooling. As Dewey often repeated in his philosophy of education, change and uncertainty is a normal condition of mankind. School leaders who deny the change dynamic rely on normal discourses to get them through the day, but they will fail to advance children emotionally and intellectually in constantly changing environments.

**Table 7.4. Normal Discourses of Schooling
(Theories, Ideas, Practices, Questions)**

Goals of Schooling
Democratic Equality, Social Efficiency, Social Mobility, Civic Involvement, Vocational Preparation, Existential Values, Humanistic Values
Teaching Traditions
Socratic, Mimetic, Apprenticeship-Based, Emancipatory
Problems of Schooling
Problem of Institutions, Problem of Goals, Problem of Pedagogy, Problem of Self, Problem of Experience
Learning Theories
Behaviorism, Cognitive Development, Constructivism, Social Interaction
Classroom
How do children learn? How should we teach?
Philosophical Systems
Perennialism, Idealism, Realism, Existentialism, Experimentalism
Curriculum
What knowledge is of greatest worth? How should subject matter be organized? How should we assess what students have learned?
Curriculum Theories
Humanism, à Progressivism, à Social Efficiency, à Developmentalism, à Social Meliorism

The dilemma today's educational leaders confront is developing processes of continual improvement within institutional environments that value stability and certainty. Innovation, or what Dewey (1958) liked to call imagination, only occurs when individuals search for novelty in daily habits and routines that are not working. Novelty, however, does not reside in normal discourses of schooling. Rather they reside in what Richard Rorty (1979) calls "abnormal discourses"(p. 320).

Engaging in abnormal discourses in education truly becomes a private journey of reading, listening, and talking to educators who travel outside the boundaries of contemporary discourses of schooling. Table 7.5 reflects my private conversations with contemporary educators whose understandings of psychology, history, philosophy, and sociology of schooling challenge the normal discourses of schooling in the United States. Each author in his or her own discipline speaks to me intellectually, emotionally, and professionally. The theories and practices put forth by each educator provided novel ways of viewing teaching, learning, and school administration. Each author's perspective on the fundamental questions of schooling was influential in constructing my instructional worldview, which has become a unique amalgam of normal and abnormal discourses of schooling. Of course this is my list, and in no way should it be considered *the* list. What Dewey would expect from administrators leading schools in uncertain environments is a commitment to a continuous process of renewal that originates with private journeys into abnormal discourses of their profession.

Strong Instructional Leaders are never satisfied with normative understandings of schooling. They feel compelled to search beyond traditional (normal) educational discourses for theories and practices, which can be anything from, in Richard Rorty's words, "nonsense to intellectual revolution" (1979, p. 320). It is in these private journeys that school administrators discover their unique instructional voices. Strong Instructional Leaders continually employ those voices to help faculties see what is nonsense in schooling, and what theories and practices in schooling possess the possibility of creating an intellectual revolution in their classrooms.

Actively Interpreting School Reform Initiatives

After gaining a private understanding of an instructional worldview, Strong Instructional Leaders embark on a private journey of actively interpreting an instructional problem in their building. They literally try out their understandings of new pedagogy by listening to how fellow administrators and teachers respond to their explanations of a new theory of instruction or a solution to an instructional problem. As these conversations progress, passive understandings of instructional theories and practices become active representations of the vocabulary, stories, experiences, and backgrounds of a particular school.

Table 7.5. Abnormal Discourses of Schooling, Contemporary Authors

Contemporary Educators

Robert Bullough; Mihaly Csikszentmihalyi; Linda Darling-Hammond; Elliot Eisner; David Elkind; Ronald Gallimore; John Goodlad; Maxine Greene; David Labaree; Deborah Meier; Nel Noddings; Seymour Sarason; Ted Sizer; Roland Tharp.

Organizational Theory (Educational Leadership)

Deborah Coburn; W. Edwads Deming; Peter Drucker; Michael Fullan; Andy Hargreaves; Jeffrey Liker; Peter Senge; Edgar Schein; Donald Schön; Thomas Sergiovanni; James Spillane; Karl Weick; Etienne Wenger; Margaret Wheatley.

Curriculum

Michael Apple; Leon Botstein; Harry Brody; Jerome Bruner; Kieran Egan; Howard Gardner; Gerald Graff; Georoge Hillocks; Walter Kaufmann; Martin Nystrand; Joesph Schwab; Ralph Tyler.

Philosophy

Ernest Becker; Nicholas Burbules; Anthony Damasio; John Dewey; Gary Fenstermacher; Stanley Fish; Jürgen Habermas; Sidney Hook; William James; Martin Heidegger; Thomas Kuhn; Reinhold Neibuhr; Frederick Nietzche; Martha Nussbaum; Plato; Michael Polyani; Karl Popper; Richard Rorty; Alfred North Whitehead.

History of Education

Larry Cuban; Lawrence Cremin; Herbert Kliebard; Diane Ravitch, David Tyack.

Social Context of Schooling

Jean Anyon; Peter Berger; Pierre Bourdieu; Michael Cole; Lisa Delpit; Penelope Eckert; Clifford Geertz; Anette Lareau; Luis Moll; Angela Valenzuela; Philip Wexler.

Inside Classrooms

Deborah Ball; Barbara Tye; David Cohen; Phil Jackson; Dan Lortie; Susan Rosenholtz.

Teaching

Marie Clay; T. F. Green; Madeline Hunter; Parker Palmer; Lee Shulman; Lev Vygotsky.

Table 7.6 summarizes the distinction between active and passive interpretations of instructional problems (Daft & Weick, 1984). Passive interpreters of instructional change initiatives assume no responsibility for explaining to faculty the theories and practices composing new approaches to curriculum and instruction. Traditional definitions of instructional leadership fall into the passive profile of policy interpretation. Instructional managers perceive their roles as administrators of resources, directors of logistics, coordinators of assignments, and supervisors of tasks. In the passive mode of interpretation, school administrators fulfill their responsibilities by distributing materials and setting up workshops. Teachers fulfill their responsibilities by following prescribed scripts and attending workshops. School administrators and teachers who adopt passive modes of interpretation are expected to mimic what is given to them by external policy bodies. No private journey is necessary in this model. No venue exists in passive modes of interpretation for teachers and administrators to engage in a deliberative process determining what theories and practices embedded in a new instructional initiative need to be adopted, modified, or discarded. The implementation of a new pedagogy becomes merely a matter of acceptance, presentation, and distribution.

Strong Instructional Leaders assume the role of active interpreters of instructional change initiatives. They do not allow any theory or practice to enter their school unfiltered—if it enters the school at all. They assume responsibility for working with faculty to make collective sense of new instructional initiatives. They understand that effective implementation of a new pedagogy has little to do with managing the logistics of a new instructional initiative and everything to do with how teachers come to understand and apply new learning theories to the real world of classroom instruction. The implementation of a new pedagogy becomes a matter of adaptation, deliberation, collaboration, and influence.

Table 7.6 identifies three interpretative acts that Strong Instructional Leaders privately rehearse before going public with a new pedagogy. In Act I of active interpretation, they identify instructional problems that are surfacing in public and private conversations with teachers. The comments uttered in hallways, lounges, and faculty meetings might point to a schoolwide problem (e.g., absenteeism) or a problem experienced by a particular group of teachers (e.g., bilingual program issues). No matter where such leaders stand in their buildings, however, they hear a problem before they construct a practical argument (Fenstermacher, 1986) to resolve a pattern of frustrations expressed by faculty.

Before they can actively interpret what teachers are saying about an instructional problem, they must discriminate between commonsense interpretations of an instructional problem and intellectual interpretations of an instructional problem. Teachers in the former mode of interpretation seek solutions based in beliefs and practices that are weakly associated with purposeful methods of inquiry, such as the belief that practice makes perfect or that positive comments motivate students to do better. Teachers in the latter mode of interpretation demonstrate a mode of thinking that is strongly informed by research and experimentation: What kinds of practice applied to what kinds of tasks produce better learning? What kinds of positive comments applied to what kinds of tasks produce better learning?

After determining where a faculty or a group of teachers falls on a continuum between common sense and intellectual interpretations of an instructional problem, Strong Instructional Leaders construct a private understanding of the beliefs, theories, and practices that intelligently explain an instructional problem. They must resolve existing gaps between how teachers are thinking about an instructional problem and what research says about the instructional problem. Teachers

Table 7.6. Acts of Interpretation

Source	Passive Interpretation	Active Interpretation
Information (Act I)		
What gets noticed	• State & federal mandates • District policies & procedures • Professional accreditation guidelines	• Social context of school (e.g., where students and teacher are coming from) • Intentional states of students • Personal observations and discussions • Reliance on anecdotal information
Interpretation process	• Reactive • Limited to what authorities & legislative bodies mandate • Rule bound • Continually asking for more information • Mimic regulations, guidelines, & procedures	• Proactive • Open to multiple viewpoints • Few rules • Develop common terminology & conceptual understandings • Analyze and evaluate
Decision-making process	• Rational • Goals à Tasks à Plan of Action • Implement program or theory	• Experimental (trial & error) • Plan à Implement à Assess à Modify à Plan
Theories, Ideas, & Practices (Act II)		
What gets noticed	• Model schools programs (e.g., Little Red School House, Success for All) • Curriculum frameworks/standards • Well-known consultant	• Pedagogies promoted by professional organizations (e.g., NCTM; NCTE) • Thematic and interdisciplinary approaches to subject matter • Non-institutionalized approaches to pedagogy (e.g., Expeditionary Learning)

Interpretation process	• Telling → Selling • Follow teaching scripts or protocols • Align or map curriculum to mandated standards or accreditation guidelines	• Listening → Facilitating • Autonomous (dependent on subject-matter specialties; social context) • Create frameworks, outlines, guides that represent common understandings of theories and practices
Decision-making process	Adopt mandated program → Present	Construct worldview → Filter programs (adopt, adapt, ignore) à Develop appropriate curriculum

Audiences (Act III)

What gets noticed	• Packaged programs • Well-known consultants • What other districts are doing	• Theories and ideas • Authorities in the field • Experimental programs
Interpretation process	• Publicize in formal media (e.g., newsletters) • Presentations for formal policy bodies (e.g., Board of Education) • Promotion	• Position papers • Program reviews • Focus groups • Influence
Decision-making process	Delegate → Monitor → Bring Into Compliance	Participate → Assess → Modify → Reinterpret → Transform

Adapted from Daft & Weick, 1984.

view what the research says as a remote world of abstract conceptions of behavior expressed in experimental designs, correlations, and confidence levels. The world that teachers live in is a situational world lodged in classrooms—where habits and folk psychology allow them to survive for another day. In Act II of active interpretation, Strong Instructional Leaders privately resolve the balancing act between theory and practice by constructing practical arguments for adopting a new pedagogy. Fenstermacher (2002) describes practical arguments as the merging of the hard world of experimental discourse and the soft world of beliefs, intentions, and purposes.

University scholars build content and methodological walls between both worlds. In the real world of schooling, active interpretation of new pedagogies requires an accommodation between theory talk and classroom practice. Pedagogies heavily laden with theoretical concepts become unapproachable in classrooms where judgments are based on personal insights, understandings, and feelings. Pedagogies devoid of theory become a random assortment of techniques and folk psychology, which eventually become hardened into routines, prejudices, and instrumentalism.

But schools are messy places where theory and practice historically do not mix well. The very natures of theoretical knowledge and practical knowledge work against their seamless integration in classrooms. In fact, the goals of generalization, predictability, and validity never integrate well with the goals of particularity, ambiguity, and spontaneity. Strong Instructional Leaders understand and accept the reality that no pedagogy effectively integrates the certainties of science with the uncertainties of the classroom. They overcome the dissimilarities of both worlds by privately creating a transformative pedagogy that works soundly in a classroom.

Sound pedagogies are coherent articulations of why a certain combination of materials, activities, strategies, organization, and subject matter result in a valued end of instruction. The why becomes the controlling question in acts of interpretation. Why questions inevitably force practitioners into thinking theoretically about how they teach—the world of generalizations meeting the world of particularities. Caught between these two worlds, Strong Instructional Leaders assume the role of instructional coach. In that role, they perform four functions in the interpretative process:

1. Articulate a valued end of schooling residing in an instructional problem.
2. Accurately describe the facts controlling an instructional problem.
3. Select theories and practices associated with an instructional problem.
4. Facilitate institutional processes, assisting teachers with
   the active interpretation of a new pedagogy.

The essence of active interpretation of an instructional problem is the private construction of a practical argument. Well-constructed practical arguments accomplish two goals. First, they dissolve the walls between the world of theory and the world of practice. Second, they challenge teachers to think differently about an instructional problem. Accomplishing the first goal requires the employment of a variety of explanatory frameworks (e.g., analogies, metaphors, vocabularies) that connect traditional and contemporary discourses on teaching and learning. The second goal promotes argumentation as a method of presenting and defending minority viewpoints regarding a particular instructional problem. Conversations employing practical argumentation ask participants caught up in a problematic instructional situation to engage each other in a respectful give and take over opposing theories and practices. Adapting Fenstermacher's (1986) model for practical argumentation, Tables 7.7, 7.8, and 7.9 present three practical arguments constructed by a Strong Instructional Leader with regard to problems existing at different levels of a school organization: building (fighting in hallways), department (admissions to higher education), and classroom (reading comprehension).

As Strong Instructional Leaders construct practical arguments, they are mindful of the tension that exists between teacher beliefs that control a particular instructional problem and theoretical understandings of the problem. This does not mean that practical judgments of teachers in the classroom must be continually scrutinized using instruments and methodologies from the research community. It does mean that practical arguments and subsequent practical actions must evolve out of deliberative processes through which teachers and administrators apply disciplined methods of inquiry (see Table 7.10) to habitual ways of thinking and acting upon an instructional problem.

Strong Instructional Leaders conclude their active interpretation of an instructional problem with private constructions of practical arguments that make sense to audiences *outside* the walls of the school. Schools are located in districts, in towns, in counties, in states, and in a nation. Each audience interprets an instructional problem differently. Teachers view a problem with reading compre-

Table 7.7. Practical Argument: Fighting in Hallways

Situation	• We are experiencing an increase in the number of fights in hallways. • Teachers and deans observe different gangs congregating in different parts of the building.
What the Research Says	• Studies of school safety conclude that violence occurs in "unowned" areas of the building (those areas where students feel no adult presence) (Astor, Meyer, & Behre, 1999). • The deans charted the locations of violence in our building and found that fights are occurring in places where teachers rarely travel.
Action	• Work with teachers' association and design an arrangement through which departments will claim ownership of different parts of the building. • Each teacher in the department will assume supervisory responsibility for "unowned" places in our building.

Table 7.8. Practical Argument: Admission to Institutions of Higher Learning

Situation	• We are experiencing an increase in the number of English Language Learners who are coming to our school with advanced training in mathematics and science. Because of their low English proficiency, we are placing these advanced ELL students in remedial or low-level courses in mathematics and science. • School achievement reports indicate that a majority of these students are dropping out because they are bored and angry about placement in low-level math and science courses. • ELL students who come to our school in college-bound tracks are unable to gain admission to higher education because they lack courses in advanced mathematics and science.
What the Research Says	• Educators mistakenly think that proficiency in conversations in English transfers into understanding the abstract vocabulary and concepts of academic subject matter. The ability of ELL students to carry on conversations in our cafeteria is very different from their ability to understand a lecture or read a textbook in biology (Bailey & Butler, 2003; Cazden, 2001; Cummins, 1991, 2000). • Although the research is mixed, learning of academic content knowledge appears to work best in dual-language environments (Thomas & Collier, 2002). • Advanced courses in core academic subjects are gateways to post-secondary education.
Action	• Actively pursue teacher candidates who are proficient in the target language and possess content majors in science, social studies, and mathematics. • Develop dual-language course offerings for advanced academic subjects.

Table 7.9. Practical Argument: Increasing Reading Comprehension

Situation	• While our students appear to be reading more, comprehension still remains a challenge for them; also our students do not seem to retain and apply vocabulary from their weekly lessons to other texts. • School achievement reports indicate that the basal reading series does not contain a systematic approach to teaching reading comprehension, and our weekly reading strategy does not appear to increase reading comprehension.
What the Research Says	• Isolated skills-based approaches to teaching reading (e.g., vocabulary, phonics) may perpetuate low literacy achievement rather than improve reading comprehension and literacy behaviors (Brause, Lee, & Moliterno, 2008). • Effective instructional pedagogy for teaching reading comprehension requires foundational knowledge of how the components of the reading process fit together and the application of those understandings to the social context of specific classrooms (Commission of Reading, 2004).
Action	• Bring together grade-level teams to discuss the following questions: (1) What are students doing when they comprehend a text? (2) What do we mean by a balanced reading program? (3) What role should basal readings play in our reading program? • Invite grade-level teams to sit down with a consultant to devise a plan to implement an effective and balanced reading program.

Table 7.10. Five Questions in the Collective Sensemaking Process

Question	Elements of Practical Argumentation
1. What is the problem?	Valued End of Schooling + Situation
2. What should we do about the problem?	Valued End of Schooling + Situation + Theory
3. How should we do it?	Valued End of Schooling + Situation + Theory + Action
4. What happened?	Valued End of Schooling + Situation + Theory + Action + Consequences
5. What do we do next?	Repeat Questions 1, 2, 3, and 4

hension (poor parenting) differently from parents (poor teaching); boards of education view the problem of reading comprehension (low test scores) differently from state officials (failure to implement model-school-reform programs); and state legislators view the problem of reading comprehension (loss of federal funding) differently from national policymakers (loss of an election).

While remaining sensitive to the various audiences they face, Strong Instructional Leaders never change the substance of the original practical argument. Audiences still hear statements about a valued end of schooling, statements about the current situation, statements about an instructional theory, and statements about a course of action. What changes in the practical argument is the depth and breadth of the statements. Boards of education, for example, do not want theory talk; they want to know about the course of action the district will pursue in implementing a new pedagogy. In this case, the practical argument is short on theory and long on the resources and organizational configurations required to accomplish a valued end of schooling. In each instance of active interpretation of an instructional problem, the ultimate goal is to not mislead an audience but to tailor a practical argument for the particular understandings and needs of particular audiences. What sustains the integrity of a practical argument is faithful attention to a valued end of schooling and to an instructional worldview that promotes what a school community values about teaching and learning.

It should be understood that active interpretation of a new pedagogy demands that school administrators stop dancing around the classroom and start entering teacher workspaces. Only in classrooms, in hallways, in lounges, and in media centers will common understandings of a new pedagogy materialize. All knowledge (theories, principles, facts) are socially constructed (Berger & Luckmann, 1966). No theory, principle, or fact is neutral—all knowledge originates from someone, located someplace, with some purpose in mind. Making sense of a theory-based instructional initiative requires high levels of joint study, discussion, and practice among teachers and administrators. Ultimately, the result of the interpretative process is an instructional reality unique to the talents, training, and social context of a school. The goal of the Strong Instructional Leader is to maintain a close relationship between newly constructed instructional realities and the original intentions of the theories they promulgate.

Implementing School Reform Initiatives

School administrators who assume the role of active interpreters of new pedagogies understand that changing deeply held beliefs, ideas, and practices about teaching and learning involves an interaction between how teachers understand a new pedagogy and how the organization supports the practice of a new pedagogy. School administrators who become active interpreters of new pedagogies become adept at orchestrating the interaction between acts of interpretation and organizational configurations (see Table 7.11) that facilitate a faculty's pursuit of collective sensemaking (Weick, 1995).

At the heart of the collective sensemaking resides a leader who continually draws teachers into conversations over the five questions listed in Table 7.10. Strong Instructional Leaders do not ask these questions from their offices. Rather, they seek out and create a variety of discourse and practice communities where administrators and teachers come together to discuss relevant questions in a collective sensemaking process. Each act of interpretation in the process carries with it the same method of inquiry (see Table 7.10). Depending on the responses of teachers, some questions are asked more frequently than others. What remains constant in the collective sensemaking process is the role of the leader. He or she keeps the logistics of the process moving along and employs vocabularies, analogies, metaphors, and stories to describe, explain, and clarify the theories and practices of new approaches to curriculum and instruction.

Table 7.11. Tasks of Collective Sensemaking

Acts of Interpretation	Organizational Configurations
• Disrupting normative understandings of an instructional problem • Introducing new vocabularies, theories, and practices governing an instructional problem • Explaining and modeling new vocabularies, theories, and practices in teacher workspaces • Becoming a participant in instructional conversations about problems evolving out of the implementation of a new pedagogy	• Providing time, expertise, and materials to experiment, interpret, and practice a new pedagogy • Providing safe spaces for teachers to fail with a new pedagogy • Providing venues where teachers clarify and challenge habits of teaching • Making available the technical and logistical support for teachers struggling with a new pedagogy

Dissolving the gap between what the research says and what works for teachers requires both an understanding of theories and practices that govern the new pedagogy and the development of practical applications for adopting a new way of teaching. School administrators who become active interpreters of new pedagogies leave behind the role of manager in order to author, together with teachers, new interpretations of teaching and learning.

8

The Public Journey:
Engaging Skeptics

In the public journey, Strong Instructional Leaders assume the public responsibility for creating organizational configurations that permit school administrators and faculty to negotiate the meaning of a new instructional initiative. The first aim of the public journey is to frame the instructional problem in such a way that applicable learning theories make practical sense to teachers. The second aim is to create activity settings in which teachers and administrators are positioned to deliberate over and practice unfamiliar theories, ideas, and practices in curriculum and instruction.

While developing an understanding of instructional problems is a private journey carried on far from the classroom, the ultimate resolution of an instructional problem occurs in classrooms. The outcomes of private journeys are instructional worldviews, practical arguments, and position papers. Classrooms filled with 25 or more students, however, are not welcoming places for theory talk or philosophies of education. Schools and classrooms are in constant motion with little time left for observation, analysis, and reflection. Teachers are pragmatists. They typically want to know what works, not why it works. In the public journey, Strong Instructional Leaders assume the public responsibility for creating venues where school administrators and faculty come together to make collective sense of the why and how of a new pedagogy.

Strong Instructional Leaders act upon the assertion that changing core beliefs about teaching and learning requires an understanding of the interaction between the theory and practice of a new pedagogy. Without understanding how theory informs practice and how practice informs theory, teachers focus on the techniques of a new instructional message rather than the theory underpinning it. In accountability cultures, where principals run around with clipboards inspecting classrooms for visible evidence of a new pedagogy (e.g., lesson plans, word walls), focusing on the how of a new pedagogy rather than the why works very well. Focusing on the how without knowing why works poorly in reflective cultures within which teachers are expected to carry out theory-based instructional initiatives. School administrators in reflective instructional environments are not running around with clipboards. Instead they enter teacher workspaces to discuss the relationships between the methods of a new pedagogy (e.g., math manipulatives) as well as the theoretical justifications for employing certain methods at certain times with certain students (e.g., students learn by constructing mathematical formulations).

Reflective instructional environments are founded on processes designed to help teachers grasp relationships between the abstractions of theory talk and the reality of classroom practice. One focus of the public journey is to design organizational configurations that facilitate collective deliberations over theory talk and practice talk. Strong Instructional Leaders accept the reality that prior understandings of teaching and learning always trump unfamiliar educational theories and practices. Abandoning the inspectorial role of accountability cultures, such leaders spend their time orchestrating an educative process that allocates time and expertise for conversations about dissatisfactions with current practices, presentations of alternative theories and practices, and opportunities to openly experiment with new pedagogies.

The process of collective deliberation involves developing discourse communities (joint productive activities settings), where teachers and faculty come together to negotiate a shared understanding of what constitutes an instructional problem, what conditions are causing the problem, what the consequences of the problem are, and what theories or practices might resolve it. Joint productive activity settings (Tharp, 1993) become places in a school building and district where time, space, materials, and expertise are readily available to generate the kinds of social processes—discussions, deliberations, coaching, and modeling—that enlarge teacher understandings and applications of a new pedagogy. Strong Instructional Leaders are a constant presence in these settings. They assume a central role in providing teachers with appropriate levels of organizational and intellectual support to move faculties to expansive ways of thinking about and acting upon instructional problems.

For example, a faculty might begin looking at the problem of poor attendance and high dropout rates of particular groups of students as a problem of poor parenting. Strong Instructional Leaders, in their private journey, however, might come to see this problem as a poor match between institutional ways of learning and individual learning styles and interests of particular groups of students. Framed in this way, the problem of poor attendance and high dropout rates might be appropriately addressed by establishing personalized learning environments accommodating the learning styles and interests of groups of disaffected students. Clearly there is a gap between what the faculty thinks ought to be done with this group of students (suspension from class) and what the Strong Instructional Leader discovered in the private journey. Bridging gap between suspending chronically absent students and accommodating their individual learning style, involves drawing faculty into a deliberative process over the causes, consequences, and theories of student alienation.

Table 8.1 lists the components of collective deliberation. Each component of collective deliberation is designed to negotiate meaning and develop an understanding among faculty of the relationship between the theory and practice of a new pedagogy. During the process of collective deliberation, it is critical to link substantive changes in teachers' thinking about an instructional problem to opportunities to practice that new thinking in classrooms. Understanding and then implementing ambitious teaching is an extraordinarily complex and difficult undertaking. Teachers who embark on such a journey require time, resources, and training to implement both the how and the why of a new pedagogy.

Instructional managers see no need to engage in a process of collective deliberation over a new pedagogy. Managers view implementation of a new instructional initiative as a problem of capacity: the capacity to fund, schedule, purchase, employ, assign, and assess a new program. Strong Instructional Leaders approach implementation of a new instructional initiative as a problem of education: how to establish a process through which teachers adopt dissonant worldviews of teaching and learning. Instructional managers view instructional change as a matter of resource allocation and logistics. Strong Instructional Leaders view instructional change as a process of making collective sense (Weick, 1995) out of theories and practices that challenge firmly held views about the fundamental questions of schooling (see Table 7.2).

Much goes on between the lines of this skeletal outline of collective deliberation. Strong Instructional Leaders devote as much attention to organizing (developing administrative systems to accommodate a new instructional

Table 8.1. Collective Deliberation

Component	Action
Leveraging	Identifying an instructional situation where preexisting teaching routines, beliefs, and theories are not achieving a valued end of schooling
Announcing	Presenting practical arguments in support of a new pedagogy in public venues (e.g., faculty meetings, board meetings, open-house nights)
Conversations	Initiating discussions in teacher workspaces (e.g., classrooms, department offices, hallways) over the conditions and consequences of a failed pedagogy and advocating for a new pedagogy
Modifying	Adjusting practical arguments to accommodate teacher interpretations of a pedagogical problem without sacrificing the integrity of the theories and practices of an instructional worldview
Organizing	Arranging school organization to accommodate a new pedagogy (securing resources, selecting staff, choosing materials, developing training regimes, and creating or modifying support systems)
Implementing	Initiating a pilot program to test a new pedagogy

worldview) as they devote to conversations (theory talk with teachers). Acquiring, planning, and scheduling the kind of expertise and staff development opportunities to assist teachers with a new pedagogy is every bit as important as negotiating the meaning of a theory or practice.

Thus far, it would appear that collective deliberation is a rational process led by a leader whose public journey focuses on connecting the dots between theory and practice. Schools, however, never stand still. In the midst of implementing a new instructional initiative, they confront continual disruptions from opposing theories and practices generated by shifts in personnel, political environments, demographics, or the crisis of the week, month, or year. Strong Instructional Leaders guard against the vagaries of school environments and the give and take of collective deliberation by continually referencing the instructional worldviews developed during their private journeys. What keeps the components of the deliberative process tied together is a compelling story that weaves together the essential questions that teachers ask about a new reform initiative:

- Why is this instructional problem important?
- What do we know about the problem?
- How do we solve the problem?

Instructional Narrative: Disarming Skeptical Publics

Solutions to instructional problems announced from stages, displayed on PowerPoint Slides, or brought into classrooms by a consultant assume that teachers care about the problem, assume that teachers know something about the problems, and assume that teachers will cooperate with the proposed solution to the problems. If one or more of these assumptions is false, the process of collective deliberation will, at best, falter and, at worst, break down in collective opposition. The sole focus of the private journey is transforming private understandings of a problem into public commitments to become part of the solution. At the center of the public journey is a narrative that takes into account what teachers care about, what they know about, and what they are willing to resolve.

Instructional narratives attempt to make sense of a problematic situation in a school. Good instructional narratives bring together in public venues a description of sources of dissatisfaction among teachers, possible strategies for eliminating the sources of dissatisfaction, and the resources the district is willing to commit to helping teachers resolve them. Figure 8.1 illustrates the components of an instructional narrative. Strong Instructional Leaders utilize a variety of communication tools to engender a public narrative that includes a problem, a solution, and a plan of action. Administrators employ metaphors and analogies that connect what teachers are experiencing in their classrooms to a well thought-out plan of action. A well-crafted instructional narrative tells a compelling story about

FIGURE 8.1. Instructional Narrative Components

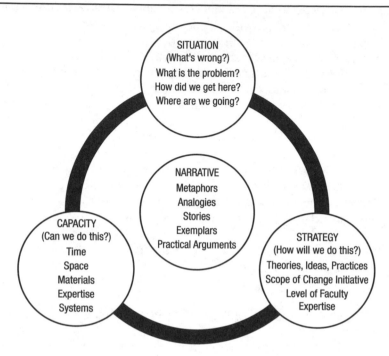

how a faculty can turn around an instructional problem they care about and that encompasses an educational goal that attracted them to the profession of teaching. Teachers do not change a core teaching belief by being told to do so. Teachers are more willing to pay attention to a new pedagogy when school leaders address an instructional problem that teachers feel strongly about and provide a plan of action teachers believe is feasible.

The power of an instructional narrative lies in its ability to draw teachers, as agents, into the resolution of an instructional problem. Instead of sitting in dark auditoriums, viewing programs from afar, Strong Instructional Leaders place themselves and their teachers in the center of the instructional problem. If the situation is described well, teachers see the problem, hear the problem, and feel the problem and envision their role in solving the problem. Ultimately, the persuasiveness of an instructional narrative does not lie in the emotional force of the story alone but in the substance of the narrative—a philosophy of education—that ties together valued ends of schooling, the theories and practices of curriculum and instruction, and realistic methods of implementing new pedagogies in the everyday routines of classrooms.

This does not mean that teachers automatically agree with an instructional narrative or that the skillful crafting of an instructional narrative induces a unified "aha!" experience among faculty. The goal of the public journey is to entice teachers into beginning "private journeys" of their own. As with the private journey of a Strong Instructional Leader, teachers require time, space, materials, expertise, and a safe environment to arrive at their personal understanding of a new pedagogy. At the same time Strong Instructional Leaders are presenting their instructional narratives, teachers proceed to "joint productive settings" to deliberate over the meaning of a new pedagogy. It is in these settings that teachers personalize the theories and practices of a new pedagogy.

Productive Collaboration

School organizations are configured as traditional bureaucratic structures with the superintendent of schools sitting at the top of the organization, principals managing the middle of the organization, and teachers implementing policies directed down from the central and main offices. Policies and procedures originate from the superintendent's office with the expectation that principals will execute the policies and teachers apply the policies. If the board of education and superintendent decide, for example, that a certain program in reading or bilingual education or mathematics should be adopted in district classrooms, principals are expected to execute the program in their buildings and teachers are expected to implement the program in their classrooms. Principals execute the new pedagogy by managing the resources and logistics allocated to their buildings from the superintendent's office. Teachers apply the new pedagogies in their classrooms by following the curricular content and methods prescribed by the board of education and superintendent. Bureaucratic schooling closes the feedback loop with a procedure for reporting up to the central office the level of teacher compliance with a new instructional program. Building principals deliver progress reports in formats documenting frequency counts of teaching practices and achievement scores. Bureaucratic schools are data-driven schools.

While the bureaucratic model of schooling ensures efficient use of resources and uniform methods for inspecting a staff's compliance with mandated programs, they are poorly designed for educating faculty on the why and how of a new pedagogy. Locating teachers in activity settings instead results in better comprehension of a new pedagogy. Joint productive activity settings can be formal meeting spaces or informal workspaces in a school building or district. What makes these activity settings productive is that workspaces can be regularly accessed, materials can be left on tables and walls, and participants can talk, observe, write, and read without being disturbed. Since schools are busy places and teachers learn best when they apply theory to practice, joint activity settings will often move out of formal and informal workspaces into classrooms, hallways, the cafeteria, the teachers' lounge, and the parking lot.

Central to the function of joint productive activity settings are safe environments where teachers, administrators, and curriculum specialists feel free to think out loud and openly practice new pedagogies that are fundamentally different from accepted practice and offer vague descriptions of the what and how of teaching a new pedagogy (Spillane, 1998). A sign that joint productive activity settings are working will come from discussions and behaviors that show a growing willingness on the part of administrators and teachers to

- acknowledge the worth of new ideas,
- accept the critiques of colleagues,
- experiment with ambitious pedagogies, and
- ground their practice in purposeful methods of inquiry.

Strong Instructional Leaders assume two responsibilities in the public arrangement and supervision of joint productive activity settings. First, they organize the school community for continuous learning: Administrators with the authority to generate organizational capacity are present in joint productive activity settings with teachers engaged in learning and practicing a new pedagogy. For a new pedagogy to make sense to practitioners, teachers and support personnel must be invited into activity settings where they receive the resources required to transform the generalities of theory into the particulars of practice. Strong Instructional Leaders bring together the right people, the right resources, and the right materials to engage in the difficult process of learning a new pedagogy.

Second, after placing the right people in the right places with the right resources, such leaders continually move in and out of activity settings to monitor teacher understandings. No matter how well conceived a joint productive activity setting may be, the constant flux of instructional situations requires continual adjustment of personnel, expertise, and resources. Strong Instructional Leaders maintain focus and clarity throughout the sensemaking process by reallocating personnel and resources to maintain the best fit between the generalities of theory and the particulars of specific situations—they connect the dots.

Connecting the Instructional Dots

When attempting to change core teaching behaviors strong leaders must "connect the instructional dots" in order to main relationships between the world of theory, the world of institutions, and the world of classrooms. In education, connecting the dots is extremely complex because administrators and teachers deal with countless human and organizational variables that make it all but impossible to establish cause-and-effect relationships. Without the ability to establish conclusive answers to the what and why of an instructional problem, there is always a certain degree of ambiguity surrounding efforts to implement new pedagogical approaches in schools.

Strong Instructional Leaders confront ambiguous instructional situations with instructional narratives designed to connect the dots of an instructional problem with appropriate theories, practices, and resources. But good instructional narratives are not enough to connect all the dots. Adapting Weick's "maxims for action" for sensemaking in organizations (Weick, 1995, p. 182), Strong Instructional Leaders expertly perform the following sensemaking actions in and around teacher workspaces:

- *Listen well*: Strong Instructional Leaders do not impose an instructional narrative on faculties. They enter teacher workspaces in a respectful manner with the purpose of jointly constructing the meaning of a new pedagogy. Rather than shutting down innovation with the imposition of contrary theories and practices, they assimilate teacher understandings into the original instructional narrative. As a new instructional initiative permeates classrooms, the instructional narrative evolves into discourse patterns that remain true to the spirit of the new pedagogy but reflect the experiences of particular faculties teaching in particular schools.
- *Facilitate understanding*: Contemporary reform initiatives carry with them an abundance of terminology that means many things to many people. Strong Instructional Leaders do not talk to teachers in mandated policy speak. When they enter teacher workspaces, they are careful to always explain what they mean by educational terms associated with a new pedagogy (e.g., critical thinking, lifelong learning, and differentiated instruction). When defining educational terms, the terminology is associated with what teachers do in classrooms.
- *Place experiences in historical context*: Strong Instructional Leaders do not place an instructional narrative on automatic pilot. The social, emotional, and intellectual complexity of school environments continually renders obsolete instructional narratives authored in private journeys. Strong Instructional Leaders continually communicate to (document for) faculties what happened, what is happening, and what will happen with the trials and errors of changing core teaching practices. What emerges from these running historical narratives is a reformulation of the original instructional narrative to fit the facts on the ground as experienced by teachers and administrators directly involved in implementing a new pedagogy. Reformulations of instructional narratives, however, always remain true to a valued end of schooling, a school's instructional worldview, and the theories underpinning the new pedagogy.
- *Create an atmosphere for good meetings*: School administrators and teachers have long harbored a strong disdain for meetings. In regulative school environments, there is justification for viewing meetings as a "huge waste of time." Bureaucratic approaches to schooling use meetings to talk at employees or to orchestrate "contrived collegiality"

(Hargreaves, 1991, p. 46). In reflective school environments, however, meetings of all kinds are the life blood of implementing a new pedagogy. Collective sensemaking in a reflective school environment is a highly social process. Strong Instructional Leaders purposefully design regular opportunities for teachers to come together to discuss the meaning and application of a new pedagogy. It is within these joint productive activity settings that teachers have the time, information, expertise, and tools of inquiry to clarify and reformulate their private understandings of new theories and practices in curriculum and instruction.

• *Hold people accountable:* In managerial and regulative school environments, instructional managers focus on moving materials and personnel and relegate the process of collective sensemaking to 1-day workshops. The deliberative process is emptied of meaning when administrators fail to make clear who is taking responsibility for seeing that teachers can successfully implement new pedagogies. Strong Instructional Leaders make sure that within the social process of developing common understandings of a new pedagogy, a teacher or school administrator assumes responsibility for reporting on the tangible outcomes arising from joint productive settings. They expect fellow administrators and teachers to end all deliberative processes with someone doing something with some theory in some classroom.

• *Ensure that joint activity settings are productive:* Talk alone does not help teachers make sense of a new teaching practice. Common understandings of unfamiliar theories and practices in curriculum and instruction evolve out of a process that integrates theory into talk about shared experiences in classrooms. An integral component of a joint activity setting is positioning teachers so they can teach together, observe each other, and talk with each other about what they do in classrooms. Collective sensemaking occurs best in environments where theory and practice talk are integrated. This integration of theory and practice transforms abstract terminology and methods into the language of everyday teaching. Teachers' eventual understandings rest solely on how expertly Strong Instructional Leaders help teachers talk theoretically about shared experiences in the classroom.

• *Author new realities:* What makes theory different from practice is the real world. Theories are often generated in experimental situations where environmental variables are statistically cleared out to focus on the study of the effects of one treatment variable. In the real world of schooling, however, school administrators and teachers possess no methodology for isolating a teaching practice from myriad environmental variables that bombard classrooms. Strong Instructional Leaders understand that no theory will ever be the same when exposed to the turbulent environments of real school settings. With this understanding, such leaders, along with their faculties, do not mirror a theory but author a new interpretation of that theory into new pedagogy. If done well, the instructional practices authored by school administrators and teachers remain faithful to the principles of the new pedagogy and, at the same time, function within the boundaries of what works in particular schools and particular classrooms.

Throughout the long and tedious process of making collective sense out of a new instructional initiative, teachers must feel that they have the time, materials, and expertise to implement a theory-driven instructional initiative. Strong Instructional Leaders assume responsibility for providing the proper mix of resources for supporting an instructional change initiative and creating environments so administrators and teachers can engage in continuous reconstruction of a school's response to the fundamental questions of learning—these leaders build organizational capacity.

Organizational Capacity: It Costs Money to Do Something Well

Early in my administrative career, I was asked to lead an innovative curriculum-writing project by the district superintendent for curriculum and instruction. As the project progressed, I became concerned with the amount of money I was spending on teachers' salaries and consultant fees. Midway through the project, I stopped by the assistant superintendent's office to report on the status of the project. I ended my progress report with the comment, "I realize that I am burning through a lot of money." He looked up from the booklets I had brought and said, "Young man, it always costs money to do something well." This brief comment summarizes decades of research on the relationship between resources and successful changes in core teaching practices. The substantial amounts of money that the private sector spends on training, research, and development is testimony to the importance that research and development play in global competition and should play in our schools.

Schools devote little of their resources to research and development. Sophisticated approaches to curriculum and instruction are implemented year after year in our schools with little more training than a 2-day workshop or a 1-week summer curriculum writing project. Implementing a change in core teaching practices requires monies for faculty release time, employment of consultants, purchase of appropriate materials, and the construction of new organizational configurations. Without appropriate resources, the willingness to learn, experiment, and transform quickly dissipates into the decades-long lament of teachers that "this too shall pass."

Strong Instructional Leaders never begin an ambitious change in curriculum and instruction without building the organizational capacity to support teachers' pursuit of a new pedagogy. School administrators, however, live in budgetary worlds in which there is little money for innovation. Strong Instructional Leaders employ four strategies to negotiate the formidable obstacle to innovation that is created by limited research and development budgets.

First, during the private journey, Strong Instructional Leaders construct an instructional worldview that prioritizes quality approaches to curriculum and instruction. No time or money is wasted pursuing the technique or program of the day. Pedagogies that enter their schools possess the curricular and instructional power to change how teachers think and practice the fundamental questions of schooling and the intellectual justification for a long-term investment in a new pedagogy or organizational configuration.

Second, such leaders create school cultures stripped down for instruction. Monies spent on the diversions of schooling, special interest projects, employment of specialists, and mandated programs are reallocated for classroom instruction.

Third, Strong Instructional Leaders become proficient at the politics of schooling—developing networks, managing information, building coalitions and collecting favors (Hoy & Miskel, 2005). They view the politics of schooling as a tactic rather than a game. As a tactic, political acumen in schools is essential for gathering resources that further a quality instructional program. Approached as a game, political machinations dissipate a faculty's commitment to changing a core teaching practice. Faculties accept the reality of school politics when school leaders use this tactic to increase the capacity of teachers to do their jobs. Faculties become cynical in school environments where leaders utilize politics to further administrative careers.

Finally, Strong Instructional Leaders always connect the request for more resources with a convincing instructional narrative. School boards and district personnel are much more willing to allocate resources for projects that reach their meetings in the form of a narrative describing a feasible organizational strategy for resolving gaps in student performance. Teachers are much more willing to enroll in ambitious approaches to teaching when they hear a feasible pedagogical strategy for resolving a difficult classroom problem. All parties in a school community who are experiencing a gap between how students are performing in classrooms and a valued end of schooling require a rationale—a compelling instructional narrative—to begin their journey toward instructional improvement.

Changing Core Teaching Beliefs

Regulative approaches to educational reform continue to misfire in our schools. While these prescriptive approaches to curriculum and instruction are attractive to accountability-minded policymakers and the strong power proclivities of instructional managers, they forget (or ignore) that teachers (and school administrators) come to their classrooms from "someplace." That someplace influences a collection of pedagogical beliefs and ideas that work for a teacher. No mandate, PowerPoint presentation, or walk-through can dislodge the cognitive, social, and emotional histories that teachers bring with them into classrooms.

Strong Instructional Leaders enter schools with an understanding that changing core teaching beliefs and practices is not a managerial function, but a pedagogical undertaking. With this mindset, such leaders view instructional or organizational problems not as situations to be managed, but as opportunities to teach faculty about theory-driven instructional initiatives. They also understand that they work in institutions designed to regulate, not to teach. The public journey becomes the vehicle for transforming institutional environments into activity settings designed for continuous learning.

Authoring a compelling instructional narrative and building organizational capacity to house that narrative is necessary, but not sufficient for seeing that narrative come alive in classrooms. The final journey of the Strong Instructional Leader occurs in daily classroom situations where instructional narratives confront the vagaries of classroom practice. The true test of instructional narratives and the understandings acquired in joint activity settings lies in the moment-to-moment interactions between teachers and students. Before embarking on the final journey into particular classrooms, with particular teachers, about particular instructional problems, one more trial awaits the Strong Instructional Leader. Even the best-conceived instructional narrative is vulnerable to assaults from "unschooled" (Gardner, 1991) understandings of teaching and learning and how schools should work. While departing the public stage, such leaders remain ready to return to the public journey to protect classrooms from public enemies capable of reducing ambitious instructional narratives to the daily grind of schooling.

9

Public Enemies

School administrators and teachers work in environments with uncertain goals, uncertain methodologies, and uncertain student bodies. Without a strong empirical and political foundation that supports what teachers and school administrators do in schools, educators become more susceptible than other professionals to colonization by the theories, ideas, and practices of what Howard Gardner calls the unschooled mind. In education there are five unschooled ideas that have charmed educators but are toxic to educational worldviews founded on expanding the thinking and practices of school faculties: truthfulness, reductionism, foreign worldviews, control, and "satisficing."

The landscape of contemporary schooling in America is littered with instructional techniques, policies, laws, and school routines shaped by "unschooled" approaches to teaching and learning. Curriculum alignment, grade retention, prohibitions against bilingual education, standardized testing, the 7-period day, and elimination of recess are just a few examples of unschooled practices that at best have proved ineffective and at worst are harmful to the emotional, social, and intellectual development of children. Journeying from the public stage to the particulars of classroom practice, Strong Instructional Leaders continually scan the educational horizon for the emergence of oppositional instructional worldviews. When an unschooled idea is introduced to their school, Strong Instructional Leaders return to the public journey to publicly oppose toxic theories, policies, and practices that possess the power to suffocate a maturing instructional narrative. The five unschooled ideas summarized here have a long history of disrupting the best-thought-out instructional narrative and the capacity for constraining a school's instructional worldview.

Truthfulness

The tradition of teaching in Western civilization is founded on the eternal search for the truth; the unexamined life is not worth living. Strong Instructional Leaders honor this belief by including in the process of collective deliberation tools of inquiry that require the substantiation of truth claims—what the research says. The toxicity of this idea, however, lies in whose version of truth an educator pursues. When Plato spoke about truth, he talked about eternal and immutable ideas or "forms" that everyone caught a glimpse of at birth but that only a chosen few (philosopher kings) would eventually "recollect." In Plato's instructional worldview, there was no need for inquiry because the student merely recollected information they already knew. Plato's version of pursuing the truth is played out every day in schools where school administrators look to content standards, standardized testing instruments, and scientific models of instruction as truths to be implemented in district classrooms. Framed this way, truth is given, never discovered; looked at, never constructed; presented, never interpreted.

John Dewey's conception of the truth was far different from Plato's. Dewey argued that the complex human and physical problems of our planet are not solved by reference to established truths, categories, or essences. Embedded in Dewey's description of intelligent thinking is an inquiry process dominated by the constant reconstruction of established truths (theories and practices) in ways that would solve, at least temporarily, the difficulties of the day. The problem of pedagogy in Dewey's instructional worldview is not one of how to transmit a given text efficiently, but rather one of mediating the private world of language, culture, personal interests, and experiences of the student with disciplined ways of knowing the world.

Approaching truth from Dewey's perspective requires teachers to venture beyond the certainties of state standards, prescribed curriculum, approved texts, and standardized assessments into the uncertain world of the needs, interests, capacities, and concerns of the individual child and the intellectual, aesthetic, and democratic values of our society. From a Deweyan perspective, schools and academic communities spend too much time teaching ideal and unchangeable Platonic truths—standards, facts in the textbook, canonical interpretations—and little or no time on developing levels of thinking and methods of inquiry that are required to solve pressing problems in society.

Strong Instructional Leaders include in their instructional worldviews organizational configurations and tools of inquiry that question mandated policies, challenge approved curricular materials, and reconstruct accepted models of teaching and learning. They facilitate processes that provide faculty with time, expertise, and forums to intelligently question the beliefs, ideas, and practices of the normal pedagogies of the day. No policy, pedagogy, curriculum, or staff development program goes unexamined. The ultimate goal of examining the truth of the day is reinterpreting that truth—theories, standards, and techniques—in the context of the problems and situations in which teachers find themselves. Examined truths, in schools led by Strong Instructional Leaders, are truths that are consistent with the schools' instructional worldview and work in the classroom.

Reductionism

Closely associated with the pursuit of truth is educators' infatuation with scientific approaches to teaching and learning. Educators look to empiricism as a way to salvage their problematic status as a profession. There is nothing like a

T-score or a day of data analysis to restore the status of a profession perceived as light on theory and heavy on intuition. The scheduling and credentialing functions of institutional schooling also align well with reducing knowledge and skills to more fundamental and smaller parts: Disciplines become standards; standards becomes subjects; subjects become objectives; and objectives become PowerPoint presentations.

Empirical approaches to teaching and learning inevitability result in reducing the child to a series of data points or the classroom to a set of variables. While such approaches appeal to researchers and policymakers, they look awful in classrooms. Teaching becomes seven steps, lessons become "I can" statements, writing becomes three paragraphs, thinking becomes taxonomies, disciplines become subjects, reading becomes decoding skills, and knowledge becomes IQ scores. The goal of reductionism is to simplify, categorize, and test.

Children learn little about the world by defining ten vocabulary words, identifying the eleven parts of the frog, naming the rivers of North America, or knowing when the Hay-Paunceforte Treaty was signed. Children learn about the world by talking about it, asking questions about it, drawing it, writing about it, reading about it, and building it. Children come to understand the world not by looking at it but by participating in it. Institutional schooling creates artificial boundaries between intelligence and emotion, reason and intuition, and theory and practice. In the real world, no such boundaries exist. Employers, family members, and fellow citizens expect action. Plans of action work best when good ideas are passionately pursued, when reason is informed by hunches, and when a theory works.

Strong Instructional Leaders see little value in pursuing curricula or pedagogies designed to reduce teaching, learning, and subject matter to manageable pieces that are then tested, aligned, and observed. Instead, they construct instructional narratives that begin with where a child comes from and proceed to where a child is drawn. The narrative ends with citizens who govern the world intelligently and individuals who remain curious about the world around them. Subjects originating from this instructional worldview become a discipline; lessons become situations; objectives become problems; and outcomes become plans of action. What continually drives strong instructional worldviews is a search for curricula, teaching practices, and organizational configurations that spark the curiosity of young people and transform an interest into disciplined ways of understanding the world.

Foreign Worldviews

Every profession carries with it a system of beliefs, values, theories, practices, and a vocabulary evolving out of particular problems in a society. Doctors solve health problems; engineers solve building problems; businessmen solve distribution problems; scientists solve cosmic problems; and teachers solve learning problems.

Each problem contains a unique set of variables to be analyzed, theorized about, and acted upon. Each profession develops distinctive frameworks that explain how select sets of variables relate to theories and how theories relate to actions.

The unique nature of the problems taken on by each profession draws natural boundaries around their explanatory frameworks. Lawyers would not think of operating on a patient; a doctor would not think of trying a case. Both professions, however, would have no problem telling teachers how to teach a class. Because of public accessibility to schools, the profession of teaching is particularly vulnerable to professional boundary crossing. Professionals cross boundaries when they seek to impose elements of their explanatory frameworks on the explanatory frameworks of another profession. When the explanatory framework of a foreign profession colonizes a profession, the colonized profession surrenders the vocabulary, tools of inquiry, and valued outcomes that define its special function in a society. Colonized professions give up their status as a profession; they no longer possess the specialized knowledge and skills a society is calling for.

Boundary crossing by the business profession has been particularly corrosive to public schooling and the profession of teaching. On the national level, the adoption of policies incentivizing more testing, school choice, and an array of accountability measures designed to reward and punish school performance reflects the dominance of business discourses over social democratic discourses (Hursh, 2007). A profession brought up in a tradition of democratic equality and critical inquiry is transformed into a profession expected to train productive workers and dole out favored programs (gifted, honors, advanced placement) to students destined to be bosses.

At the local level, educators are dominated by vocabularies, theories, and practices straight out of corporate America. Superintendents become CEOs, principals become directors, teachers become coordinators, and students become data points. Educators no longer look to Plato, Dewey, or Tyler for guidance but to the "Seven Steps," One-Minute Remedies, and Baldridge Quality Awards. Inundated with mounds of data, teachers and school administrators have little time to review texts, analyze proposed curricula, or study a new instructional strategy. A profession founded on excellence, optimization of difference, and creativity (uncertain outcomes) becomes an orphan in a worldview within which definitions of quality are reduced to customer satisfaction, standardization, and measurable outcomes.

During the private journey, Strong Instructional Leaders realize the moral purpose of schooling. If we are a society and not a market, then our private search for meaning and our public pursuit of a livelihood incorporate instructional worldviews that examine how we can live together in a decent way and preserve the dignity of human beings (reduce fear and humiliation). Such leaders ground instructional worldviews in the moral purposes of schooling. They remain ever vigilant in protecting their schools from attempts at colonization by instructional worldviews that denigrate the right to be different, the right to participate, and the right to serve.

Control

Strong Instructional Leaders oppose the culture of control with an instructional worldview composed of three core principles. First, administrators and faculties should do no harm. Strong Instructional Leaders assume the role of ombudsman in all procedures and judgments regarding student discipline. They actively intercede in any case where students are denied due process or where a punishment inflicts fear or humiliation on a student. Knowing that quite a lot of student discipline goes on without their knowledge, in their public and situational journeys, Strong Instructional Leaders draw boundaries around acceptable and unacceptable approaches to discipline. When it comes to student discipline, all participants—students, parents, teachers, and fellow administrators—enter the office on an equal playing field. School officials enter the office of such leaders understanding that no matter what the infraction, the involved student was listened to, was never threatened, and never felt humiliated. If any of these rules have been violated, teachers and fellow administrators know that things will not go well in the main office.

Second, administrators and faculties will not blame the victim for poor school performance. Depending on where you stand in the organization, the blame always moves downward: The board of education blames the superintendent for not developing a policy; the superintendent blames the principal for not knowing about the situation; the principal blames the teacher for not retiring a year ago; the teacher blames the administration for not testing the student for special education services; and all of the above blame the parent for not reading to the child.

Strong Instructional Leaders take a step back from this chain of blame and ask the question, "Are institutions designed to educate young people or regulate their movement through a bureaucracy?" The answer arrived at during their private journey is the recognition that schools are more suited to granting "grades, credits, and degrees" (Labaree, 2000, p. 3) than developing a student socially, intellectually, and emotionally. Every day in our nation, students attend schools with many rooms, many teachers, many bells, and many subjects. Children and adolescents spend most of the day sitting, listening, taking notes, and taking tests. There are brief moments in a school day when students become truly engaged with their environments (e.g., before school, passing periods, lunchtime, and after school). But these moments rarely involve what is going on in classrooms.

The collateral damage to teaching and learning caused by institutional worldviews of schooling leads to the third core principle of Strong Instructional Leadership—place an emphasis on the pull of schooling rather than the push of schooling. Instructional worldviews designed to draw students into schools assume that when students are fearful or bored, mischief occurs. To counter the dysfunctional behaviors brought on by unwelcoming and monotonous environments, Strong Instructional Leaders work with faculties to develop instructional environments that are meaningful, personalized, and provide authentic options for students. Students are pulled towards instructional environments when

- they find the subject they are studying meaningful;
- they believe the teacher wants them to succeed;
- the subject is organized in a way that makes sense to them;
- the subject relates to a personal goal;
- they are permitted multiple options for demonstrating proficiency; and
- they possess the appropriate knowledge and skills
  to perform at higher levels in a discipline.

Creating instructional environments that honor the substance of schooling rather than the forms of schooling is a formidable undertaking, especially in policy environments that dole out rewards and punishments based on the efficient performance of the forms of schooling. While Strong Instructional Leaders employ different mixes of organizational and instructional configurations to draw students toward school, they remain loyal to W. Edwards Deming's (1986) first commandment of leadership—all perceived human failures in organizations are caused by a dysfunctional system. Strong Instructional Leaders, like Deming, search for causes of poor school performance in the systems of schooling, not in their victims.

"Satisficing"

Organizing a school for teaching and learning is a complex undertaking. School administrators expend a great deal of energy and thought on putting students, books, curricula, and teachers in the right classrooms at the right times. Unlike their counterparts in the private sector, school administrators assume this management responsibility in organizations with unclear goals, unsure teaching methods, and no control over consumers (students). Despite uncertain goals, teaching technologies, and suppliers, school administrators are still expected to apply the same rational decision-making models used in the private sector. In the real world of schooling, administrators never possess enough time, information, or expertise to consider all of the possible alternatives and consequences of a decision. Instead, school administrators settle for a solution that works rather than adopt the best solution—that is, they "satisfice" (Simon, 1947).

All school administrators, even Strong Instructional Leaders, satisfice. The political, organizational, cultural, and technical systems that move in and around a school each day are too complex for one individual to fully comprehend or rationally act upon. The buses arrive, the day begins, and decisions must be made. School administrators draw on past experience, training, and intuition to just keep the organization moving. These decisions may not be the best, but they almost always keep the school doors open.

While satisficing is an administrative fact of life, Strong Instructional Leaders know when they have satisficed and know when they have made the right decision. The distinction is an important one because it signals the ability to differentiate between aims, diversions, and functions. What works (diversions) gets you through the school day; what is best (aims) creates an instructional worldview that advances quality learning environments.

Strong Instructional Leaders resist succumbing to the uncertainties of the social context of schooling. In their private journeys, they develop a clear understanding of the instructional worldview they are pursuing. Along the way, the political, cultural, technical, and organizational pressures of the day sometimes require a decision that just works. However, if one looks below the surface of the multitude of decisions made by a Strong Instructional Leader, a pattern of decision-making emerges. In subtle ways, each decision aligns with a particular instructional worldview. No decision serves as an obstacle to realizing a particular instructional worldview in classrooms. Teachers in schools led by such leaders know when school administrators have satisficed. At the same time, teachers also know that whatever decision required satisficing, the school's instructional worldview was not compromised—never satisficed.

Strong Instructional Leaders are not idealists; they are pragmatists. They are well aware of the power of unschooled minds to reduce classroom instruction to taking timed tests, learning best-guess strategies for multiple-choice tests, and writing state standards on chalkboards. When confronted with a powerful public enemy, Strong Instructional Leaders seek out a middle ground between the valued ends and means of their instructional worldviews and the public enemy of the day. If they have become comfortable with who they are educationally—the private journey—they are capable of authoring a response to the public enemy of the day that preserves a school's intellectual culture as well as satisfies state mandates.

Strong Instructional Leaders are guided by the response to two questions: (1) What is the intellectual quality of what students are doing and producing in classrooms? (2) How do I organize time, space, materials, and personnel to achieve high levels of thinking, reasoning, and communication? Administrators who complete the private, public, and situational journeys will know what high levels of intellectual quality look like and how to move a faculty towards that goal. No public enemy can penetrate an instructional worldview that defines the intellectual culture of a school.

There will come those times in the career of a Strong Instructional Leader when a public enemy forces its way through the schoolhouse door. It is at these rare times when the listening, framing, and facilitating stops and being "alone at the top" begins. Developing an intellectual culture in a school demands that at certain times and places administrators walk into boardrooms and classrooms and say: "No, we aren't doing that." A school administrator becomes a strong instructional leader when that "no" resonates with the school community they serve. The journeys in this book describe a process for acquiring the knowledge and determination to say no to those mandates, policies, and procedures that would undermine a school's instructional worldview. The signature of Strong Instructional Leadership is protecting their school from unschooled minds.

The Myth of Failing Schools

Standing alone, the unschooled beliefs about schooling in America could be largely ignored by Strong Instructional Leaders. Drawing attention to these beliefs are the election cycles that feature unschooled politicians perpetually calling for more accountability from teachers and school administrators working in failed school systems. Since the publication of *A Nation at Risk* (1983), teachers and school administrators stand accused of not teaching Johnny how to read, not believing that all children can learn, and leaving children behind. These allegations are followed up with urgent calls from the media and governing bodies to raise students' achievement, or else. To support these allegations and calls for action, media "experts" and politicians reference a collection of "facts" about student achievement in U.S. schools that appear to prove the case for tougher accountability mandates. When examined closely, however, the "facts" of educational decline in America are myths manufactured for short-term political purposes. Some of the more common myths used to justify harsh accountability legislation include the following (Berliner & Biddle, 1995, pp. 5–6):

- Student achievement in U.S. primary schools and colleges
  has recently declined.
- America's schools always come up short when compared
  with schools in other countries.
- The United States spends a lot more money on its schools
  than do other nations.
- Investing in the schools has not bought success—indeed money is
  unrelated to school performance.
- Recent increases in expenditures for education have been wasted or have
  gone merely into unneeded raises for teachers and administrators.
- The productivity of U.S. workers is deficient, and this reflects the
  inadequate training they receive in U.S. schools.
- America produces far too few scientists, mathematicians, and engineers.
- Our schools are not staffed by qualified teachers.
- Because they are subject to market forces, private schools are
  inherently better than public schools.

Each myth focuses attention on the inadequacies of teachers, school administrators, tenure, unions, and certain parenting styles and turns attention away from the influence of social, political, and economic forces on student achievement. In addition to serving as powerful talking points for particular political agendas, the myths of schooling in America support an instructional worldview that treats students, teachers, administrators, and school communities as objects to be assigned, assessed, scripted, rated, monitored, and sanctioned. There is little room in accountability-driven instructional worldviews for intentionality, agency, or professionalism. The theme running through the "manufactured crisis" of schooling in America, is do what we tell you to do or we will impose some sanction on you.

The prevailing worldview perpetuated by the myths of schooling in America is particularly dispiriting for individuals who entered the profession of teaching knowing they would be working in less-than-ideal conditions for less-than-ideal compensation. We became teachers because we were passionate about some disciplined approach to thinking and acting and we deeply believed young people should enter their lives knowing something about our subject. Teaching in a so-called nation at risk, however, introduced us to the politics of fear in classrooms, administrative offices, and district boardrooms. Knowing the dysfunctional outcomes of fear-based approaches to leadership, Strong Instructional Leaders aggressively protect their schools from educational worldviews and instructional narratives that threaten the lifeworld of students, teachers, and fellow administrators. Such leaders wall off their schools from the myths of schooling by continually educating the publics they serve. In hallways, classrooms, open houses, newsletters, boardrooms, and governmental meetings, they communicate an instructional worldview that challenges unschooled assumptions about teaching and learning. Depending on the audience and the particular unschooled belief in play, they expand upon one or more of the following *schooled* frameworks for thinking about and acting upon curricula and instruction.

Schooled Ideas

The last decade of school reform has been dominated by policies and practices that mandate a continuum of sanctions and mandates for schools that do not attain state-prescribed levels of student achievement—what gets measured, gets done. The ideas that are steering school accountability discussions originate from unschooled policymakers offering unschooled practices to fix a myth of schooling. For unschooled publics, policymakers appear to be doing the right thing when they write state content standards (unschooled idea) to reverse the decline in student achievement (a myth of schooling).

Strong Instructional Leaders grasp the power of accountability-driven narratives to endanger or defeat instructional initiatives that run counter to the myth of the day. They also know that myths of schooling and unschooled ideas come and go. What remains constant in schooling is a parent's deep desire for schools to nurture their child socially, emotionally, and intellectually. With this constant in mind, Strong Instructional Leaders offer a counter-instructional narrative composed of three schooled ideas that are unique to schooling in the United States. Each schooled idea reassures parents that the classrooms in their communities are designed to nurture, challenge, and respect their children.

Forgiving schools. For the most part, the story of public schooling in America is about the search for policies, methods, and organizational configurations that offer children, adolescents, and adults second chances to obtain an education. Unlike their counterparts in Europe and Asia, U.S. schools provide multiple opportunities to develop talents and abilities—opportunities missing in systems designed to establish vocational destinations before the end of grammar school. Despite higher graduation requirements, high standards, and high-stakes testing, teachers and school administrators in the United States continue to find creative ways to keep disaffected youth progressing toward a personal dream—as remote as that dream may be. Those who enter the teaching profession deeply believe in the power of education to unleash the diverse talents and abilities of the young people seated in front of them. This is the strength of American public schooling. Every teacher and school administrator tells a story of their personal role in helping a student make it against all odds. While these stories are often too few and far between, the willingness to give second and third chances to discouraged young people is a core belief of teaching professionals.

When unschooled notions about what to do with students who are not making the grade appear on the horizon, Strong Instructional Leaders weigh in with an instructional narrative that pays tribute to the diversity of talents entering their schools. This narrative also confirms how a school's instructional worldview supports multiple pathways to realizing the giftedness of each student. Along with believing in an instructional worldview that values the unique abilities of children, Strong Instructional Leaders act upon this belief by creating curricula, designing systems, interpreting rules, and working with teachers in ways that strengthen strategies promoting uniqueness and weaken strategies enforcing conformity.

Excellence. In accountability-driven-policy environments, excellence is pictured as a pyramid with students receiving high test scores standing on top of the pyramid and students receiving low test scores sitting on the bottom of the pyramid. Unschooled definitions of excellence proclaim that there is plenty of room for all children at the top of the pyramid. Teachers and school administrators, however, live out a very different reality in their schools. Institutional schooling is designed to restrict access to the top of the pyramid to a few academically talented students and to accommodate, in some way, most of the student population at the wide bottom of the pyramid. As much as our society proclaims a belief in equal opportunity for all, that belief has no place in schools organized to discover, program, and reward a selected few students whose talents and dispositions align well with assign-and-assess modes of instruction. For the last century, middle- and upper-class children have been seated in college-bound courses, while their poorer friends from the lunchroom have been seated in basic skills courses.

Strong Instructional Leaders resolve the dueling definitions of excellence with a paradigm of schooling that allows equality and equity not only to exist side-by-side but to mutually reinforce the knowledge and skills associated with each goal of schooling. Instead of policies, procedures, curricula, and pedagogy designed to support a pyramid, such leaders locate the schools they lead in the center of concentric circles. Each circle represents a level of participation in activities in which children express an interest in an instructional program or programs designed to develop that interest. By viewing excellence as concentric circles, all students can participate in the same activity despite having varying levels of talent. Students who become more expert in a given activity gravitate toward the center of the circles while those with less expertise will participate in the outer circles. The concentric-circle interpretation of excellence accommodates both the development of personal meaning and public displays of excellence. When an individual serves a public function (e.g., doctor, electrician, lawyer, teacher), there is a certain level of knowledge and skills that one must possess to perform a job well or to participate meaningfully in a civic function. Personal satisfaction in performing a given activity, however, may be achieved at different levels of proficiency.

Unschooled beliefs and practices associated with pyramids support contemporary requirements for all students to achieve the same outcomes with respect to common standards. Schooled beliefs and practices also encourage standards and excellence, but there is a significant difference. If you develop talent within a pyramid, you narrow the levels of excellence and restrict the definition of standards. Strong Instructional Leaders, using a concentric-circle interpretation of excellence, are comfortable with many levels of excellence, thus, expanding the definition of standards. Instead of pursuing a narrow definition of excellence (or a standard), at the center of the circle, students are able to pursue many levels of excellence in the outer rings of the concentric circle.

Strong Instructional Leaders argue that all citizens in a democracy, including students in schools, should be encouraged to participate in a broad range of activities (e.g., algebra, athletics, home repair). Schools configured as concentric circles offer an expansive collection of activities and help young people understand what excellence looks like in that activity. Depending on the activity, a student may not possess the talent, the time, the money, or the physiology to become excellent in that activity. Does that mean that certain groups of students should not take algebra or play basketball? Schools structured as pyramids say yes. Schools structured as concentric circles say no.

Strong Instructional Leaders endorse an instructional worldview within which the diverse talents of all young people are respected and nurtured. Such an instructional worldview calls for increasing the breadth of activities offered by schools and broadening the definition of achievement in activities into which children are drawn. Schools designed around an inclusionary instructional worldview provide pathways for young people to become excellent in an activity while not excluding students whose talents conflict with pyramid definitions of talent development in that activity.

Unschooled goals of schooling emphasize preparation for the real world. The real world for unschooled minds is a pyramid—a lot will try, but only the best will reach the top of the pyramid. Strong Instructional Leaders offer an entirely different goal for real-world schooling. Societies that are dynamic and continue to mature are constantly infused with new ideas and ways of doing things. Growth in a society, as well as in education, occurs only in environments where diverse interests and talents are nurtured. Strong Instructional Leaders protect the schools they lead from policies, procedures, and programs that narrow the pathways for young people to find personal meaning and public achievement. In their public journey, Strong Instructional Leaders call for expanded visions of schooling within which teachers and school administrators continually work at broadening opportunities for young people to do what they like to do and find meaningful.

Ambitious teaching. Public perceptions about teaching are learned over 12 or more years of direct experience in classrooms with mimetic forms of teaching. Unschooled publics expect that children in schools will sit quietly in desks for 6 hours each day, listening to an adult at the front of the classroom telling them to memorize this, copy that, and recite from something assigned the day before. Mimetic teaching focuses on the recall and repetition of facts with little attention to how facts connect to the interests and experiences of students. The goal of mimetic teaching is quantity, not quality. Mimetic teaching finds a welcoming home in policy environments where test scores become the measure of successful teaching and school leadership. Teaching in such environments is no longer viewed as disciplined improvisation but the efficient execution of scripts and routines. The goal of teaching in the mimetic tradition is transformed from seeking the truth to acquiring knowledge, skills, and credentials that possess a cash value—high test scores, admission to colleges, and diplomas.

Strong Instructional Leaders cultivate an entirely different model of teaching in their schools. What they look for in the teachers they interview, observe, and work with is a commitment to experimenting with and becoming proficient at *ambitious teaching*. To teach ambitiously means to design lessons that fully respond to the following questions (Jackson, 1986):

- How will knowledge be used by the learner?
- How will knowledge be related to what was learned before?
- How will knowledge become personalized into the learner's language?
- How will knowledge be applied to new situations?

The goal of ambitious teaching is to transfer the responsibility for learning from the teacher to the student. For students to assume the sole responsibility for learning, however, translates into classroom environments where students are given substantial control over how they learn, what they learn, and how they demonstrate what they have learned.

Whether you call this pedagogy transformative (Jackson, 1986), or teaching for understanding (Elmore, Peterson, & McCarthey, 1996), or constructivist (Windschitl, 2002), ambitious teaching poses two public problems for Strong Instructional Leaders. First, ambitious teaching promotes curricular and pedagogical practices that are dramatically different from what unschooled publics experienced in their classrooms when they were students. Second, ambitious teaching is founded on teaching theories and practices that are largely underdefined (Spillane, 1998). Publics become concerned with school administrators who tamper with traditional understandings of the role teachers and students should be playing in a classroom.

There is no easy answer to responding well to unschooled publics over what they perceive to be "progressive" approaches to curriculum and instruction—remember the legacy of modern math. For Strong Instructional Leaders, however, there is no way around the model of teaching they sponsor within their schools' instructional worldviews. A focus of the public journey is persuading parents that ambitious teaching is the best way to prepare their children for a global economy. Even unschooled publics understand that memorizing, copying, and reciting have little value in organizations that are looking for young people who are fluent in accessing, managing, integrating, creating, and communicating information. These 21st-century thinking skills are different from the ones that appear on standardized tests—the ones that are rewarded in assign-and-assess classrooms and are credentialed by institutional schooling. Unschooled minds will value ambitious teaching when they see student outcomes mirroring the kinds of thinking and doing expected in global economies.

Strong Instructional Leaders will fail at persuading unschooled publics of the worth of ambitious teaching if they are not personally prepared (private journey), publicly organized (public journey), and correctly situated (situational journey). The three journeys are phases in a process of making collective sense out of ambitious approaches to teaching and learning. When each phase of the sensemaking process is done well, ambitious teaching becomes the agreed-upon norm in the school and community. The last phase of strong instructional leadership, the situational journey, is where detailed examples of ambitious pedagogy are discussed in teacher workspaces and practiced in classrooms. It is during the situational journey that "weakly defined" (Spillane, 1998, p. 52) teaching practices find voice and where the voice of the Strong Instructional Leader assists in delicately transforming core teaching beliefs and practices into new ways of thinking and teaching ambitiously.

The Real World of Work

The most powerful unschooled belief in this country always involves the ability of schools to prepare young people for successful careers in the working world. No school referendum drive begins with espousing the value of a liberal education. Requests for more monies for schools are couched in terms of a school's facility for preparing young people for a career.

Throughout the public journey, Strong Instructional Leaders take into account the powerful desire on the part of parents to see that their children do well in the working world. At the same time, however, these leaders hold in common with the teachers they supervise a strong commitment to teaching young people intangible skills: "to think effectively, to communicate thought, to make relevant judgments, to discriminate among values" (Harvard University, 1945, p. 65). When teachers and school administrators feel really good about their jobs, they refer to a comment, a note, or a class discussion where they observed a student doing a task that requires an intangible skill. Given the numerous goals set forth by policymakers, the teaching profession always converges on the goal of helping young people acquire the knowledge and skills for examining the unexamined life.

The credentialing function of institutional schooling and the career ambitions of parents often mask the deep desire on the part of teachers and students to study subject matter and engage in conversations that pursue in depth the question "What is living for?" Strong Instructional Leaders view as artificial the century-long struggle over being trained to do something well versus being educated to judge something. Both goals of schooling, about which Dewey wrote endlessly, are not mutually exclusive but mutually reinforcing. Character values (What is fairness?), intellectual values (What is truth?), and aesthetic values (What is good taste?) permeate the facts we learn in class, the actions we take in our jobs, and our conduct in our homes and communities. Whatever career young people decide to pursue, employers want to hire someone who can think well, communicate well, judge well, and value well, and someone who works well with others. At the same time employers are expecting workers to perform these goals well, they also are expecting their employees to produce quality products, provide quality services, and generate quality ideas. The operative term in global economies is quality, which is never far removed from questions of worth and thoughtfulness. The instructional worldview of Strong Instructional Leaders is never bashful about exposing the relationship between values and public action. Embedded in all strong instructional narratives is a commitment to developing curricular and teaching practices that help young people reach the important goal of seeing and experiencing the relationships between fact and value, conduct and action, and theory and practice.

Traditional school values of hard work, self-control, and thrift have been replaced with questions of how children learn best and how we should assess student achievement. This psychological turn in today's schools pits constructivists against behaviorists over what techniques will best help students achieve high test scores and earn credits toward graduation. The philosophical questions of what knowledge is of greatest worth and what students value in their jobs, homes, and communities receives little attention in faculty lounges, schools of education, and boardrooms. Knowledge in today's schools is viewed as a commodity to be traded for a grade, a credential, and eventually a well-paying job. The commoditization of education assumes that what students want is placement in high-status courses, good grades in these courses, and acceptance into post-secondary schooling that furthers the acquisition of money, power, and fame.

Strong Instructional Leaders hold very different assumptions (or philosophies) about the goals of schooling. Instead of focusing teachers on the psychology of learning—the technique of the day—Strong Instructional Leaders draw faculties into discussions of purpose and worth: What are the valued ends of schooling? They believe that the values, knowledge, and dispositions of knowing how to do a task well should interact with the values, knowledge, and dispositions of what tasks are worth doing. Both goals of schooling should interact and transform each other. Whether in the tight logic of the natural sciences, the interaction of complex variables in the social sciences, or the creative images of the humanities, curricula become sources of meaning and action and not merely subjects to be counted and tested.

Not only do curricula become infused with purpose and meaning in schools led by Strong Instructional Leaders, but the culture, organization, and relationships with outside publics reflect the valued ends of the schools' instructional worldviews. Questions of school discipline, the dispensing of honors, the placement of students, the awarding of grades, and what subjects become privileged are all subject to questions of meaning and purpose. But how does a school administrator identify and then answer questions of meaning and purpose? School administrators for the last half-century relied on vocational goals—training for occupations and acceptance to post-secondary schooling—as the primary goal of schooling. Civic, aesthetic, and creative goals were relegated to an occasional course here and there and elective course offerings. In the last decade, the manufactured call for increased standards in schools translated into more required courses ("college-bound" courses) and fewer elective courses in the arts and humanities.

During their private journey, Strong Instructional Leaders spend considerable time reading, thinking, and talking about the purpose of schooling. Questions of purpose—the valued ends of schooling—are what philosophies of education are all about. Table 9.1 summarizes how two systems of values would address the domains of truth, knowledge, education, democracy, and mass communications. A school leader could construct an instructional worldview that reflects values associated with the goal of material success and enjoyment (desire) or an instructional worldview that reflects values associated with self-understanding and service (worth). A school curriculum and school organization dedicated to pursuing

Table 9.1. Two Philosophies of Schooling

Values Domain	Worth (common good)	Desire (self-interest)
Truth	• Accessible • Knowing • Inquiring • Influencing • Disputing	• Inaccessible • Believing • Outcomes-based • Coersive • Disloyal
Knowledge	• Understanding • Judgment • Discipline • Critical	• Power • Technique • Skill • Instrumental
Education	• Accommodate • Emancipate • Perform • Dialogue	• Differentiate • Conform • Credential • Monologue
Democracy	• Equality • Community • Responsibilities • Serve • Checks and Balances	• Mobility • Individuality • Rights • Satisfy • Majority Rule
Mass communication	• Educate • Inform • Serve	• Manipulate • Entertain • Profit

knowledge and skills for the sake of one's self-interest is different from a school curriculum and school organization "devoted" to pursuing knowledge and skills for the common good.

Table 9.1 is just one way of framing valued ends of schooling. The private journeys of school administrators who choose to become Strong Instructional Leaders will doubtless reflect other ways of reframing a philosophy of curriculum and instruction. Private journeys are unique to the academic backgrounds and educational experiences of a school administrator. What remains constant among such leaders is the understanding that no instructional worldview is neutral. Accepting the purposes of schooling as one of achieving material success and enjoyment commits school administrators and teachers to policies, procedures, and an instructional program that will be very different from the experiences of children in schools where school administrators and teachers are devoted to the educational goals of self-understanding and service. What sets Strong Instructional Leadership apart from traditional instructional leadership is the private understanding and public embodiment of a coherent pattern of values that continually informs organizational and pedagogical decision-making.

Although a compelling vision of what students should become is necessary, it is not sufficient for galvanizing a faculty around an educational mission and the expected changes in core teaching practice associated with a clearly articulated purpose of schooling. The focus of the private and public journeys is to create a sense of mission among faculty over particular instructional problems and offering practical arguments for resolving those problems at the classroom level. The abstractions of values statements, theories, and research practices, however, still leave teachers with little guidance regarding what they should be doing in their classrooms on Monday morning. The final journey for Strong Instructional Leaders is connecting the abstractions of mission statements and what the research says with the tasks of teaching—what teachers do in classrooms on Monday. Constructing connections between theories of learning and the tasks of teaching do not happen during the private journey or during public explanations of a new direction in curriculum and instruction. Changes in core teaching practices come about when school administrators help teachers understand, experiment with, and practice particular teaching tasks, in particular classrooms, in particular instructional situations. This situational journey, the final journey of Strong Instructional Leadership, functions as the final link between private and public understandings of a new pedagogy and the particular tasks of teaching.

10

Creating a
Professional-Growth Culture

The final destination of the private and public journeys of Strong Instructional Leaders is the classroom. The formidable challenge of this part of the journey (the situational journey) is changing the hearts and minds of those most directly working with children—persuading teachers to abandon pedagogical beliefs and habits that have stopped working and to adopt new theories, ideas, and practices of which they may have little understanding.

No matter how well thought-out an instructional worldview may be, or how well that worldview is publicly framed, Strong Instructional Leaders judge the success of their private and public journeys by how accurately teachers practice structural understandings of a subject. Do teachers, for example, believe the subject of mathematics requires the memorization of procedures and accurate computation, or should students be focusing on mathematical concepts proving the application of mathematical procedures? Do teachers conceive of the subject of science as completing cookbook experiments or as requiring the application of theories to problematic situations in the universe? Do teachers perceive reading instruction as word recognition skills or the ability to comprehend the meaning of a text? Do teachers believe learning history is recalling names, places, and dates, or the ability to interpret the significance of historical events? How teachers respond to these questions influences what kinds of materials, activities, discourses, and assessments students experience in classrooms.

Instructional managers rarely ask these questions; they believe that their job is to implement change in the form of programs, textbook series, model reform programs, or the technique of the day. Strong Instructional Leaders know that distributing boxes to teachers, requiring attendance in 1-day workshops, or mandating a lesson-plan format may regulate an instructional initiative, but directives issued from offices will change neither teachers' intellectual understandings of a subject nor how that subject is taught in classrooms. Before distributing materials, planning workshops, or hiring consultants, Strong Instructional Leaders participate with teachers in a process of making sense of the theories and ideas of new pedagogies—the why of an instructional initiative—and then consider how those theories and ideas should look in classrooms.

Of the three journeys described in Chapters 7 through 13, the situational journey is the most complex one to undertake because it involves questioning competing beliefs and theories about teaching and learning. Teachers do not arrive at schools as pedagogical blank slates. Teachers enter their classrooms with well-developed worldviews of how students should behave, what students should be doing in class, what the curriculum should look like, and how a subject should be taught. Questioning a personal instructional worldview not only examines the integrity of deeply help beliefs about teaching and learning, but will inevitably breed tension between the certainties of classroom practice and the uncertainties of theory-based pedagogies.

Traditional approaches to instructional leadership, in reality, result in instructional management. These approaches avoid the complexity and trauma of mediating conflicting instructional worldviews by emphasizing the forms of a new instructional initiative: Teachers are encouraged to increase the frequency of employing certain instructional techniques (e.g., cooperative learning, math manipulatives); teachers are directed to reorganize their rooms (e.g., using learning centers); and faculties are mandated to adopt a new program (e.g., Success for All). While each of these reform initiatives may increase student interest, engagement, or time spent on a subject, they do not fundamentally restructure how students think about or do mathematics, science, or history (Spillane & Callahan, 2000).

Emphasizing the forms of a pedagogical change initiative removes instructional managers from processes—instructional situations—in which teachers interact with colleagues, experts, students, and supervisors over new understandings of a subject or a problematic area in curriculum or instruction. Instead of inserting themselves into networks where beliefs, strategies, or materials are questioned, instructional managers assume the role of distant observer and transmitter of orders. Instructional managers judge the progress of an instructional change initiative by noting quantitative increases in the use of certain techniques (e.g., cooperative learning, word walls) and the efficient distribution of resources to support the technique or program of the day. Absent a well thought-out instructional worldview acquired during the private journey, instructional managers have little to offer but classroom inspections for the technique of the day and managing the distribution of instructional materials.

Strong Instructional Leaders do not view an instructional change initiative through binoculars from afar. Rather they place themselves directly into situations where teachers are asked to make sense of unfamiliar ways of thinking about and teaching a subject. Electing to show up in the classroom, however, is not the same thing as being invited into the classroom. Being invited to participate with teachers in solving problematic situations in curriculum and instruction may not happen right away. These invitations are the result of a process, a series of administrative moves designed to change how teachers think about how to solve instructional problems.

Table 10.1 summarizes the situational moves that Strong Instructional Leaders make to guide a faculty away from teaching practices that are not working and toward theories and practices that better address the causes and consequences of a problematic situation in curriculum and instruction. Each instructional situation requires that Strong Instructional Leaders participate (join) with teachers in making sense out of an instructional initiative (educating). Most importantly, Strong Instructional Leaders do not leave an instructional situation until they select a participant who possesses the knowledge and leadership skills to follow through on agreed upon outcomes (delegating).

Strong Instructional Leaders do not allow the external and internal constraints of institutional schooling to derail teachers from fully pursuing the goals, ideas, methods, and practices of a new instructional initiative. What keeps the situational journey moving forward is a commitment to valued ends of schooling—the moral purposes of schooling. When Strong Instructional Leaders insert themselves into a problematic situation in curriculum and instruction, they pay little attention to the managerial role of checking on the gaps between a method of teaching and measures of institutional learning. Instead, they provide their teachers with organizational structures and intellectual tools to examine the disparity between the talents, abilities, and dreams that children bring to school each day and institutional structures that stand in the way of who that child can become—the moral purpose of schooling. Strong Instructional Leaders understand that pursuing the moral purpose of schooling requires an educational pro-

Table 10.1. Situational Moves

Move	Tasks
Joining	• Establish trust in teacher workspaces. • Resolve situational dilemmas.
Educating	• Establish connections between an instructional problem, selected learning theory, valued end of schooling, and existing understandings of the affected pedagogy. • Provide direct guidance on substantive implementation of the new pedagogy (e.g., what teachers and students are doing when they construct meaning). • Provide staff with multiple opportunities to understand and apply the new pedagogy. • Move faculty and the organization along when they become stuck. • Protect a school's instructional worldview from opposing worldviews or cultural influences opposed to serious academic study.
Delegating	Select, train, mentor, and authorize teacher leaders to achieve full implementation of new pedagogy.

cess: providing teachers and administrators with the time, materials, and expertise to make collective sense of ambitious strategies for teaching a subject or resolving institutional constraints that stand in the way of nurturing children's intellectual, social, and emotional growth. Teachers are willing to change very deeply held beliefs about what works in their classrooms when instructional initiatives make sense to them, when they see organizational commitment (e.g., time, materials, space, and expertise) to a new pedagogy, and when the instructional environment trusts their best efforts.

Cycle of Reform Failure

Before school administrators insert themselves into particular instructional problems, they must first resolve, in some way, the social, institutional, and cultural obstacles that stand between them and the teachers they are assisting. Elements of these obstacles were referenced in the first part of this book. Some of them are problems and some are dilemmas. Problems in school administration are typically resolved by applying a rational planning process. If administrators possess the proper mix of resources, expertise, and plans of action, then the problem goes away—at least temporarily. Systems problems in schools (e.g., scheduling, budgeting, grading) are usually fixed with a minor revision to a process, appropriate applications of a resource, or correct employment of personnel skills. School administrators like to spend their days solving problems. Improving routine tasks with specific processes, materials, and personnel provides tangible results (the process works better) and a demonstration of know-how (I am good at what I do).

School administrators do not share the same enthusiasm for solving dilemmas. Unlike a problem, the source of a dilemma is difficult to identify, the dilemma is not solved with a resource, and, when action is taken, results are often ambiguous. The source of the dilemmas of schooling is the conflict between societal expectations for schooling in America and professional understandings of how schools ought to operate. No mix of resources, expertise, and plans of action fully resolves this historical conflict. The best that a school administrator can hope to accomplish when confronted with a dilemma of schooling is to prevent societal and institutional expectations for schooling from undermining the aims and functions of a new pedagogical initiative.

Instructional managers treat conflicts between societal and institutional expectations for schooling and professional understandings of teaching and learning as a problem of schooling, not a dilemma. Problems of schooling are fixed with a plan of action designed to adopt the one best program, curriculum, or pedagogy for resolving dissatisfactions with student performance. Misinterpreting a dilemma for a problem, however, leaves cultural, pedagogical, or institutional sources of an instructional problem unaddressed. When a dilemma is translated into a problem of schooling, the instructional change initiative adapts to the societal and institutional expectations of schooling. While seeming to resolve an "instructional problem," the underlying dilemma of schooling eventually reappears, generating the cycle of reform failure (see Figure 10.1).

Homework is often the focus of a Cycle of Reform Failure. In this case, we have a public that expects homework to be assigned (societal expectation) and teachers who expect homework to be handed in (institutional expectation). The dilemma is that our professional understanding of homework practices calls into question these societal expectations and institutional expectations. Public perceptions of the value of homework are questionable because the relationship between homework and achievement is inconclusive. Teacher practices for assigning homework are also suspect: We know that there is a relationship between different types of homework assignments and how different groups of students respond to those assignments.

Figure 10.1. Cycle of Reform Failure (CRF)

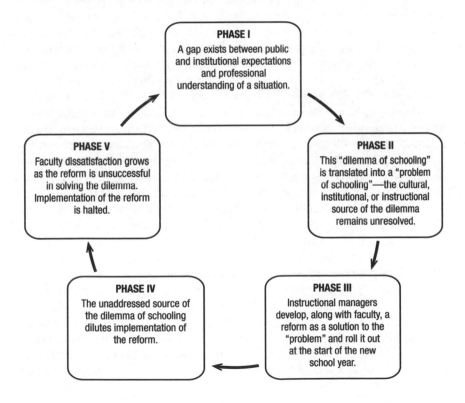

The cycle of reform failure (CRF) is set in motion by the gap that exists between public and institutional expectations for homework and what educators know empirically about homework (Phase I of CRF). The two beliefs about homework completion demonstrate a true dilemma—societal and institutional demands to sanction recalcitrant homework completers clash with educational theories that call for proper practices of assigning homework. Instead of addressing effective ways to assign homework, instructional managers translate this "dilemma of schooling" into a "problem of schooling"—a problem seen as the lack of enforcement of homework policies (Phase II of CRF). Representing the institutional goal of documentation and enforcement of homework rules, instructional managers develop, along with faculty, a reform to solve the problem: a range of punishments for noncompletion and rewards for completion of homework (Phase III of CRF). Instructional managers are far more comfortable with developing processes for enforcing rules and punishments (solving a problem) than convincing teachers to change how they assign homework (addressing a dilemma).

By November, within a few months of initiating the "get tough" homework policy, Phase IV of CRF is in full force. Not only are students not doing their homework, but failure rates are climbing dramatically (as a result of zeros for no homework) and suspensions are climbing dramatically (as a result of students not showing up for homework detentions). Teachers and administrators are entering Phase V of CRF. Administrators respond to alarming failure and suspensions rates with directives to modify grading practices (stop counting homework into final grades) and eliminating the homework detention room (teachers may, if they desire, hold their own after-school detentions in their rooms).

The gap still exists between societal and institutional expectations for homework and professional knowledge of homework practices (Phase I). The source of the dilemma remains unexamined and unresolved (Phase II). Frustrated with student disregard for homework and poor implementation of homework rules, teachers and administrators meet in March to address (again) the problem of homework and so design a new homework policy for the coming school year (Phase III)—a policy with some teeth in it. In August of the new school year, continuing Phase III, the principal introduces a PowerPoint presentation on the new program—zero homework tolerance. While examining newly distributed zero tolerance referral forms, teachers turn to each other and say, "Haven't we done this before?"

Strong Instructional Leaders acknowledge the power of institutional goals of schooling (see Chapter 6) to contaminate professional understandings of teaching and learning. Instead of looking for a program or technique that conforms to societal or institutional expectations for how schools should operate, such leaders search out theories and practices that transform societal and institutional expectations for how schools ought to operate. They transform societal and institutional expectations for schooling by instilling a sense of mission into a proposed instructional change initiative. In their private and public journeys, they develop practical arguments and action plans that include (1) an appeal to a valued end of schooling (purpose); (2) a call to be excellent; and (3) an invitation to be a contributing member of a professional community. In whatever venue they find themselves, Strong Instructional Leaders weave a sense of mission into all public pronouncements and private conversations over the resolution of an instructional problem.

Infusing a sense of mission into an instructional change initiative finds fertile ground in schools where teachers see administrators join them in making sense of a new pedagogy and where teachers see administrators protect classrooms from the corrosive effects of unschooled ideas about teaching and learning. A sense of mission becomes lost in schools where teachers see administrators sitting in offices reviewing test scores and surrendering professional understandings of teaching and learning to unschooled ideas of how a subject should be taught.

Sitting with Teachers at Even Tables

The principal activity of the situational journey occurs when Strong Instructional Leaders leave their offices and auditorium stages for locations where teachers practice their craft. They understand that changing deeply held beliefs about teaching and learning requires leaders to position themselves in times, places, and relationships in which they are able to focus teachers' social, emotional, and intellectual attention on developing personal insights into how to apply the theories and practices of a new pedagogy.

Before discussing the specifics of the process for focusing teacher attention on particular theories and practices of a new pedagogy, school administrators must recognize that while understanding the functions of a new pedagogy (the private journey) and developing organizational capacity (the public journey) are necessary, they are not sufficient for working collaboratively on instructional problems. Teachers will not invite administrators into their workspaces if they feel that their professional knowledge and classroom experience will be ignored, that they are "sitting at uneven tables" (Kritek, 1994). Teachers are more willing to critique their teaching, listen to new ideas, and experiment with new pedagogies when administrators seated across from them arrive with no hidden agendas, no plans of action, and no administrative edicts—when they come to them on an equal playing field—an even table.

Strong Instructional Leaders establish three ground rules to "flatten the table" in teacher workspaces. First, Strong Instructional Leaders frame instructional problems as a fact of schooling, not a source of blame. Western approaches to organizational accountability traditionally look for someone to blame for failing to reach a projected goal. In the case of schools, teachers and school administrators are blamed for low test scores. Strong Instructional Leaders never blame teachers for poor student achievement. They frame gaps between valued ends of schooling and student performance in terms of a purposeful process for identifying the problem, reviewing the research, stating a hypothesis, and developing an action plan. The chosen methods of inquiry are grounded in the belief that solutions to instructional problems do not rest solely in classrooms but with changes in organizational configurations, quality staff development, and a commitment of resources. Administrators operating in a problem-solving mode—instead of the blame mode—assume equal responsibility for resolving the discrepancy between a school's instructional worldview and student performance.

The assumptions inherent in a professional culture that is grounded in study, reflection, and experimentation are listed in Table 10.2. Although the table summarizes Western versus Eastern (Toyota) cultural assumptions for solving manufacturing problems in the automobile industry, the values and practices listed in the table are applicable to educational settings. The traditional Western approach often results in climates of distrust between administrators and teachers. This approach to school supervision is more interested in documenting the presence of prescribed teaching behaviors and coverage of mandated subject matter. It is clear in Western classrooms who is the boss and who will be held accountable for low test scores.

Eastern approaches to supervision are concerned with fostering a culture of critical inquiry. Toyota, for example, supports a culture of continuous improvement (critical inquiry) in three ways. First, employees are trained to know when an established standard of performance is compromised. Second, employees, no matter where they sit in the organization, are required to call attention to deviations from established standards of performance. Lastly, employees are expected to enroll in courses and training opportunities to continually improve their problem-solving skills. The *Toyota Way* (Liker, 2004) asserts that organizational prob-

Table 10.2. Western Versus Toyota View of Problems

Organizational Problem	Traditional Western Culture	Toyota (Eastern) Culture
What is the cause of the problem?	Who can we blame?	Why did the system fail?
Who is responsible?	Person who caused the problem	Management
What should the person who causes the problem do?	Solve problem on own if possible	Call attention to the problem for assistance and to avoid the problem in the future
Assumptions about people	They will not accept blame unless forced to	They will feel empowered if they get positive support for solving problems

From Liker & Hoseus, 2008. Reprinted with permission.

lems are solved when managers and workers sit down at even tables to resolve deviations from established standards of performance. No one is blamed; all team members are expected to contribute to a solution.

The second ground rule for leveling uneven tables in teacher workspaces is to generate the organizational capacity to support teachers in their journey to change core teaching behaviors. Teachers become enormously frustrated with administrators when they are asked to adopt a new pedagogy without adequate resources or organizational configurations to fully learn or practice new approaches in curriculum and instruction. Table 10.3 summarizes common requests teachers make when asked to implement a new instructional initiative.

Table 10.3. Building Organizational Capacity

Managerial Functions	What Teachers Ask for
Scheduling	• Common planning times • One room assignment • Limited number of preparations • Appropriate times allocated to accommodate new approaches in curriculum and instruction
Personnel	• Appropriate academic backgrounds in targeted subject areas designated for instructional change
Physical Environment	• Room configurations that align with new approaches in curriculum and instruction • Building infrastructure that is designed to accommodate a new approach in curriculum and instruction
Organizational	• Policies and procedures that align with the requirements of new approaches in curriculum and instruction • Administrative responsibilities that are aligned with new approaches in curriculum and instruction
Budget	• Monies allocated in the budget for purchase of materials, employment of consultants and additional staff, attendance at conferences, and physical modifications to the building
Staff Development	• A purposeful plan to train teachers • Appropriate expertise to help teachers understand and apply new theories and practices • Availability of consultants, lead teachers, and district coordinators who possess a deep understanding of theories and practices of a new approach in curriculum and instruction and the interpersonal skills to coach teachers • Release time granted to teachers to work in teams, observe other teachers, and develop instructional units • Attendance by teachers at in-state and out-of-state conferences and workshops that focus on methods and content of a new approach in curriculum and instruction

Instructional managers view the teacher requests listed in Table 10.3 as nego-tiable—some requests are fully granted, some are partially granted, while others are completely ignored. The goal of instructional managers here is to demonstrate to superiors and external agents of accountability that forms of a new pedagogical initiative are up and running: Teachers are using math manipulatives, word walls, and "I can" statements.

Strong Instructional Leaders view the teacher requests listed in Table 10.3 as non-negotiable—all requests must be granted and fully implemented before new pedagogical initiatives are implemented. The goal of such leaders is not to gain control over the implementation of a new pedagogy, but to create the possibili-ties for teachers to understand and experiment with new instructional theories and practices. Providing access to consultants, time, space, expertise, and materials communicates a willingness on the part of administrators to support teachers in the risky undertaking of abandoning what has worked for them in exchange for uncertain methodologies in teaching and learning.

The third and final ground rule for constructing even tables in teacher workspaces is to listen respectfully. The norms governing conversations with teachers at even tables include fully listening to participant contributions (no interruptions), setting aside judgments, asking questions for clarification, and searching for personal connections to personal narratives. Strong Instructional Leaders learn in their private journeys that all theories, especially those in the social sciences, are merely conjectures—best guesses about observed patterns in nature or society. Theories in education are even more suspect because those originating from rigorous experimental designs or speculative philosophy are either too fragmented or too abstract to make any sense to classroom teachers faced with the weekly question "What do I do on Monday?" Strong Instruc-tional Leaders emerge from their private journeys with the humility to listen to alternative theories of how children learn.

Gathering perspectives on teaching and learning, however, is only one leg of the table. Leg two reveals how intensely teachers feel about an instructional problem. Too often administrators label teacher expressions of discontent as just another example of a profession prone to whining and intransigence. Adminis-trators hear a teacher complaint, but they often miss the intensity of discontent. Beneath the perfunctory calls for more resources, more administrative supports, and better parents are teachers struggling with their professional identity—the gap between their professional expectations and what they are experiencing in their classrooms. Before talking about an instructional problem, administrators must first acknowledge that the complaints are legitimate expressions of frustra-tion with a career or a classroom that is not working the way it is supposed to, according to teacher preparation programs. This does not mean that adminis-trators stand by while the collective sensemaking process becomes bogged down in an ongoing rendition of what administrators, kids, and parents are not doing.

The primary task of administrators sitting at even tables is to move the sensemaking process along. Administrators will not succeed at this task, however, unless they pay attention and, if necessary, address in a meaningful way what administrators, kids, and parents are not doing.

Leg three of the table reveals levels of understanding of new theories and practices associated with an instructional problem. The literature on school reform documents an ongoing frustration with the discrepancies that arise between how researchers understand a theory-driven instructional initiative and how teachers apply that theory in classrooms. When administrators sit down at even tables, they listen respectfully to idiosyncratic interpretations of instructional theories, ideas, and practices. Administrators understand that what appears to be a shallow or mistaken understanding of a theory, idea, or practice is a vital component of making collective sense out of often undefined terminology and uncertain approaches to teaching a subject. Making sense out of how to teach a subject well requires that administrators assume the role of participant in the active interpretation of an instructional theory. Administrators use these interpretative conversations as a means for clarifying their personal understandings of a theory-driven instructional initiative and a source for assessing what educational supports their staff will require to effectively implement a new instructional initiative.

Leg four reveals what teachers require from the organization to begin their own instructional journeys. Teachers will never hold back when it comes to articulating what they will need to implement a new pedagogy. Some of what teachers will ask for (e.g., "I need windows in my classroom") is clearly beyond the resources and power that administrators bring to the table. Sitting at even tables, however, means a willingness on the part of administrators to make changes to organizational routines and grant access to resources that will be viewed by teachers as a good faith effort to support their instructional journey.

Orchestrating even tables is a necessary condition for preparing teacher workspaces, but it is not sufficient for carrying out a sustained culture of professional learning. The school floor that the table sits on must also be even. That even floor sits on a school foundation that values teacher collaboration and respects the experiences that teachers bring to the table. Strong Instructional Leaders balance out the foundation by designing feedback systems to assess progress with an instructional initiative and providing the time, space, materials, and access to expertise that help teachers over the "dips" in enthusiasm for a new theory-driven instructional initiative.

Collective sensemaking is the most difficult process that Strong Instructional Leaders will encounter during their private, public, and situational journeys. It is a lot to ask a teacher to unlearn what has worked for them in the classroom and learn new pedagogies that research says might work better. Rather than participate in the complex process of asking (sitting at even tables), administrators are easily drawn to telling teachers to change this practice, adopt that program, or hand in this report. If there is one lesson we have learned from the literature on school reform, it is the futility of telling teachers to change what they do in classrooms. At best, telling results in a compliance mentality; at worst it creates an antiintellectual environment where conformity is rewarded and reflection is punished. Originating an instructional worldview requires an organizational environment that thrives on openness to new ideas, respectful disagreements, and experimentation—what I have described as sitting at even tables.

Sitting at even tables in teacher workspaces is a humbling experience. The certainty of implementing the program of the day—what instructional managers do— is replaced with the fundamental uncertainty of instructional change initiatives. No educational theory or practice exits a classroom the same way it enters a classroom. Teachers reformulate theories and practices in education based on institutional influences (e.g., class sizes, resources), their personal histories (e.g., family backgrounds, educational experiences), and cultural norms of the school they work in.

At the same tables where Strong Instructional Leaders are learning how fragile theories and practices are in education, they come to understand that institutional schooling is malleable. The goals and practices of institutional schooling are not givens but are authored by teachers and administrators working together on theories and practices of a new pedagogy.

Authoring new institutional realities will not occur in administrative offices. Only by sitting at even tables are administrators and teachers able to reach common understandings of the meaning and implementation of a new pedagogy. The convergence of teachers and administrators on the interpretation and implementation of new methods of teaching anchors the activities of the situational journey. Instead of conforming teaching practices to the constraints of the organization, Strong Instructional Leaders mold the organization to the theoretical and practical demands of implementing a new instructional initiative.

Instructional managers continually ask teachers compliance questions. Are we implementing the new pedagogy according to prescribed methods and outcomes? Strong Instructional Leaders continually ask teachers "enactment" questions. What are we doing? What should we be doing? How do we get better at what we should be doing? Questions of compliance set the table for monologues; questions of enactment—questions of meaning—set the table for dialogues.

Schools become instructional communities when teachers and school administrators sit at even tables wrestling with the meaning and application of new theories and practices in curriculum and instruction. The process of establishing even tables creates an instructional environment into which a wide continuum of ideas and interpretations of a new pedagogy are invited. In schools led by Strong Instructional Leaders, teacher workspaces become messy social and intellectual places to sit. These leaders foster messy instructional environments with the knowledge that such environments generate ideas and ideas generate possibilities for understanding and practicing ambiguous instructional theories.

Sitting at even tables in messy intellectual environments can be uncomfortable for school administrators. The understandings achieved during private and public journeys have little influence in schools where the relational trust between teachers and school administrators has been diminished by a focus on implementation and accountability. Only by sitting at even tables in teacher workspaces can school administrators establish instructional environments where teachers feel safe enough to think about, talk about, and act upon new theories and practices in education. It is a leap of faith for teachers to depart from conventional ways of interacting with students, selecting and organizing subject matter, and assessing student performance. Teachers must enter their workspaces every day believing and feeling that however far they leap, school administrators will make sure they land softly.

11

Understanding the How and Why of School Reform Initiatives

The educational process for interpreting theory-based instructional initiatives is wholly different from traditional workshops designed to train teachers to implement a particular technique. The challenge of this part of the situational journey is to interpret theory-based pedagogies in workspaces inhabited by teachers who are at different places in their careers, coming from different experiences in classrooms, and working in different school environments. Instead of mirroring a theory-based pedagogy, Strong Instructional Leaders, along with teachers, author a new instructional reality.

The foundation for changing core teaching beliefs and practices is the existence of trusting places where teachers feel their beliefs about teaching and learning are respected and where they are encouraged to experiment with unfamiliar pedagogies. When teachers leave even tables, they require the intellectual tools and organizational structure to understand the how and why of a theory-based instructional initiative. Without a firm understanding of the core principles of new pedagogy, teachers resist or unknowingly practice "lethal mutations" (McLaughlin & Mitra, 2001, p. 307) of a new practice in curriculum and instruction.

Educating teachers to faithfully represent the theories and practices of a new pedagogy is a process constrained by social, political, and professional beliefs and practices that endanger the faithful representation of a theory-based instructional initiative. Table 11.1 summarizes how each external reality of schooling constrains administrative efforts to generate instructional systems that are conducive to representing accurately the principles of a theory-based instructional change.

The external realities summarized in Table 11.1 permeate school environments. Strong Instructional Leaders confront the external constraints of schooling with a strong instructional worldview. All policies, personnel, theories, and practices that enter the doors of schools led by Strong Instructional Leaders conform to staff beliefs about how knowledge should be treated, how classroom instruction should be organized, how student thinking should be acknowledged, and how student learning should be assessed. Policies, procedures, theories, and practices that support the school's instructional worldview are welcomed in the front door; those that do not support the school's instructional worldview are ignored or ushered off into places where they can do no harm.

Table 11.1. External Realities of Schooling

External Reality	Constraints
Instructional Problem	• An ongoing problem in classrooms is attributed to forces beyond the control of the teacher (e.g., poor parenting, poverty, incompetent administrators). • Efforts to address an instructional problem with a purposeful method of inquiry or a theory-based reform are viewed as a waste of time. Faculties urge administrators to take action now using simple cause-and-effect reasoning to develop a commonsense response.
Profession of Teaching	• Teachers view their profession as an art, not a science. They take pride in a job function practiced in highly individualistic ways behind closed classroom doors. • Classrooms are viewed as the domains of teachers, not school administrators.
Social Context of Schooling	• Each school community contains social, economic, and political capital that correlates with the resources, educational experiences, and influence students bring with them to classrooms. The social and intellectual capital of some communities aligns very well with the institutional goals of schooling. In other communities, the social and intellectual capital is in opposition to the institutional goals of schooling. • Most schools in the United States possess a culture devoted to materialism and celebrity. • Historically, Americans have distrusted intellectuals and laud the wisdom of the common man.
Opposing Instructional Worldviews	• Particular communities and particular reform initiatives respond to the fundamental questions of schooling differently: How do children learn? What knowledge is of greatest worth? How should knowledge be organized? How should we assess what students learn? How should we teach? • Some communities and reform initiatives support mimetic traditions of teaching, while others support transformative traditions of teaching (see Chapter 6, Table 6.2). • Teachers and students will have different educational experiences in schools where knowledge and skills are transmitted to students by teachers and in schools where students construct knowledge and skills with teachers.

Table 11.2 summarizes the qualities of two instructional worldviews (A and B) that a school might adopt. Students sitting in A classrooms experience fundamentally different learning environments than do students sitting in B classrooms. Teachers standing in A classrooms select, organize, and present knowledge and skills in fundamentally different ways from teachers standing in B classrooms. School administrators leading A schools organize instruction, allocate resources, and train staff in fundamentally different ways from administrators leading B schools.

Tables 11.3 and 11.4 summarize student experiences with different instructional worldviews in particular classrooms. Applying Cohen and Ball's (2000) definition of teaching to two subject areas, students in A classrooms learn mathematics and language arts very differently from students in B classrooms. Teachers in A classrooms think about, talk about, and practice mathematics and language arts very differently from teachers in B classes.

Table 11.2. Two Instructional Worldviews

Fundamental Questions of Schooling	Practices Based on Instructional Worldview A	Practices Based on Instructional Worldview B
How do students learn?	• Memorization • Practice	• Social interaction • Discovery
What knowledge is of greatest worth?	• Facts • Procedures/Routines • Definitions	• Big ideas • Big questions • Concepts
How should knowledge be organized?	• Units (in textbooks) • Chapters (in textbooks) • Course objectives • Breadth (rather than depth)	• Themes • Interdisciplinary studies • Depth (rather than breadth)
How should we assess student learning?	• Test questions aligned with unit objectives • Test objectives • Number of correct and incorrect answers	• Performance reflecting understanding of theory, concept, idea • Responses to divergent questioning • Projects/exhibitions/performances
How should we teach?	• State objective • Present information • Check for understanding • Reteach • Practice	• Focus students on a problem or event in their lives • Question student understandings of the problem or event • Present big ideas, metaphors, analogies, theories, concepts (explanatory frameworks) to resolve "schooled" and "unschooled" understandings of the problem or event • Have students solve problems by applying one or more explanatory frameworks

Table 11.3. Teaching Mathematics: Two Instructional Worldviews

Teaching	Instructional Worldview A	Instructional Worldview B
What a teacher does	Stands in front of the room to define terms, explain procedures, and assign practice problems	Walks around the room and asks students to explain and justify the application of a mathematical concept
What a teacher says	"While I am checking your homework write down the definitions on the board."	"Yesterday we looked at the relationship between angles and parallel lines. Today, I want you to make up your own problems by changing the position of angles between parallel lines."
The kind of mathematical thinking a teacher expects from students	How fast and accurately can my students solve assigned problems?	What connections can my students make between mathematical concepts, procedures, and principles?
What materials a teacher uses	• Textbooks • Worksheets	• Math manipulatives • Computer simulation of real-world problems
What tasks a teacher assigns	Complete practice problems on an already demonstrated mathematical procedure.	Justify to the class your reasoning for a problem with multiple solution strategies.

Table 11.4. Teaching Language Arts: Two Instructional Worldviews

Teaching	Instructional Worldview A	Instructional Worldview B
What a teacher does	Works from a computer at a desk in front of the room to display PowerPoint slides defining tragedy	Presents learners with a set of problem-based scenarios that present situations that could be construed as tragedies
What a teacher says	"As I display the elements in the definition, I want you to record the elements in your notes."	"Working in your groups, determine in each case if the situation is a tragedy, and explain why it is or isn't."
The kind of literary thinking a teacher expects from students	Students should be able to recall the criteria that define the idea of tragedy in literature.	Students should be able to derive a definition of tragedy, which we can compare to a classical definition and apply to our reading of drama.
What a materials a teacher uses	• Notes • Text of a play	• Set of problem-based scenarios • Notes • Text of a play
What tasks a teacher assigns	On a quiz, without reliance on notes, write an accurate definition of tragedy. On an essay test, explain how the given definition applies to the features of an assigned play.	Write an extended definition of tragedy, exploring a set of defining criteria, supported by examples to illustrate each criterion statement. Apply the derived definition to an analysis of a play, both in discussion and in written response.

143

Instructional worldviews can develop by accident, or they can be the out-growth of an intentional process of research, discussion, reflection, and, ultimate-ly, the institutionalization of how teachers and administrators think about and act upon the fundamental questions of schooling. Instructional managers allow instructional worldviews to develop by accident in their schools. Programs, text-books, consultants, state mandates, and district administrators fly through their schools at a dizzying pace. Each school year begins and ends with instructional managers sitting in their offices managing an instructional worldview composed of some of this theory, some of that program, and some of what works in teachers' classrooms. What instructional managers are shaping is not a coherent instruc-tional worldview, but an instructional puzzle. Managing instructional puzzles places school administrators in the uncomfortable position of either telling teach-ers to adopt (or selling them on) pieces of an instructional puzzle (programs, text-books, organizational routines, etc.) that do not fit together. It is not surprising, then, that trying to fit square textbooks into round theories, instructional manag-ers look harried and uncertain about the instructional programs they are charged with implementing. At some point in the process of trying to explain to teachers the inexplicable relationship between different pieces of different instructional puzzles scattered around the building, school administrators throw up their hands and move on to the implementation of the newest instructional puzzle piece. The cycle of reform failure (see Chapter 10) begins anew.

Strong Instructional Leaders, on the other hand, do not experience the va-garies of weak instructional worldviews. Strong instructional worldviews are not puzzles, but coherent instructional frameworks within which all the fundamen-tal questions of schooling fit together. Instead of forcing puzzle pieces into place, these leaders spend their time facilitating and teaching theories and practices of the common instructional worldview. Whatever instructional problems arise in their schools, they employ a common instructional framework for understanding and resolving instructional problems and teaching new pedagogies.

Tables 11.3 and 11.4 illustrate the power of instructional worldviews to guide the situational journey. When teachers express dissatisfaction with student achievement in language arts or mathematics, a Strong Instructional Leader looks to the school's instructional worldview to guide the discussion of the problem, to examine educational theories and practices, and, ultimately, to develop a plan of action to resolve the problem. Time and resources are not wasted on the adoption of incompatible instructional programs that make little collective sense to facul-ties. More importantly, from the perspective of the leader, coherent instructional frameworks serve as a firewall against the disruptive influences of foreign instruc-tional initiatives that interfere with the process of continually improving and mak-ing sense of theories and practices that support a school's instructional worldview.

Strong instructional worldviews evolve out of the private and public journeys of Strong Instructional Leaders. The situational journey shifts their attention from con-structing a common conceptual framework for understanding teaching and learning to applying the agreed-upon conceptual framework to particular instructional situations. In these particular situations, a school's instructional worldview is embodied in the what, why, and how of resolving an instructional problem. The remainder of the situational journey calls upon Strong Instructional Leaders to make sense of theory-based instructional strategies for teachers who have become dissatisfied with programs, methods, and curricula that are failing to achieve a valued end of schooling.

Interpreting an Instructional Problem: Winding the Watch

When experiencing an aircraft emergency, professional pilots are trained to "wind the watch" before doing anything in the cockpit. Wind the watch means stop, think, think again, and then act. This maxim of airline safety teaches the lesson that acting before thinking always makes bad situations worse. The same lesson holds true for the situational journey. When school administrators enter classrooms to work on an instructional problem, teachers expect action. The proclivity of instructional managers is to do something: add a teacher's aide; change a schedule; impose a new rule; employ a consultant; or order new materials. All of these actions mute teacher complaints for a while. Soon, however, the complaints begin anew (see Cycle of Reform Failure in Chapter 10). The instructional problem continues to recur until someone in school leadership stops to wind the watch.

The situational journey begins with reflection, not action—winding the watch. Just doing something assumes that teachers come from nowhere and, with little or no guidance, can be directed to go somewhere. Teachers make sense of their daily classroom practices based upon what they learned in college, what they practiced during student teaching, and what they experienced in their teaching careers. Where teachers come from serves as a powerful filter for what elements of a new theory-based reform initiative they choose to adopt, modify, or ignore. Teachers ignore theories that are far removed from where they come from and quickly adopt techniques that keep the daily grind of schooling moving along. A we-they mentality (teachers versus administrators) evolves from the intellectual need on the part of teachers to understand a change initiative and the instrumental need on the part of administrators to efficiently implement it. This clash of instrumentalism and intellectualism ends badly when, in frustration, instructional managers run around with clipboards checking to see if teachers are implementing surface features of a new instructional initiative (e.g., plan books, word walls).

Strong Instructional Leaders break the cycle of reform failure by acknowledging the filter that all educators apply when confronted with unfamiliar instructional theories and techniques. If completed in a conscientious fashion, the private journey of such leaders generates an intellectual environment that questions, reorganizes, and transforms how teachers think about instructional problems. Without the benefit of the same educational process (private journey), teachers naturally resist pedagogical changes that threaten their comfortable teaching routines. Strong Instructional Leaders view the subtle and not-so-subtle opposition that teachers mount against a new instructional initiative as normal responses to theories and practices that make little sense to them and mediate teacher resistance to theory-based instructional initiatives by inviting teachers into a learning process similar to the one experienced during the private journey. These leaders organize times and places where teachers, administrators, and experts come together to negotiate the meaning of a new pedagogy.

Figure 11.1 illustrates the complex set of intellectual moves the leaders and teachers negotiate to develop common understandings of a theory-based instructional change initiative. Each move in the process requires three distinct, but interrelated, shifts in teacher thinking: first, from looking outside the classroom (Figure 11.1, circles A and B) for solutions to the instructional problem to looking inside the classroom (Figure 11.1, C); second, from formulaic remedies of theory-based pedagogies to their purposeful applications (Figure 11.1, D and E); and, finally, from the mechanics of implementing a new theory to developing an understanding of it (Figure 11.1, F and G).

Figure 11.1. Interpreting an Instructional Problem

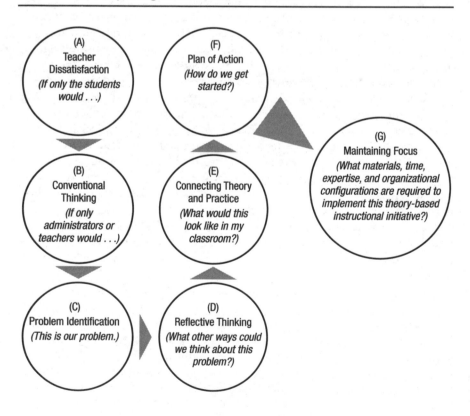

The educational process for interpreting a theory-based instructional initiative pictured in Figure 11.1 is wholly different from traditional workshops designed to train teachers to implement a particular technique. Instructional techniques are procedures, steps, or routines designed to achieve specific outcomes: quiet classes, decoded vocabulary words, grouped students, or planned lessons. Instructional managers are comfortable with organizing workshops designed to train teachers to follow procedures, steps, or routines. The glaring omission in these workshops is a reason why teachers should implement the newly arrived technique. Merely understanding how to use an instructional technique, without understanding why it is being used, promotes simplistic responses to complex instructional problems: how to teach children and adolescents to read well, compute well, write well, and think well. A program, a technique, or curriculum grows out of theory-based explanations for instructional problems. Explanatory theories provide a conceptual framework that imposes order on instructional methods introduced into messy classroom environments.

Teachers who actively interpret an instructional problem are educated to understand underlying theoretical justifications for applying particular methods in particular instructional situations. Teachers who passively interpret an instructional problem are trained to replicate a procedure or routine in their classrooms. Teachers leave the interpretative process pictured in Figure 11.1 with an understanding of how a particular technique, step, or routine relates to an instructional worldview (how children learn; how we should teach; what knowledge is of greatest worth; how knowledge should be organized; and how we should assess what students understand). Teachers leave training workshops on Friday with a set of techniques they are expected to implement on Monday: using word walls, constructing activity centers, or posting classroom rules. The necessary act of interpreting the when, where, how, and why of a word wall or activity center becomes the responsibility of consultants or the guru of the day—both of whom are far removed from the classroom.

Instructional Conversations

School administrators, involved teachers, and experts in the field interpret an instructional problem through a series of conversations. Figure 11.1 and Table 11.5 summarize the types of conversations Strong Instructional Leaders conduct in teacher workspaces to transform teacher thinking about the causes of and solutions to an instructional problem. Each interpretative move requires a different type of conversation. They initiate different types of conversations based on where teachers are coming from (their social, emotional, and intellectual levels of functioning and their prior experiences with theories associated with the new pedagogy) and on external constraints impacting the school. The challenge of the situational journey is to interpret theory-based pedagogies in workspaces inhabited by teachers at different places in their careers, coming from different experiences in classrooms, and working in particular school environments.

Table 11.5. Types of Conversations in the Interpretive Process

Interpretative Moves (as seen in Figure 11.1)	Type of Conversation	Conversation Patterns
A Teacher Dissatisfaction	Type I If only students would . . .	• Do their homework • Take notes in class • Take state tests more seriously • Attend school more often • Speak English
B Conventional Thinking	Type I If only administrators or teachers . . .	administrators would . . . • Get tougher with kids • Give us more resources (smaller classes, add teacher aides) • Adopt this method, textbook, program (what works for me) teachers would . . . • Focus on their teaching instead of how to run a building • Act more professionally • Take staff development more seriously • Treat kids better
C Problem Identification	Type I This is our problem.	• What is the problem? • What theories and practices under our control govern this problem? • What theories and practices governing this problem are not working?

D *Reflective Thinking*	*Type II* *What other ways could we think about this problem?*	• What explanations might be offered for this problem? • What theories and practices govern these explanations? • Do any of these theories and practices offer possible solutions for the problem?
E *Connecting* *Theory to Practice*	*Type II* *What would this theory look like in my classroom?*	• Which theory or practice would work in our classrooms? • Does this theory agree with the school's instructional worldview? • What knowledge and skills would teachers need to apply this theory or practice in their classrooms?
F *Action Plan*	*Type III* *How do we get started?*	• Who is responsible for what? • How do personnel know what they are responsible for? • Who supervises a standard of performance? • How do we know if we are effective?
G *Maintaining Focus*	*Type III* *This is where we are going.*	• What resources do we need? • What organizational changes should accompany this instructional change? • What influences outside of the school constrain implementation of this instructional change? • What ideas and practices are (and are not) working for me/us? • What knowledge and skills do we need to better represent the theories grounding this instructional initiative? • Does this instructional initiative promote our instructional worldview?

Strong Instructional Leaders assume responsibility for determining which conversations occur with particular teachers, regarding particular classrooms situations, under particular school circumstances. Some teachers, for example, come to an instructional problem blaming low student achievement on forces outside their classrooms (e.g., parents, TV). For these teachers, such leaders employ a discourse pattern that originates from Type I conversations. The goal of Type I conversations is to move the locus of responsibility for an instructional problem from outside the classroom to inside the classroom.

For other teachers expressing personal dissatisfaction with a program or instructional technique, these leaders employ a pattern that originates from Type II conversations. The goal of Type II conversations is to formulate connections between teacher perceptions of how a subject should be taught and alternative interpretations of how a subject should be taught. Teachers in this same conversation may have already embraced a new theory or practice in the field. With these teachers, Strong Instructional Leaders delicately revisit Type II conversations to make sure that their enthusiasm has not resulted in a lethal modification of the new pedagogy.

No matter where teachers locate themselves on a continuum between Type I and Type II conversations, all teachers involved in the implementation of a new instructional initiative ask the persistent question of school reform: "How are we going to do this?" Variants of the question begin with the word *Where?*

- Where do we get the money?
- Where do we get the materials?
- Where do we get the time?
- Where do we get the help we need?

Teachers continually pose "where" questions in the midst of Type I and Type II conversations. The response to a where question becomes the standard by which teachers judge administrative commitment to implementing a new instructional initiative. How school administrators should respond to where questions is the subject of the next chapter. Within the context of an instructional conversation, without a plausible Type III response, Type I and Type II conversations become contentious. Teachers are unwilling to experiment with new pedagogies until they trust administrators to deliver on where questions. The questions asked in Type III conversations are answered based on the organizational capacity that Strong Instructional Leaders developed during the private and public journeys. The goal of Type III conversations is to maximize the time and energy teachers spend on learning and practicing a new pedagogy and minimize the time and energy teachers spend on asking where questions.

Talking with Teachers—Not at Them

For explanatory purposes, Figure 11.1 and Table 11.5 present a rational process of inquiry that begins with problem identification and ends with an action plan. As described throughout this book, however, school administrators work in messy instructional environments characterized by uncertain goals, uncertain pedagogies, and uncertain student bodies. Added to this mix of instructional uncertainty are teachers' perceptions of the causes and solutions to problems they are experiencing in the classroom. Teachers' perceptions of what is going wrong and what should be done in their classrooms overrule any attempt to utilize logical methods of inquiry. The emotional and intellectual strain of responding to the learning needs of large groups of students narrows teachers' perceptions of teaching and learning to the sole question "What works?"

Schools offer no time, no venue, no expertise, and no materials to promote what the management literature calls the reflective practitioner (Schön, 1983). Instead of interpreting daily classroom practices within disciplinary guidelines— reflection on practice—teachers spend their days refining classroom and instructional routines that work for them—reflection on action (Schön, 1983). Busy classrooms transform purposeful methods of inquiry and conceptual understandings of curriculum and instruction into a mode of thinking and conversation that

- reduces instructional problems to single causal explanations based on a series of personal observations and/or adjoining instructional facts (e.g., test scores, absenteeism);
- relies on "gut" feelings about problematic classroom situations;
- feels comfortable with what works rather than what the research says;
- feels uncomfortable with technical vocabulary;
- demands short-term solutions (fixes); and
- looks for data confirming individual perceptions of an instructional problem.

Simply put, concepts do not work in classrooms; techniques do. One of the biggest challenges of the situational journey is to make sense of the confusing messes (Schön, 1983) of classrooms within well-defined educational research. What the research says provides school administrators and teachers with a vocabulary and analytical tools to classify and analyze myriad variables that swirl around crowded classrooms: reflection on practice. What the research leaves out are the social interactions and emotional undercurrents that dominate classroom practice and discourse: reflection on action. In research-methods courses, it is accepted practice to discard variables that researchers are unable to quantify. In messy classrooms, teachers care most about those unquantifiable variables (fear, humiliation, anger, and joy). It is no surprise that teachers uniformly disregard what the research says in favor of what works on Monday.

Strong Instructional Leaders adhere to two principles in responding to the theory-practice divide: First, they remain respectful to the purposeful methods of inquiry outlined in Figure 11.1 and Table 11.5. What the research says imposes an order and regularity to the uncertainty of classroom practice. Theory-based instructional initiatives serve as buoys for navigating uncertain waters of classroom practice. Second, they remain respectful to the idiosyncrasies of classroom practice. What works in classrooms serves as a safe harbor for anchoring a theory-based instructional initiative. Effectively negotiating a meaningful relationship between the empirical realities of theory-based initiatives and the practical realities of classroom instruction empowers teachers to author a personal instructional reality.

Constructing meaningful links between the analytical world of research and the personal world of classrooms calls for a mode of discourse that Shotter (1993) calls conversational realities. When teachers talk about instruction, they talk about what is working and what is not working. Teachers begin grading papers when conversations turn to what the research says. Acknowledging the realities of talking about classroom practice, Strong Instructional Leaders condense the interpretative moves listed in Table 11.5 to four strategies of conversation pictured in Figure 11.2. Each style of communication is designed to elicit different perceptions of classroom realities and move teacher talk from *describing* what they are doing to *justifying* what they are doing. What follows are descriptions of each style of communication employed in conversations about classroom realities. Each style, however, should not be viewed as discrete or as progressing in a linear sequence from listening to authoring. Conversations with teachers about classroom realities are messy conversations. As conversations initiated in teacher workspaces progress, each style loses its distinctive qualities in an ongoing dialogue about what is working and what is not working in classrooms. In talks about classroom realities, Strong Instructional Leaders move the conversation from descriptions of what is not working in classrooms toward explanations of what might work better in classrooms.

Listening. Strong Instructional Leaders begin discussing the realities of classroom instruction by listening for stories, descriptions, complaints, questions, and demands that express a deep gap between student performance and a valued end of schooling (educating responsible citizens, productive workers, and critical thinkers; cultivating humanity). What resonates in teacher workspaces are conversations about gaps between cherished ideals of schooling and the realities of student performance.

Questioning. While conversations about ideal goals and classroom realities serve as a catalyst for the conversational dynamic pictured in Figure 11.2, the emotional attachment to valued ends of schooling overwhelms talk about actual classroom practice. Frustrations generated by the gap between valued ends and

Figure 11.2. Talking with Teachers—Not at Them

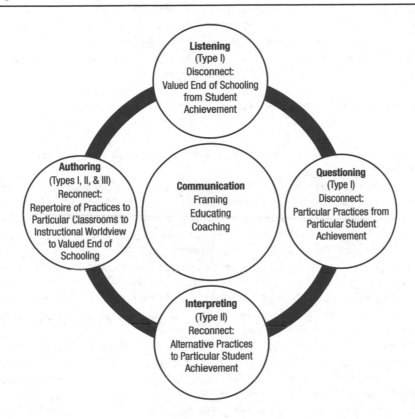

real performance impel teachers to look outside classrooms for forces that are corrupting the foundations of their profession. Strong Instructional Leaders respond to gaps between teacher ideals and classroom realities with questions that focus on the particulars of classroom practice and the particulars of student achievement. The questions posed by such leaders are not accusative ("What are you doing?" "Why aren't you doing this?"), but inquisitive ("Compare your intentions and practices with actual outcomes."). Questioning teachers about their interactions with students and materials turns the conversation away from blaming circumstances far removed from the classroom and holds up a mirror to ineffective instructional practices.

In their questioning conversations with teachers, Strong Instructional Leaders use the concepts, terms, and practices that represent a theory-based instructional initiative. These have greater explanatory power than the concepts, terms, and practices that teachers sometimes talk about and perform in their classrooms. Such leaders, however, are careful not to stray too far from how teachers are making sense of an instructional problem. Alternative concepts, terms, and practices that are introduced into questioning conversations must be understandable. Teachers must see connections, no matter how faint, between what is working, what is not working, and what might work better.

Interpreting. When teachers are ready to look at alternative theories and practices to resolve gaps between what they expect from students and how students are actually performing, the conversation changes. Instead of simply describing the achievement gaps, teachers are ready to look at strategies to resolve them.

Presenting alternative explanations for gaps in student achievement is not a matter of replacing one program with another program. Teachers must be educated on the why and how of practices that have greater promise for resolving their dissatisfactions with student achievement. Strong Instructional Leaders serve as interpreters for translating theory-based instructional initiatives into a language that is understandable to practitioners in action. Interpretative conversations are composed of three discourse patterns. First, teachers describe their perceptions of which teaching behaviors are working and which are not working in their classrooms. These leaders probe teachers for the rationales that support their perceptions of effective and ineffective teaching behaviors.

Second, Strong Instructional Leaders provide a theory-based critique of practices teachers are currently employing in their classrooms. Listening to teachers describe what practices are working and which are not working in their classrooms, such leaders mentally note which of the practices are supported (and which are not) by research. The statement, what the research says, is never mentioned in these conversations. Instead, the leaders explain, using theory-based rationale, why a particular teaching technique is more or less effective than another.

When assessing teaching practices, Strong Instructional Leaders use terms, concepts, and practices that are familiar to teachers. Teachers become confused or resistant when they are told that Technique X (e.g., round robin reading) is ineffective because it does not agree with Theory Y (e.g., constructivism). Such a comment does not explain to teachers how round robin reading relates to constructivism and fails to identify what practices might be more effective. Instead of relating actions to abstract theories or philosophies of education, such leaders explain why round robin reading (a favored technique) is not increasing student comprehension (and may be causing discipline problems). During this conversation, a Strong Instructional Leader might determine that teachers are incorrectly using round robin reading. School administrators with an understanding of how reading should be taught might question teachers on the reading strategies they are employing before, during, and after the round robin activity. If teachers are not employing reading strategies to enhance engagement and comprehension, a Strong Instructional Leader would describe reading strategies that increase the effectiveness of the favored reading method (round robin reading). Depending on teachers' background knowledge of the teaching of reading, such leaders may further explain particular methods and strategies of teaching reading by relating a technique or group of techniques to a theory of reading and to the school's instructional worldview.

Third, throughout the interpretative process, Strong Instructional Leaders continually press teachers to establish common understandings of educational terminology. Teacher workspaces are cluttered with vocabulary and techniques (such as thematic instruction and reciprocal reading) that are left over from past reform initiatives. Unintended consequences of the rapid turnover of yearly reform initiatives are confused lists of concepts and terminology that are never clearly defined in practice. Over time, teachers are left with an incoherent mix of instructional strategies that represent conflicting instructional worldviews. For example, teachers can be required to complete a seven-step lesson plan for a problem-based curriculum. It is at this point in the interpretative process that Strong Instructional Leaders break out markers and butcher paper and begin recording publicly what teachers are saying and doing in their classrooms.

Whatever method the leader chooses to represent the way teachers think about an instructional problem, the resulting organizational framework prioritizes and aligns instructional concepts and practices with a coherent instructional worldview. Table 11.6 represents one way of mapping teacher conversations about low reading achievement. Throughout the conversation, Strong Instructional Leaders record teachers' thoughts and actions on paper and, more importantly, guide the conversation by imposing a conceptual framework on what teachers are thinking and doing about low reading achievement.

Table 11.6. Conversation Chart for Low Achievement in Reading

Method	Key Elements	Instructional Goals	Materials and Skills	Instructional Worldview	Sources
Reading in the Content Areas					
Guided Reading					
Differentiated Instruction					
Cooperative Learning					
Word Walls					

Strong Instructional Leaders establish common understandings of instructional practices in conversations aimed at what teachers practice (methods), what teachers understand (key elements), what teachers hope to accomplish (instructional goals), and what teachers actually do in classrooms (materials and skills). Intentionally left out of the conversation are references to an instructional worldview and sources that support the methods brought up by teachers: what the research says. Interpretative conversations are focused on teachers making sense of what they are doing in classrooms—the how of teaching.

Interpretive conversations are not void of references to instructional worldviews or how teachers learned a teaching method. Strong Instructional Leaders, however, steer the conversation away from specific references to an instructional worldview until all ideas and practices are charted and prioritized. After teacher responses have been recorded, Strong Instructional Leaders return to questioning conversations to assess teacher understanding of practices they employ in their classrooms and what practices teachers feel comfortable with. As these questioning conversations proceed, Strong Instructional Leaders subtly guide the interpretative process by choosing where ideas and practices are placed on the chart and which elements, goals, and materials accurately represent a method favored by teachers.

In this conversation of low reading achievement, teachers and administrators reach consensus about a method that shows promise (e.g., reading in content areas); a method that is not working (e.g., word walls); methods that increase reading achievement (e.g., differentiated instruction, cooperative learning); and what particular actions, materials, and goals faithfully represent a favored method of teaching reading.

The final conversation chart of an instructional problem should represent what teachers believe is a pattern of best practices in the field. What remains unfinished in interpretative conversations is connecting the list of practices, goals, and materials to a generalized theory of how a subject should be taught. Teachers become authors of a new instructional reality when they are able to articulate relationships between particular practices, particular theories of instruction, and a school's instructional worldview.

What the Research Does Not Say

Throughout the give-and-take of discussing the instructional realities of the classroom, Strong Instructional Leaders focus on what teachers feel comfortable talking about and what practices are working or not working in their classrooms. The desired outcome of these conversations is an organized representation of practices that govern the teaching of a particular subject matter and explanations of why particular techniques are working or not working. Left out of these conversations are references to instructional theories that justify methods discussed in teacher workspaces.

The disconnect between theory and practice in teacher workspaces exemplifies the natural differences between the two traditions in education: (1) a teaching tradition focused on personal relationships, practical applications, and moral undertakings and (2) a research tradition focused on analytical relationships, general understandings, and generation of ideas. The difference in these two traditions is in the generalized and specialized approaches to knowledge creation. Generalized approaches to knowledge creation (research tradition) employ research methodologies to generate theories, principles, or laws that apply across cases. Specialized approaches to knowledge creation (teaching tradition) employ routines, steps, and methods to increase the efficiency and effectiveness of a practice.

Theory-based reform initiatives provide coherent frameworks for understanding how a repertoire of instructional methods works to address particular instructional problems. Methods-driven reform initiatives provide the skills to execute practices expertly. When doing the right things interacts smoothly with doing things right, teachers and school administrators acquire both the flexibility of thought to choose the right repertoire of techniques for resolving an instructional problem and the required proficiencies to expertly implement a coherent body of instructional methods.

The culminating strategy of talking about classroom realities is the establishment of common vocabularies, metaphors, exemplars, and stories that fuse together the repertoires of methods teachers choose to apply to an instructional problem and the underlying justifications for their selection. Discussing the relationships between the how and why of instructional techniques, as mentioned already, is uncomfortable for teachers. The daily grind of managing large groups of students strips teachers of the vocabulary, conceptual frameworks, and academic sources necessary for seeing relationships between a technique that works and justifications for employing a workable technique. Merely saying to a teacher that Technique X agrees with Theory Y leaves the teacher with no understanding of how Technique X originates in the variables studied in Theory Y and, more importantly, how Techniques X and Z work together to realize the predictions of Theory Y.

Strong Instructional Leaders continually experiment with metaphors, stories, and cases that have the vocabulary and imagery to connect the generalities of theory-based instructional initiatives with particular techniques employed in classrooms. As these experiments in collective sensemaking progress, the leaders rely on a series of conversational strategies that generate an instructional dialogue allowing teachers to freely wander back forth between preexisting beliefs about curriculum and instruction and alternative explanations of how subject matter should be taught. What evolves out of these theory-practice conversations is not a direct representation of theory-based pedagogies in classroom practice. Instead of mirroring a theory-based pedagogy, Strong Instructional Leaders author, along with teachers, a new instructional reality.

Table 11.7 describes the goals and tasks of authoring a new instructional reality. The conversational strategies described in Table 11.7 proceed eclectically and persistently, with Strong Instructional Leaders employing different strategies in response to different concerns of teachers. At various times, conversations call for defining and explaining (educating); reinterpreting teacher perceptions (framing); reflecting on action (coaching); or creating action plans (structuring). Throughout these conversations, the original instructional problem, the agreed-upon theory-based instructional initiative, and the plan of action are continually revised and ultimately transformed into an instructional narrative that makes collective sense to teachers.

Authoring an instructional narrative is a long process of listening, questioning, interpreting, and ultimately constructing new understandings of theories and practices in education. The process requires a commitment on the part of school administrators to sitting with teachers and articulating the relationships between teachers' expressed dissatisfaction with student achievement and implementation of alternative perceptions and realities of a theory-based pedagogy. For the authoring process to succeed, the leader must possess personal mastery of the pedagogical content knowledge in question and the organizational know-how to provide teachers with the time, materials, and expertise to make sense of the new pedagogical initiative. Missing either attribute, conversations about classroom realities are reduced to daily confrontations over the rationale and implementation of using this technique or that material.

An instructional narrative resonates with teachers when they understand how an instructional theory works to close gaps in student achievement. Teacher enthusiasm for a theory-based pedagogy, however, can quickly turn sour when the reality of managing and teaching large groups of students clashes with an intellectually appealing instructional narrative. The remaining task of the situational journey is to marry the enthusiasm for a theory-based pedagogy to the skillful application of techniques that grow out of newly authored instructional narratives: the complex task of transforming concepts into practice.

Table 11.7. Authoring Instructional Realities

Strategy	Goal(s)	Tasks
Frame	• Shift locus of the problem from outside the school to inside the classroom. • Shift solutions to the problem from conventional wisdom to formal methods of inquiry and theory-based instructional interventions. • Reinterpret teacher perceptions of why theory-based initiatives will not work in their classrooms.	• Identify instructional problems that resonate with teachers. • Elaborate on connections between theory-based pedagogies and teacher perceptions of instructional problems. • Employ metaphors, stories, and cases to establish connections between classroom experiences and theory-based pedagogies. • Provide alternative explanations or solutions for teacher dissatisfaction with a theory-based pedagogy (e.g., too difficult for students; do not understand it; do not have the materials; philosophically opposed).
Educate	Identify alternative theories and practices to resolve expressed dissatisfactions with student achievement.	• Present alternative theories of instruction and ways of thinking about the subject matter (e.g., math is computation; reading is word recognition). • Explain philosophy, goals, and techniques associated with theory-based instructional initiatives. • Define terminology associated with alternative theories of instruction. • Identify alternative theories that best address an instructional problem and align with a school's instructional worldview. • Describe what the theory looks like in the classroom. • Present practical arguments for discarding ineffective methods of instruction and adopting effective methods of instruction. • Establish relationships between particular techniques, theory-based pedagogies, and an instructional worldview.
Coach	• Identify strengths of teachers. • Identify gaps between intended and actual performance of students.	• Respectfully listen to teacher experiences with theory-based instructional initiatives. • Paraphrase teacher understanding of the how and why of a theory-based instructional initiative. • Summarize gaps in understandings of relationships between theory and practice. • Construct instructional strategies that are sensitive to particular classrooms and particular understandings of a theory-based instructional initiative.
Structure	Develop organizational capacity to support a theory-based instructional initiative.	• Allocate time, space, materials, and expertise. • Supervise a plan of action that results in authoring a new instructional reality.

12

Developing
Master Teachers

Master teachers are in abundant supply in our schools. What are not in abundant supply are the instructional environments and training opportunities to develop masterful approaches to curriculum and instruction. Strong Instructional Leaders assume the responsibility for designing staff-development programs that place teachers in positions to properly "enact" theory-based reform initiatives.

Deep down, teachers believe the profession they entered should be practiced as an art, not a science. National and state accountability mandates oppose this belief—legislators believe teaching is a science. Scientific teaching, as mandated by government policy, reduces scientifically based reform initiatives to series of steps, routines, and procedures that teachers are expected to consistently execute in their classrooms. Teachers in this model align curriculum, transmit facts, follow scripts, implement techniques, analyze data, and hand out grades. The goal of scientific teaching is to acquire testable knowledge and master skills. School administrators who adopt scientifically based reform initiatives believe that what teachers do in classrooms and what is expected of students are easily observable. Teachers employed in these "production schools" are considered technocrats who expertly implement programs characterized by low task variety and low task uncertainty (Wilson, 1989). Administrators in production schools are considered managers who implement supervisory systems that monitor teacher compliance with prescribed program tasks.

On the other end of the teaching continuum, there are schools that promote artistic approaches to teaching and learning. Artful teaching is a highly intuitive affair: Teachers are expected to continually create and adjust instructional activities based on the interests and talents of the students sitting in their classes. The goal of artful teaching is to create an enthusiasm for learning and develop individual talent. School administrators who coordinate artful approaches to curriculum and instruction believe that what teachers do in classrooms and what is expected of students are not observable (Wilson, 1989). Teachers employed in these progressive schools are considered artists who create individual learning environments characterized by high task variety and high task uncertainty (Wilson, 1989).

Administrators in progressive schools are considered facilitators who assume responsibility for creating instructional environments where experimentation, flexibility, and innovation are honored qualities of the teaching profession.

The decades-long dispute between those who believe teaching is a science and those who believe teaching is an art plays out each year in the policy arena. Reformers who seek to turn schools around by enticing into the teaching profession the best young minds in our universities are on the teaching-is-art end of the policy continuum. According to this group of reformers, only the best and brightest graduating from our universities are capable of implementing ambitious curricular and instructional designs necessary to produce the kinds of thinking and dispositions for effective participation in the 21st century. These idealists believe that finding the best and letting them loose in classrooms is our last best hope for transforming schooling in the United States.

Reformers on the teaching-is-science end of the policy continuum acknowledge artistry in teaching but contend that the teachers we remember in schools are few and far between. Realistically, assert these reformers, administrators should stop looking for artists and start making sure the teachers they now employ do things right. These realists believe that improving education in the United States is a matter of holding teachers accountable for implementing scientifically based reform initiatives.

Strong Instructional Leaders understand that true artistry in teaching is rare. Even if artistry in teaching were in abundant supply, they believe that idiosyncratic approaches to teaching disrupt the cumulative effects of carefully thought-out sequences of knowledge and skills. Instructional programs make sense to students when teaching methods, classroom activities, instructional materials, curricular organization, and assessment instruments form a coherent approach to curriculum and instruction (Newmann, Smith, Allensworth, & Bryk, 2001). Strong Instructional Leaders also acknowledge that technocratic approaches to curriculum and instruction generate deadening teaching routines and intellectual morbidity. To avoid the twin evils of incoherent and mechanical approaches to curriculum and instruction, they proceed down the middle path of school improvement—they seek out and develop teachers who are masters.

Table 12.1 summarizes an adaptation of Pitcher's (1995) description of leadership styles (technocrats, masters, and artists) to the teaching profession. The core competencies of teaching as a craft (mastery) are summarized following Table 12.1. What sets master teachers apart from artists is their willingness to engage in disciplined approaches to minimize the weaknesses and maximize the strengths of their instructional repertoire. What sets master teachers apart from technocrats is their willingness to expand their instructional repertoire beyond comfortable habits of teaching. Master teachers possess the knowledge and skills to do things right and the craft experience (reflection on action) to do the right things.

Table 12.1. Technocrats, Masters, and Artists

Characteristics of Instruction	Technocrats "doing things right"	Masters "doing the right things well"	Artists "doing the right things"
Goals & outcomes	Tightly coupled	Coupled	Loosely coupled
Valued outcomes	Mastery	Proficiency	Creativity
Decision-making	Rule bound	Experience-based	Eclectic
Knowledge	Standardized	Interpreted	Constructed
Valued intelligences	Intellectual	Social, emotional, intellectual	Social, emotional
Risks	Minimize	Calculate	Maximize
Valued materials	Textbooks	Problems	Social context
Tasks assigned	Low variety	Reasonable variety	High variety
Task outcomes	Predictable	Developmental	Unpredictable
Teaching	Routine	Reflective	Intuitive
School outcomes	Award credential	Produce responsible citizens & productive workers	Cultivate humanity

Adapted from Pitcher, 1995.

Core Behaviors of Master Teachers

- Possesses deep knowledge of subject matter
- Knows pedagogical strengths and weaknesses
- Is receptive to educational theories and practices
- Reflects on action continually
- Takes disciplined approach to thinking about curriculum and instruction
- Is willing to experiment

Master teachers are in abundant supply in universities and schools. What are not in abundant supply are the instructional environments and training opportunities to develop master approaches to curriculum and instruction. Figure 12.1 pictures the training program that Strong Instructional Leaders adopt to instruct master teachers. The proposed model for training master teachers uniquely connects the what of curriculum (A + B + C) with the how of teaching (D + E + F + G). Table 12.2 describes the tasks teachers and administrators are expected to perform during the master training program.

Figure 12.1 Master Training Program

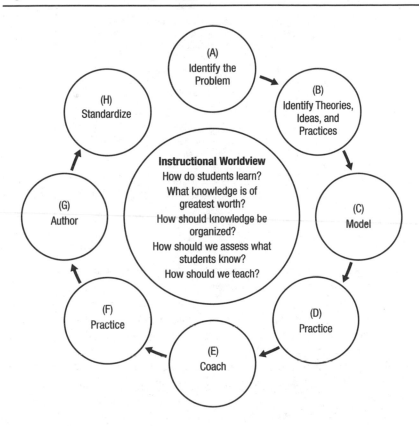

Table 12.2. Tasks of the Master Training Program

	Component	What Teachers Are Asked to Do
A	*Identify the Problem*	Identify gaps between a valued end of schooling and actual student performance.
B	*Identify Theories & Practices*	Identify alternative explanations for the instructional problem.
C	*Model*	Observe expert performance of theory-based methods.
D	*Practice*	Under the supervision of a mentor/consultant, apply theory-based methods in classroom.

(continued)

Table 12.2. *(continued)*

E	*Coach*	Participate in ongoing conversations with mentor/consultant on gaps between the intentions of theory-based methods and actual performance of those methods in classrooms.
F	*Practice*	Under the supervision of a mentor/consultant, continue to employ feedback from coaching sessions to close gaps between intentions of theory-based method and actual performance of those methods in classrooms.
G	*Author*	Construct pedagogical approaches and a plan of action that agree with a school's instructional worldview, the social context of the school, and preexisting experiences of teachers.
H	*Standardize*	Normalize a set of teaching methods that make sense to teachers, are working for teachers, and accurately reflect the application of a theory-based method of instruction.

Teachers who enter master training programs proceed at their own pace through each stage of the program; no teachers, however, are permitted to skip a stage. The dynamic of the program moves teachers from conceptual understandings of theory-based instructional initiatives to accurately practicing theory-based methods in their classrooms (teachers understand how to use math manipulatives to teach concepts in mathematics).

Employing, training, and nurturing master teachers provide administrators with the best parts of the two paradigms of the teaching profession: the accurate representation of the form and substance of theory-based methods of instruction and the judgment to know when and where to pursue or discard a theory-based method. At the end of each classroom session, master teachers habitually ask themselves the following questions:

- What methods were employed in class today?
- How were the methods employed?
- Why were the methods employed?
- Did the methods work?
- How do I know the methods worked?
- Why did the methods work?/Why didn't the methods work?
- What is my plan of action for tomorrow?

Technocratic training programs discard the substance of a theory-based reform initiative (A + B). Instead, technocratic training begins and ends with replicating techniques embedded in a theory of instruction (C + H). Technocratic training programs ignore the rationale for adopting a theory-based initiative (why we are doing this). Absent a rationale for a new instructional initiative, instructional managers see little need to provide time, expertise, and venues to observe, practice, and reflect upon the implementation of a theory-based method (how the techniques accurately reflect a theory of instruction). Partial understandings of theories that govern ambitious teaching practices coupled with inadequate time and expertise allocated for practicing theory-based methods result in surface representations (or lethal mutations) of theory-based instructional initiatives.

Artistic approaches to improving student achievement emphasize under-standing the rationale for theory-based instructional initiatives (A + B + C); pay little attention to the mundane routines for expertly performing theory-based methods (D + E + F + G); and dismiss any effort to standardize teaching meth-odologies (H). In schools that value artistic approaches to teaching, there are no pathways to expanding creativity. Energy and innovation generated in a few class-rooms fail to enter other classrooms in the building.

True innovation in education does not occur when the technique of the day leaps over the theories that justify new methods of instruction. Nor does true in-novation in education occur in leaps from interesting ideas to idiosyncratic class-room practices. True innovation in schooling occurs when theory and practice inform each other, and when teaching experience informs both theory and prac-tice—the formula for master teaching.

Historically, instructional change initiatives that propose radical breaks with the institutional norms of schooling are diluted or repudiated. Reform in U.S. schools will always be a gradual affair—a master activity that values the intelli-gent integration of theory, practice, and experience. No obstacle to master reform initiatives is as formidable as developing the organizational capacity to a theory-based instructional initiative. Without the organizational capacity to elaborate a theory-based instructional initiative, master approaches to practicing a new peda-gogy dissolve into teachers routinely applying the technique of the day or passion-ately trying to seize the day.

Changing Core Teaching Beliefs and Practices

Instructional managers favor technocratic and artistic approaches to implement-ing theory-based instructional initiatives. Both approaches require little cost, little time, little expertise, and little organizational change. Technocratic reform initia-tives reduce the situational journey to one or two half-day workshops followed by some type of evaluation tool that supervisors use to check for the presence or absence of the mandated technique of the day. Artistic reform initiatives reduce the situational journey to sending the best and brightest among a teaching staff to hear inspirational speakers followed by inspirational presentations by the chosen few sent to the conference. Both strategies remove instructional managers from the complex and arduous tasks of changing core teaching beliefs and organizing school environments to faithfully represent intellectually ambitious curriculum (Cohen & Ball, 1999). Both strategies free up time and resources for instructional managers to pursue what they perceive as the real job of school administration—the diversions of schooling.

The journeys of Strong Instructional Leaders, however, commit school administrators to developing and leading processes that educate and train teachers to faithfully represent theory-based pedagogies in their classrooms. The remaining component of realizing accurate representations of the substance and the methods of a new pedagogy is the design of an instructional reform initiative's implementation. Building the organizational infrastructure to accommodate theory-based instructional initiatives is strictly an administrative matter. Only school administrators have access to the resources and organizational systems to execute the kinds of educating and training necessary to faithfully replicate theory-based instructional initiatives.

Cohen and Ball (2000) described the roles that "elaboration" (p. 15) and "development" (p. 17) play in the school improvement process. Adapting those descriptions, Figure 12.2 is a conceptual representation of the interaction between the components of a training program designed to educate as well as train faculty to accurately represent theory-based instructional initiatives. A strong training program accurately reflects the interaction between materials, methods, assessments, and activities embedded in a theory-based pedagogy.

Elaboration. The vertical elaboration arrow represents the level of explanation, education, and training needed to accurately implement an instructional reform initiative. The adoption of ambitious approaches to curriculum and instruction requires varying degrees of educating and training. If the initiative is very sophisticated (e.g., a constructivist mathematics program), Strong Instructional Leaders know that the depth and breadth of the tasks of master training will be highly elaborate. If the initiative is straightforward and uncomplicated (e.g., new grading software), a much lower level of elaboration is required.

Development. The horizontal development arrow represents the different levels of resources needed to accurately implement an instructional reform initiative. To accurately implement a sophisticated pedagogy in classrooms (e.g., a constructivist mathematics program), a Strong Instructional Leader must create substantial organizational capacity (e.g., materials, time, expertise, and space) to transform how teachers think and practice the subjects they teach. Implementing a simple change (e.g., new grading software) requires very little in the way of expertise and changes in organizational arrangements.

Figure 12.2. Training Program

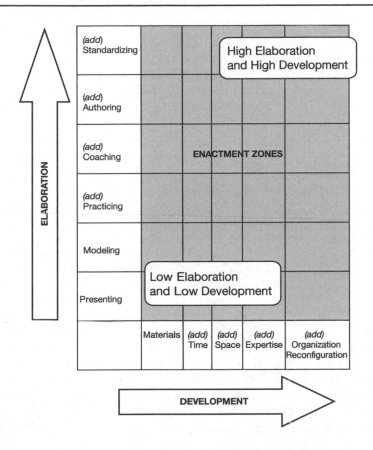

Enactment Zones. The interaction between the level of training required to understand and apply a theory-based reform initiative (elaboration) and the amount and kind of organization resources (development) occurs in what Spillane (1999) calls enactment zones. Strong Instructional Leaders situate themselves in these enactment zones to mediate the relationship between levels of training and levels of organizational capacity. Table 12.3 gives some examples of factors that influence the implementation of a theory-based pedagogy. Throughout the situational journey, Strong Instructional Leaders monitor and adjust an implementation design in response to teachers' understanding and execution of a change initiative and the complexity of the theory-based pedagogy.

Table 12.3. Examples of Elaboration and Development Levels

School Context and Complexity of Reform Initiative		Elaboration and Development Levels
If the initiative is . . .	CLOSELY aligned with current school practices & instructional worldview, you need . . .	Low elaboration and Low development
	POORLY aligned with current school practices & instructional worldview, you need . . .	High elaboration and High development
If the staff is . . .	WELL prepared in the subject matter, you need . . .	Low elaboration and Low development
	POORLY prepared in the subject matter, you need . . .	High elaboration and High development
If the initiative is . . .	HIGHLY sophisticated, you need . . .	High elaboration and High development
	NOT sophisticated, you need . . .	Low elaboration and Low development

Table 12.3 simplifies a complex decision-making process embedded in the day-to-day conversations and the training programs of the situational journey. Determining the proper quantity and quality of resources to support a theory-based initiative is accomplished in many ways. Figure 12.2 and Table 12.3 represent only one way of evaluating the proper mix of training and resources. In addition to the factors listed in Table 12.3, a Strong Instructional Leader must also assess the pervasiveness of the initiative in the school. Will every faculty member need training and resources or will only a small subset use the new initiative?

However one depicts the interaction between levels of elaboration and levels of development, the attention paid to the instructional-reform-implementation design remains constant during the situational journey. Without the proper mix of organizational capacity and training, theory-based instructional initiatives have little chance of being accurately represented in classrooms.

The situational journey is coming to an end. Providing the education and training needed for master approaches to solving instructional problems is a complex and lengthy process. At a minimum, Strong Instructional Leaders remain situated with a complex instructional problem for several years. At some interval in the process of implementing a theory-based pedagogy, school administrators must move on—schools are messy places where messy problems keep moving in. Before moving on, however, these leaders make sure that institutional norms, organizational capacity, and proper supervision are firmly in place to sustain and spread a theory-based instructional initiative and guard against "implementation dip."

"Implementation Dip"

What is often overlooked in the public and situational journeys is Fullan's (2001) observation that most school reform initiatives fall victim to "implementation dip." Fullan describes implementation dip as the erosion of an organization's capacity over time to sustain the kind of energy, resource allocation, and leadership focus necessary to institutionalize an ambitious instructional initiative. The implementation dip is a natural outcome of a process that requires substantive changes in the way teachers think and practice instruction. Each journey described in this book requires both the intellectual capacity to create meaningful instructional frameworks for teachers, the managerial capacity to generate the organizational structure for teachers to learn and practice ambitious pedagogies, and the energy to overcome fatigue and frustration. All of this must happen in policy and institutional environments that are antagonistic to ambitious pedagogies and in school configurations that are structured around the century-old–assign-and-assess model of teaching and learning. It is easy to see why leadership dips occur in instructional situations that require high levels of intellectual understanding and high levels of organizational capacity over extended periods of time. While instructional managers remain in offices occupied with the diversions of school administration, the energy that accompanied the introduction of new pedagogy is lost, as seen in the equation for implementation dip:

Loss of Focus + Loss of Capacity + Loss of Support = IMPLEMENTATION DIP

The same implementation dip happens to teachers, other school administrators, boards of education, and parents. Reorganizing schools for learning and experimenting with innovative approaches to curriculum and instruction requires constant intellectual openness to new ways of teaching and learning, trust in the administrator's ability to do the right thing, and freedom from diversions of schooling. All of these requirements for successful instructional innovation easily disrupt school environments that are under constant siege from external attackers of schooling (see Chapter 11) and the internal realities of the daily grind of bureaucratic schooling. Strong Instructional Leaders convert the equation of the implementation dip into a formula for continually infusing energy into new teaching ideas and practices:

INSTRUCTIONAL ENVIRONMENT to welcome new ideas
+ ORGANIZATIONAL CAPACITY to implement ideas
+ TRUSTING CULTURE to support staff experimentation with new ideas
+ STRONG INSTRUCTIONAL LEADERSHIP to maintain integrity of new ideas

SUCESSFUL IMPLEMENTATION

The ultimate goal of Strong Instructional Leaders is to translate abstract theories and ideas into everyday classroom practice. Implementation dip creeps into reform initiatives when ideas and practices become disconnected from each other. Instructional managers are susceptible to implementation dip because they pay little attention to the theories and ideas that drive particular methods of instruction. Instructional managers do not develop an allegiance to a particular instructional worldview. In schools led by instructional managers, theories and methods float around in hallways and classrooms without an instructional framework for understanding the why and how of a newly introduced instructional initiative. Teachers lose energy and focus in the confused comings and goings of this theory and that method. Administrators lose support and capacity when they are unable to demonstrate how a theory-based instructional initiative fits into a larger vision of increased student performance—their schools' instructional worldview.

Figure 12.3 pictures the tasks (A + B + C + D + E) of implementing an instructional change initiative. All tasks interact with each other, forming a shield from the external constraints of schooling and forming the organizational capacity to move teachers to higher levels of understandings and applications of a theory-based instructional initiative. While the effective implementation of each task is most visible in the situational journey, the final elaboration of a theory-based instructional initiative in classrooms originates in private understandings of theories and practices in education and the public marshaling of resources and rationale to support ambitious departures from the daily grind of schooling.

Table 12.4 provides details of the tasks and functions Strong Instructional Leaders carry out on a daily basis to maintain a sustained focus on accurately representing a theory-based instructional initiative in classrooms.

A process for bringing together the tasks and functions of implementation is missing from Figure 12.3 and Table 12.4. That process is not found in formal meeting structures or products of those structures (policies, procedures, or mandates). Rather, sustaining an instructional change initiative is a highly informal process embedded in teacher workspaces where teachers and school administrators come together to talk about the goals, the frustrations, the successes, and understandings associated with learning to practice a theory-based instructional initiative.

Responding to the Common Complaints of Reform Initiatives

The implementation of an instructional-reform initiative is played out each day in ongoing instructional conversations with teachers working to understand theories and practices foreign to their normal classroom repertoire. Establishing a discourse pattern that respects the prior experiences of teachers while continually pressing teachers to rethink those prior experiences in light of new theories in teaching and learning makes these conversations awkward and complex. An instructional con-

Figure 12.3. Tasks of Instructional Reform Implementation

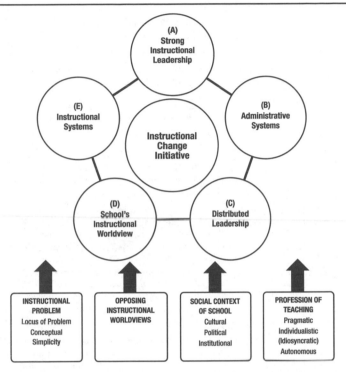

versation is composed of two components. First, the Strong Instructional Leader acknowledges the prior experiences—the private realities—of teachers. Second, the Strong Instructional Leader reframes the core instructional practices that are important to teachers in ways that adhere to best practices in the field. At the same time Strong Instructional Leaders are authoring a new instructional reality with teachers who are struggling with seemingly intractable instructional problems, they immerse themselves in conversations with other administrators, support personnel, and potential teacher-leaders to gain support for a theory-based instructional initiative. All the tasks and functions of implementation revolve around numerous instructional conversations about a theory, practice, system, or procedure. No conversation wanders far from the school's instructional worldview.

There are no scripts for instructional conversations. Training exists in various forms of interpersonal communication that coach rather than impose meaning on teachers. Certainly, these types of training programs should become an ingredient of the private journey. But process should never overwhelm substance. The substance of these ongoing conversations, and what anchors all conversations

Table 12.4. Tasks and Functions of Implementation

Phase of Implementation	Task	Functions
A	*Strong instructional leadership*	• Control employment and induction processes. • Build organizational capacity to sustain training programs. • Reframe theories and ideas to align with school's instructional worldview. • Introduce theory-based instructional initiatives. • Require rational methods for examining instructional problems. • Question preexisting assumptions and practices about teaching and learning.
B	*Administrative systems*	• Develop support systems within which the aims of the system align with the functions of the system. • Develop support systems within which the aims of the system align with the functions of a theory-based instructional initiative. • Monitor support systems for deviations from agreed-upon aims and functions. • Immediately resolve discrepancies between aims and functions of support systems.
C	*Distributed leadership*	• Apprentice teachers and administrators who demonstrate the potential to (1) acquire a deep understanding of a theory-based initiative; (2) coach colleagues; and (3) manage organizational capacity. • Provide resources, organizational support, and authority for teachers and administrators who assume leadership roles in particular instructional situations. • Monitor leaders embedded in an instructional situation..
D	*School's instructional worldview*	• Align theory-based instructional initiatives with a school's instructional worldview (initiatives that do not align are not welcomed into the school). • Align organizational capacity (e.g., materials, time, space, expertise, and configuration) with school's instructional worldview.
E	*Instructional systems*	• Normalize a purposeful approach to curriculum development. • Normalize a purposeful approach to staff development. • Normalize a purposeful approach to professional performance review. • Align processes for curriculum development, staff development, and performance reviews with school's instructional worldview.

Table 12.5. Conversational Realities

Reality	Question	Substance of Conversation
Private Reality	What is not working?	Dissatisfaction with student performance
Public Reality	What is the problem?	Content, organization of content, methods, & assessment
Professional Reality	What do we know about the problem?	Theories, ideas, & practices
Institutional Reality	What do we need to solve the problem?	Materials, time, space, expertise
Management Reality	What do we do next?	Action plan

conducted by Strong Instructional Leaders, are the five questions listed in Table 12.5. Each reality presents a different question that is integral to changing core teaching practices and executing a theory-based instructional initiative. The goal of these instructional conversations is to transform private dissatisfactions with student achievement into courses of action that reflect the best practices in the field. Drawing together private understandings of an instructional problem and a theory-based instructional plan requires a school environment where each reality is talked about and acted upon. Teachers are more willing to learn and practice an unfamiliar pedagogy if they understand how each reality contributes to executing the new pedagogy and how school leaders plan to administer each reality. In other words, progress toward the successful implementation of an instructional initiative is dependent on a fair exchange of realities: No reality can be ignored; no reality is permitted to usurp other realities. When administrators fail to faithfully respond to the realities of implementing ambitious approaches to curriculum and instruction, the conversations in teacher workspaces become adversarial exchanges between teachers expressing confusion about the what and how of a new instructional initiative and administrators expressing frustration with a stubborn adherence to tried-and-true ways of teaching that are not working anymore.

In order to fairly acknowledge all the conversational realities in teacher workspaces, Strong Instructional Leaders adhere to three principles of Strong Instructional Leadership. First, they are clear about the intent and implementation of a new pedagogy. Second, they help teachers author a new instructional reality by paying attention to what parts of a theory-based instructional initiative teachers understand and what parts of a theory fall beyond their private understandings. Lastly, they look upon requests for more resources as a reality, not an excuse for inaction. Holding each principle in place in frenetic workspaces promotes a free exchange of realities and, ultimately, the authoring of a new instructional reality.

13

Transforming the Daily Grind
of Schooling

The combined private, public, and situational journeys of Strong Instructional Leadership is truly a personal journey of authoring, advocating, and executing an instructional worldview that has the intellectual power and organizational capacity to transform the daily grind of schooling. Each journey is driven by five qualities of leadership that generate the kind of focus, energy, and direction necessary for executing imaginative configurations of schooling—what schools could be.

John Dewey (1958) defined imagination as the distance between what is and what could be. In the world of contemporary schooling in the United States, "what is" are school hallways, administrative offices, classrooms, and teacher workspaces that are foundering in the face of accountability mandates, the hoarding of credentials, and the enforcement of the rules of institutional schooling. "What could be" lies in the mischievous eyes and endless energy of my 5-year-old grandson, whose talents and intelligences have yet to be ignited.

Chapters 1 through 6 described what is happening in schools today. School administrators spend their days enforcing the rules of institutional schooling; teachers spend their days talking at students; and students spend their days "doing school." Leadership in schools that grind out the routines of institutional schooling amounts to managing systems, documenting the mandate of the day, and mediating disputes over resources. In the midst of handing out detentions, handing out diplomas, and handing out textbooks, instructional managers periodically emerge from their offices to enunciate "what could be" phrases lifted from district mission statements. Teachers sitting in the audience, who once believed in what could be, know that soon they will return to classrooms that are controlled by what is. The missing link between the high-sounding rhetoric of school mission statements and the daily grind of schooling is the combination of knowledge and skills necessary to fully execute a coherent instructional worldview of what could be. Without a coherent strategy to ask and answer the fundamental questions of schooling, school administrators and teachers wander aimlessly from one reform idea to another, one mandate to another, one program to another, one crisis to another, and one year to the next.

Chapters 7 through 12 describe a series of journeys for developing and executing an instructional worldview. The journeys begin with the personal and private development of a coherent response to the fundamental questions of schooling. They become public with a narrative that applies an instructional worldview to a particular instructional problem. The journeys end in classroom situations in which theory-based solutions to instructional problems are woven into the everyday routines and understandings of a school community. Each journey is designed to move school administrators and teachers to shared resolutions of the fundamental questions of schooling and eventually to common representations of theory-based instructional initiatives in classrooms.

The goals and practices of institutional schooling stand in the way of executing coherent instructional worldviews. On a daily basis, administrators arrive at the crossroads of what is happening in their schools and what should be happening in their schools. School administrators who choose not to embark on the journeys described in chapters 7 through 12 remain managers. Instructional managers see no crossroads—just highways. Each year, there is a new highway to be driven, signs to be obeyed, and frequent stops to pick up new programs.

Strong Instructional Leaders choose to journey off these highways—they venture down the least traveled roads pursuing questions of purpose, questions of practice, and questions of implementation. Their journey is made more difficult because there are many roads and no maps to guide them. The private, public, and situational journeys of Strong Instructional Leadership are truly a personal journey of authoring, advocating, and executing an instructional worldview—what could be in schools becomes what is.

Chapters 7 through 12 chronicle the processes that Strong Instructional Leaders undertake to acquire the knowledge and skills to create school environments that care and educate. What is missing from the descriptions of the three journeys of Strong Instructional Leaders are the qualities of leadership necessary to reignite intellectual energies that lie dormant in our schools, what the literature on organizational behavior calls "leadership style." The process for becoming a Strong Instructional Leader is not about style, however, but substance: what you know; how you know it; how you communicate it; and how you execute it. Style matters little in the journeys of Strong Instructional Leadership. What does matter are five qualities of leadership embodied in private study, public arguments, and situational conversations: passion, curiosity, discipline, entrepreneurship, and humility.

All five qualities are present in each journey of becoming a Strong Instructional Leader. Together these qualities enable the kind of focus, energy, and direction necessary for executing imaginative configurations of schooling—what schools *could be*. Although Strong Instructional Leaders express these qualities differently based on their particular personalities and their particular situations, they display them all in what they say and how they behave.

Passion

Strong Instructional Leaders possess a genuine passion for teaching and learning. It is a good day for such a leader when he or she observes skilled teaching, sits with teachers to write meaningful curriculum, or reviews student products that demonstrate an understanding of disciplined ways of knowing the world. With passion comes the energy to keep moving a school community toward a valued end of schooling and the perseverance to resist the corrosive effects of institutional schooling.

Curiosity

Strongly associated with passion for teaching and learning is a curiosity about why some pedagogies are working and why some pedagogies are not working. Strong Instructional Leaders view teacher dissatisfactions with student performance as opportunities to improve their instructional programs—to find solutions by exploring theories and practices not yet examined. With curiosity comes an eagerness to look at problems in new ways and the determination to experiment with new approaches to curriculum and instruction.

Discipline

Strong Instructional Leaders possess the discipline to pursue an in-depth study of an instructional problem. They never act before they understand—they "wind the watch." Developing a deep understanding of an instructional problem requires hours and hours of private time specifically devoted to reading research, talking to experts, observing model programs, and documenting in some way one's private thoughts about an instructional problem. No program goes forth, no money is allocated, no personnel is assigned, no schedules are changed, and no materials are distributed until Strong Instructional Leaders fully understand the substance and methods that govern an instructional change initiative. With discipline comes patience with faculty experimentation with new theories and practices in education and the capacity to continually frame and reframe a theory-based instructional initiative in ways that make collective sense to teachers struggling with an instructional problem.

Entrepreneurship

Passion, curiosity, and discipline naturally form a disposition to try new things—really new—in education. If there is a program, theory, or practice in education that holds the potential to realize an "ought" of schooling, Strong Instructional Leaders are willing to take a look. Not only are they willing to try something really new, but they are willing to risk public scorn for creating wholly new configurations of schooling that faithfully nurture a child emotionally, socially, and intellectually.

Entrepreneurship as practiced by Strong Instructional Leaders is not a reckless affair of trying out this theory or that program. Strongly associated with entrepreneurial approaches to curriculum and instruction are disciplined ways of studying and developing solutions to an instructional problem. Embedded in the quality of entrepreneurship is the courage to try something really different in schooling—to do the right things—and the organizational expertise to do them well.

Humility

Finally, each journey of Strong Instructional Leadership teaches anew the ambiguous relationship that exists between teaching and learning. No theory, idea, or practice in education will ever free itself from a profession that is unable to control inputs, unable to define what is effective teaching, and unable to define the goals of schooling. Unlike their counterparts in the private sector, Strong Instructional Leaders do not hesitate to say: "I don't know."

What they do know is that the certainties of "No Child Left Behind" (test scores, content standards, and scientifically based instructional methods) continue to produce, and in fact accelerate, the low levels of thinking characteristic of teachers doing lessons by rote and students "doing school." Strong Instructional Leaders are cautious when executing an ambitious instructional initiative—they are always attuned to the unintended consequences of the best intentions of what the research says. With humility comes an understanding of the limits of knowledge and the openness to start over again.

Conclusion

A recent study of student performance in college (Arum & Roksa, 2011) gives voice to John Goodlad's (1984) observation, nearly 30 years ago, that schools are places where students have become "academically adrift" (p. 3) in institutions largely designed to grant a credential, enforce the daily routines of schooling, and prize completion of work over understanding and reflection. For the last 3 decades, schools have been subjected to waves of reform initiatives attempting to change the daily grammar of schooling (Tyack & Tobin, 1994) and raise the level of intellectual thinking of high school graduates. Whether one looks at teacher performance in classrooms or student performance after high school, the impact of 3 decades of reform is negligible. A constant theme running throughout research studies of failed school reform efforts is the central role school leaders must play in identifying, framing, and executing effective instructional programs.

Confronted with the ingenuity gap between what schools are and what they could be, school administrators have three choices: they can retreat to their offices and manage the diversions of schooling; They can manage the reform program of the day (be instructional managers); or they can enter classrooms as Strong Instructional Leaders. Administrators choosing to enter classrooms truly embark on a difficult path of discovering who they are educationally, what educational theories move faculty toward realizing valued ends of schooling, and how to build organizational capacity to support ambitious teaching. The pathways into classrooms are littered with decades of failed school reform initiatives. Entering the classroom—becoming a Strong Instructional Leader—is the only remaining opportunity to fully develop the creativity, intelligence, and competence of the next generation of students.

References

Arum, R., & Roksa, J. (2011). *Academically adrift: Limited learning on college campuses.* Chicago: University of Chicago Press.

Astor, R. A., Meyer, H. A., & Behre, W. J. (1999). Unowned places and times: Maps and interviews about violence in high schools. *American Educational Research Journal, 36,* 3–42.

Bailey, A. L., & Butler, F. A. (2003). *An evidentiary framework for operationalizing academic language for broad application to K–12 education: A design document.* Los Angeles, CA: National Center for Research on Evaluation, Standards, and Student Testing.

Benford, R. D., & Snow, D. A. (2000). Framing processes and social movements: An overview and assessment. *Annual Review of Sociology, 26,* 611.

Bennis, W. G. (1989). *On becoming a leader.* Reading, MA: Addison-Wesley.

Berger, P. L., & Luckmann, T. (1966). *The social construction of reality: A treatise in the sociology of knowledge.* Garden City, NY: Doubleday.

Berliner, D. C., & Biddle, B. J. (1995). *The manufactured crisis: Myths, fraud, and the attack on America's public schools.* Reading, MA: Addison-Wesley.

Bobbitt, J. F. (1915). *What the schools teach and might teach.* Cleveland, OH: Survey Committee of the Cleveland Foundation.

Brause, R. S., Lee, S., & Moliterno, A. A. (2008). Childhood reading and literacy engagements: Curricular concerns, contexts, and challenges. In S. B. Kucer (Ed.), *What research really says about teaching and learning to read* (pp. 124–154). Urbana, IL: National Council of Teachers of English.

Cazden, C. (2001). *Classroom discourse: The language of teaching and learning* (2nd ed.). Portsmouth, NH: Heinemann.

Coburn, C. E. (2001). Collective sensemaking about reading: How teachers mediate reading policy in their professional communities. *Educational Evaluation and Policy Analysis, 23*(2), 145–70.

Coburn, C. E. (2004). Beyond decoupling: Rethinking the relationship between the institutional environment and the classroom. *Sociology of Education, 77*(3), 211–244.

Cohen, D. K., & Ball, D. L. (1999). *Instruction, capacity, and improvement* (CPRE Research Report Series, PR-43). Philadelphia, PA: Consortium for Policy Research in Education.

Cohen, D. K., & Ball, D. L. (2000). *Instructional innovation: Reconsidering the story.* Working paper for the Study of Instructional Improvement. Ann Arbor: University of Michigan.

Collins, J. C. (2001). *Good to great: Why some companies make the leap . . . and others don't.* New York, NY: HarperBusiness.

Commission on Reading of the National Council of Teachers of English. (2004). *On reading, learning to read, and effective reading instruction: An overview of what we know and how we know it.* Retrieved from http://www.ncte.org/about/over/positions/categeory/read/118620.htm

Cremin, L. A. (1961). *The transformation of the school: Progressivism in American education, 1876–1957.* New York, NY: Knopf.

Csikszentmihalyi, M. (1997). *Creativity flow and the psychology of discovery and invention.* New York, NY: HarperCollins.

Cuban, L. (1984). *How teachers taught constancy and change in American classrooms, 1890–1980.* Research on teaching monograph series. New York, NY: Longman.

Cummins, J. (1991). Language development and academic learning. In L. M. Malave & G. Duquette (Eds.), *Language, culture, and cognition* (pp. 161–175). Clevedon, UK: Multilingual Matters.

Cummins, J. (2000). *Language power, and pedagogy.* Clevedon, UK: Multilingual Matters.

Daft, R. L., & Weick, K. E. (1984). Toward a model of organizations as interpretation systems. *Academy of Management Review, 9*(2), 285–295.

Deming, W. E. (1986). *Out of the crisis.* Cambridge, MA: Massachusetts Institute of Technology, Center for Advanced Engineering Study.

Dewey, J. (1958). *Experience and nature.* New York: Dover Publications.

Dewey, J. (1966). *Democracy and education: An introduction to the philosophy of education.* New York, NY: Macmillan. (Original work published 1916)

Dewey, J. (1969). *The educational situation.* New York, NY: Arno Press. (Original work published 1906)

Drucker, P. (2006). What makes an effective executive. In T. A. Steward (Ed.), *Classic Drucker: Essential wisdom of Peter Drucker from the pages of Harvard Business Review* (pp. 115–125). Boston, MA: Harvard Business School.

Elmore, R. F., Peterson, P. L., & McCarthey, S. J. (1996). *Restructuring in the classroom: Teaching, learning, and school organization.* San Francisco, CA: Jossey-Bass.

Fenstermacher, G. D. (1986). Philosophy of research in teaching: Three aspects. In M. C. Wittrock (Ed.), *Handbook of research on teaching* (3rd ed., pp. 37–49). New York, NY: Macmillan.

Fenstermacher, G. D. (2002). A commentary on research that serves teacher education. *Journal of Teacher Education, 53*(3), 242–247.

Friedman, T. L. (2005). *The world is flat: A brief history of the twenty-first century.* New York, NY: Farrar, Straus and Giroux.

Fullan, M. (2001). *The new meaning of educational change* (3rd ed.). New York, NY: Teachers College Press.

Gardner, H. (1991). *The unschooled mind: How children think and how schools should teach.* New York, NY: Basic Books.

Goodlad, J. I. (1984). *A place called school: Prospects for the future. A study of schooling in the United States.* New York, NY: McGraw-Hill.

Greene, M. (1995). *Releasing the imagination: Essays on education, the arts, and social change.* The Jossey-Bass education series. San Francisco, CA: Jossey-Bass.

Hargreaves, A. (1991). Contrived collegiality: The micropolitics of teacher collaboration. In J. Blasé (Ed.), *The politics of life in schools: Power, conflict, and cooperation* (pp. 46–77). Newbury Park, CA: Sage.

Harvard University. (1945). *General education in a free society: Report of the Harvard committee.* Cambridge, MA: Harvard University Press.

Hersey, P., Blanchard, K. H., & Johnson, D. E. (1996). *Management of organizational behavior: Utilizing human resources.* Upper Saddle River, NJ: Prentice Hall.

Hoy, W. K., & Miskel, C. G. (2005). *Educational administration: Theory, research, and practice* (7th ed.). Boston, MA: McGraw-Hill.

Hursh, D. (2007). Assessing No Child Left Behind and the rise of neoliberal education policies. *American Educational Research Journal, 44*(3), 493–518.

Jackson, P. W. (1968). *Life in classrooms.* New York, NY: Teachers College Press.

Jackson, P. W. (1986). *The practice of teaching.* New York, NY: Teachers College Press.

Katz, L. G. (1988). What should young children be doing? *American Educator: The Professional Journal of the American Federation of Teachers, 12*(2), 28–33, 44–45.

Kliebard, H. M. (1987). *The struggle for the American curriculum, 1893–1958.* New York: Routledge & Kegan Paul.

Kridel, C. A., & Bullough, R. V. (2007). *Stories of the eight-year study: Reexamining secondary education in America.* Albany: State University of New York Press.

Kritek, P. B. (1994). *Negotiating at an uneven table: A practical approach to working with difference and diversity.* San Francisco, CA: Jossey-Bass.

Labaree, D. F. (1997). *How to succeed in school without really learning: The credentials race in American education.* New Haven, CT: Yale University Press.

Labaree, D. F. (2000). Resisting educational standards. *Phi Delta Kappan, 82,* 28–33.

Levine, A. (2005). *Educating school leaders.* Washington, DC: Education Schools Project.

Liker, J. K. (2004). *The Toyota way: 14 management principles from the world's greatest manufacturer.* New York, NY: McGraw-Hill.

Liker, J. K., & Hoseus, M. (2008). *Toyota culture: The heart and soul of the Toyota way.* New York, NY: McGraw-Hill.

Lortie, D. C. (2002). *Schoolteacher: A sociological study* (2nd ed.). Chicago, IL: University of Chicago Press.

McLaughlin, M. W., & Mitra, D. (2001). Theory-based change and changed-based theory: Going deeper, going broader. *Journal of Educational Change, 2,* 301–323.

Morris, V. C. (1966). *Existentialism in education: What it means.* New York, NY: Harper & Row.

National Commission on Excellence in Education. (1983). *A nation at risk: The imperative for educational reform: A report to the nation and the Secretary of Education, United States Department of Education.* Washington, DC: Author.

Newmann, F., Smith, B., Allensworth, E., & Bryk, A. (2001). Instructional program coherence: What it is and why it should guide school improvement policy. *Educational Evaluation and Policy Analysis, 23*(4), 297–321.

Nussbaum, M. C. (1997). *Cultivating humanity: A classical defense of reform in liberal education.* Cambridge, MA: Harvard University Press.

Olson, D. R. (2003). *Psychological theory and educational reform: How school remakes mind and society.* Cambridge, UK: Cambridge University Press.

Phelan, P. (1992). Speaking up: Students' perspectives on school. *Phi Delta Kappan, 73*(9), 695–96, 698–704.

Pitcher, P. C. (1995). *Artists, craftsmen, and technocrats: The dreams, realities and illusions of leadership.* Toronto, Canada: Stoddart.

Pope, D. C. (2001). *"Doing school": How we are creating a generation of stressed out, materialistic, and miseducated students.* New Haven, CT: Yale University Press.

Quay, J. (2004). Knowing how and knowing that: A tale of two ontologies. In A. Brookes (Ed.), *Conference papers of the International Outdoor Education Research Conference: Connections and Disconnections.* Bendigo, Australia: Latrobe University.

Richardson, V. (1990). Significant and worthwhile change in teaching practice. *Educational Researcher, 19* (7), 10–18.

Rorty, R. (1979). *Philosophy and the mirror of nature.* Princeton, NJ: Princeton University Press.

Rousseau, J.-J. (1979). *Emile: Or, on education.* New York, NY: Basic Books. (Original work published 1762)

Sarason, S. B. (1982). *The culture of the school and the problem of change.* Boston, MA: Allyn & Bacon.

Sarason, S. B. (2004). *And what do you mean by learning?* Portsmouth, NH: Heinemann.

Schön, D. A. (1983). *The reflective practitioner: How professionals think in action.* New York, NY: Basic Books.

Schwab, J. J. (1978). *Science, curriculum, and liberal education: Selected essays* (I. Westbury and N. Wilkof [Eds.]). Chicago, IL: University of Chicago Press.

Scott, W. R. (2008). *Institutions and organizations: Ideas and interests.* Los Angeles, CA: Sage.

Senge, P. M. (1990). *The fifth discipline: The art and practice of the learning organization.* New York, NY: Doubleday/Currency.

Sergiovanni, T. J. (1996). *Leadership for the schoolhouse: How is it different? Why is it important?* San Francisco, CA: Jossey-Bass.

Sergiovanni, T. J. (2005). *Strengthening the heartbeat: Leading and learning together in schools.* San Francisco, CA: Jossey-Bass.

Shotter, J. (1993). *Conversational realities: Constructing life through language.* Inquiries in social construction. London, UK: Sage.

Simon, H. A. (1947). *Administrative behavior: A study of decision-making processes in administrative organization.* New York, NY: Macmillan.

Spillane, J. P. (1998). A cognitive perspective on the role of the local educational agency in implementing instructional policy: Accounting for local variability. *Educational Administration Quarterly: EAQ, 34*(1), 31.

Spillane, J. P. (1999). External reform initiatives and teachers' efforts to reconstruct their practice: The mediating role of teachers' zones of enactment. *Journal of Curriculum Studies, 31*(2), 143–175.

Spillane, J. P., & Callahan, K. A. (2000). Implementing state standards for science education: What district policy makers make of the hoopla. *Journal of Research in Science Teaching, 37*(5) 401–25.

Stein, M. K., & Nelson, B. K. (2003). Leadership content knowledge. *Educational Evaluation and Policy Analysis, 25*(4), 423–448.

Stigler, J. W., & Hiebert, J. (1999). *The teaching gap: Best ideas from the world's teachers for improving education in the classroom.* New York, NY: Free Press.

Tharp, R. (1993). *Institutional and social context of educational practice and reform.* In E. A. Forman, N. Minick, & C. A. Stone (Eds.), *Context for learning: Sociocultural dynamics in children's development* (pp. 269–283). New York, NY: Oxford University Press.

Thomas, W. P., & Collier, V. P. (2002). *A national study of school effectiveness for language minority students' long-term academic achievement.* Washington, DC: Center for Research on Education, Diversity & Excellence.

Tyack, D. B., & Hansot, E. (1982). *Managers of virtue: Public school leadership in America, 1820–1980.* New York: Basic Books.

Tyack, D. B., & Tobin, W. (1994). The "grammar" of schooling: Why has it been so hard to change? *American Educational Research Journal, 31*(3), 453.

Valenzuela, A. (1999). *Subtractive schooling: U.S.-Mexican youth and the politics of caring.* Albany, NY: State University of New York Press.

Vygotsky, L. S. (1962). *Thought and language.* Cambridge, MA: MIT Press.

Weick, K. E. (1995). *Sensemaking in organizations.* Foundations for Organizational Science Series. Thousand Oaks, CA: Sage.

Wilson, J. Q. (1989). *Bureaucracy: What government agencies do and why they do it.* New York, NY: Basic Books.

Windschitl, M. (2002, January 1). Framing constructivism in practice as the negotiation of dilemmas: An analysis of the conceptual, pedagogical, cultural, and political challenges facing teachers. *Review of Educational Research, 72*(2), 131–175.

Index

About the Author

Dr. Alan C. Jones is currently associate professor of educational administration for Saint Xavier University, Chicago, Illinois. His teaching career includes teaching English at Du Sable Upper Grade Center in Chicago, Illinois, and social studies at Thornton Township High School in Harvey, Illinois. He began his administrative career as an activities director at Thornton Township High School and went on to become an assistant principal at Bremen Township High School and served as principal of Community High School District 94, in West Chicago, Illinois, for 17 years. Under his leadership, Community High School was awarded the Blue Ribbon School of Excellence in 1993 and was recognized as a 1995 School of Excellence by *Hispanic* magazine. He has published a number of articles in educational journals on instructional leadership and school reform.